A SUCCESSFUL LIFE—GUARANTEED!
Personal and Relationship Fulfillment

A SUCCESSFUL LIFE—GUARANTEED!

Personal and Relationship Fulfillment

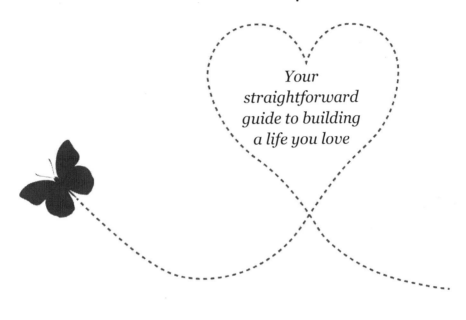

Your straightforward guide to building a life you love

Dr. Stathas shares, inspires and challenges the reader with pragmatic lessons for a life well lived. Personal enrichment, romance, marriage and family fulfillment are attainable!

John J. Stathas, Ph.D., LMFT

Printed in the United States of America

First Printing, 2019

ISBN: 978-179918756-1

Book design by Jean Boles
https://www.upwork.com/fl/jeanboles

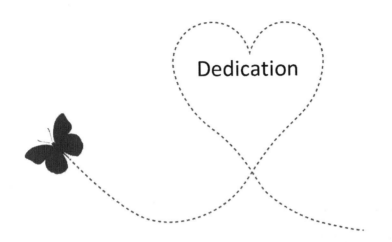

Dedication

I dedicate this effort to my beautiful loving wife, Sherry, for whom my love is everlasting. Sherry has been an incredible lifetime partner. And to our children, Kris and Brittany, for their continuing love, support, and joy shared so abundantly with me. Extended family, certain friends, and professional colleagues also deserve credit for helping me become a better person and therapist. I am most grateful. The quest continues!

Contents

Chapter Three: Men's Challenges In Relationships

Chapter Six: Marriage Success Strategies

Chapter Nine: Communication Skills

Preface

Dr. John J. Stathas is a successful Psychotherapist, licensed Marriage and Family Therapist, and newspaper columnist. He currently lives at Lake Oconee in Georgia with his wife, Sherry. This book is a selection of some of the published newspaper articles he has written over the past years.

In *Chapter One: Personal Sharing*, Dr. Stathas shares some personal information with you, his Respected Reader, as an introduction to the man and his beliefs. In the following chapters, he shares his experience and knowledge obtained in helping many people through difficult times during his many years as a Psychotherapist and a Marriage and Family Therapist. It is his hope that these essays will serve to enlighten subjects that may affect your life and provide answers to some questions that are in the forefront of many of us today as we search for a better understanding of how to have a happy and rewarding life.

Chapter One: Personal Sharing

A Personal Journey From Naïve Dreamer To Pragmatic Idealist

Have you ever had your dreams shattered? Hopes dashed? Had a life-changing wake-up call? Found out you were naïve? If so, perhaps you can understand, perhaps learn from, my experience.

Recently I heard a song that took me back in time—with some emotion. The song is entitled 'Get Together' by the Youngbloods. It brought back memories of why and when I transported my body, mind, and ideals from Green Bay to Atlanta. I came to Atlanta as a naïve idealistic Catholic priest. Ecumenism and social justice were my big dream causes. I was an enthusiastic proponent of each and I was primed to do my part to move these issues forward while performing my priestly duties.

I chose Atlanta primarily because of two men, Archbishop Hallinan and the spirit of hometown Martin Luther King. Atlanta was to be my Mecca, an opportunity to build on the ideals and leadership that these two espoused and died for. Atlanta was popularly seen as a city of unity, a city "too busy to hate" as Mayor Ivan Allen, Jr. proclaimed.

Ecumenism was an effort led by Hallinan to bring together the commonalities of the Christian religion, regardless of denominational division. King's efforts were about bringing the races together into a peaceful harmony. I brought my Christian faith ideal to these efforts.

As a priest I preached ecumenism and social justice, as well as performing my other priestly responsibilities such as baptizing, forgiving sins, marrying, burying, and counseling. I married the first interracial couple in Georgia, who still live happily married here in Lake Country. I instituted and celebrated a folk Mass which brought together people of all faiths, and agnostics as well. One of the songs sung at this celebration was 'Get Together.' It was emotionally spiriting and motivating. I share some of the lyrics here. You may want to Google and hear it. It will get you moving!

> "Love is but a song to sing. Fear's the way to die. You can make the mountains ring, or make the angels cry. Though the bird is on the wing, and you may not know why.
> Some may come and some may go. We shall surely pass when the one that left us here returns for us at last. We are but a moment's sunlight, fading in the grass.
> If you hear the song I sing, you will understand. You hold the key to love and fear all in your trembling hand. Just one key unlocks them both. It's there at your command.
> Come on people now. Smile on your brother. Everybody get together. Try to love one another. Right now."

It was a beautiful and meaningful time in my life. However, change was on the horizon. Archbishop Hallinan died. A new Archbishop replaced him who was a throwback to such idealistic change. He did not like what I was doing and sent me packing to a place no priest would want to go. I went. Briefly.

This punishing banishment precipitated my looking at my life in a more enlightened manner. My Catholic enculturation through 12 years of parochial education and five years of seminary began to not make much sense in certain areas of dogma and practice. A more objective view of the Scriptures and Church history helped me realize that I could no longer continue to believe and practice certain aspects of these teachings—and celibacy was no fun!

So I moved on to Higher Education. I earned a Ph.D. in Counseling Psychology from Georgia State University. I began this part of my journey as a Counselor/teacher at DeKalb College in Georgia. From this entry point I "Peter Principled" my career all the way to being a Dean at Kennesaw University.

I was not happy in this latter position, however. I felt I had compromised my ideals. I was no longer a change agent putting my idealism and talents into making this world a better place. I was a bureaucrat, although somewhat enjoying the status, perks, and financial remuneration. But this was not why I was put on Earth! Again, a move was in order.

It was time to get back to my core ideals—the purpose of my life. I had to face my fears and begin a new career—a psychotherapist in private practice and motivational writer. With a supportive wife, I started my practice. This was a fit. Again I was, and still am, an idealistic change agent, but this time at a pragmatic level.

It has been very satisfying to touch people's lives in very profound and personal ways through therapy and written articles. I find it extremely rewarding to help a couple create a life of love together, to help people successfully parent, to assist kids with their developmental challenges, to assist individuals to know themselves and a fitting vocation, to help people deal with their mental health issues, and other varied concerns that people trust unto me.

I am grateful beyond what words can express that I have found the balanced pragmatic idealist life I was searching for. I have an incredible wife, two awesome kids and their wonderful spouses, and four beautiful grandgirls—along with a profession that is meaningful and impactful every day of my life!

C'mon people now, let's "Get together"!

My Journey From Loneliness to Solitude

Many moons ago, in a previous lifetime, I had a life-changing way of being. I made a transition from feeling lonely to experiencing solitude when experiencing alone time. Let me elaborate. I was raised a Catholic in Green Bay, Wisconsin. There are two—and only two "religions" in Green Bay—Catholicism and the Packers. The order of importance may fluctuate based on how the Packers were doing in a particular season!

My growing up in Green Bay, attending Catholic schools from first grade through high school, and having a father as a Director of the Packers, "enculturated" me, deep in my being, to love both and see them as my future vocation. I didn't make the team of my first choice, the Packers, so I "chose" to be on the priestly team of Catholicism. I had been told by many of the priestly and nun faculty that I was "called" by God to serve him as a priest. Who could renounce such a sacred calling!

Thus, after an attempted diversion of a four year degree in Economics (what was I thinking!) from the University of Wisconsin in Madison, I headed off to the seminary in St. Paul, Minnesota. Brrrrrr! It was like a prison there for my five years of matriculation. We got up at 6 a.m. and walked in darkness through the snowdrifts to the Chapel where we meditated, chanted, and worshiped this God who "called" me into His service. We were not allowed to talk much ("magnum silentiam") and we could not leave the hallowed ground except for Wednesday and Saturday afternoons. (I do have to admit that I did sneak out on occasion. I missed Wisconsin brew and brat!)

My point in sharing this background with you is to make two points. One, that your background, growing up experience, deeply enculturates you, wires you, toward a "programmed" future

6

involving significant choices made. The second point that I want to make is the feeling that you experience when you are alone, I mean really alone!

Living such an isolated monastic life left me feeling extremely lonely! I missed certain people—family, friends, a romantic relationship—and a more robust life of adventure. Over time I moved from painful loneliness to satisfying solitude. I began enjoying my alone time. I read voraciously. (One of the books that I read was *How to Be Your Own Best Friend* By Mildred Newman. It worked!) Becoming manager of the bookstore allowed me to import literature that was beyond the bounds of my Catholic indoctrination—the party line. I came to better understand how religions were formed, how the various Christian sects developed and divided, how the notion of God had changed over time. This was freeing to me. However, after wearing the priestly collar for a while I decided that I could no longer preach that which I did not believe. This was not an easy choice, leaving the opulence of clerical life to the squalor of a $50 dollar a month garage apartment while in Graduate School. Solitude was my friend as I moved forward, though moments of loneliness crept in during this transition.

My choice of solitude has served me well over the years. It has helped me dig deep inside of myself to make significant life changes. Loneliness or solitude is a choice. Solitude is a better place to be!

Be your own best friend!.

My Wife Has "Manipulated Me for Forty Years—and I like it! Positive Reinforcement Works!

After reading this headline I suppose you are wondering what kind of wimp that I must be. But not so fast. Let me give you the whole story behind such a headline.

Webster's offers three definitions for "manipulate." Two of them are:

1. To manage or utilize skillfully.
2. To change by artful or unfair means so as to serve one's purpose.

For purpose of this writing, I am using definition number one.

My wife Sherry is a very positive person. She sees the good in everyone and does not have a critical bone in her body. She has, from day one of our getting together, seen the best in me and offered it up as a compliment. (Thank goodness she has a "blind spot" or two or just knows how to keep her mouth shut when experiencing my less than wonderful side.) She "catches" me doing helpful things and thanks me consistently.

Now any of you who might have taken Psychology 101 will immediately recognize that she is employing Skinnerian Operant Theory. In essence, it is a reinforcement theory. It says if you want a behavior to continue and get stronger you reward the desired behavior on a consistent basis.

Because Sherry has continually reinforced my positive behaviors I have become a better man, husband and father. (You should have known me before she started her manipulation!) I certainly have a ways to go but I am on the right track.

I wish more couples would follow her example. In my counseling sessions I hear individuals complain that all they get from each other are criticisms. Guess what the response is to criticism? Usually it results in an angry confrontation or a silent withdrawal takes place. Criticism rarely creates change to a positive behavior.

So, perhaps you are wondering what a spouse is to do when she/he observes a behavior that is most bothersome and is in need of changing? This is where refined communication needs to take place. In my sessions with couples I focus on the issues present and the needs of each. This approach sets the stage for a more constructive dialogue on how each can better bring his or her best self to the other.

I believe that if you love someone—notice the "given" here—you want to meet that person's needs. This presumes, of course, that one's needs are within the realm of reality given the best intentions and capacities of each other. If you are trying to meet the needs and desires of your loved one you will make positive progress and then, hopefully, the other will notice and compliment the effort. This should result in each person doing his or her best and being recognized for it.

This method focuses on a "fresh start" and going forward rather than re-hashing yesterday's complaints and criticisms. Needs are offered and explained. A person commits to doing his or her best to meet that need. Positive reinforcement is offered and a person accepts the effort believing the other is doing his or her best to meet the need requested.

It is my hope that this writing has helped some people "manipulate" and be "manipulated" so that each person may positively grow into a better person and that a more loving union may result. If you need any assistance with this you can call the expert, my wife Sherry, or me, and I will do my best to teach you the art of "manipulation!"

40 Years Together: "I've Got You Babe"!

Sherry and I recently celebrated our 40th anniversary of marriage! There we were at an open-air chapel overlooking Lake Lanier in Georgia. Our simple wedding included our guitarist who played our chosen songs ('Time in a bottle,' 'Wedding Song,' and 'Follow Me.') Our rent-a-preacher did his job witnessing the happy couple sharing our creative vows of love and commitment with each other.

Over our 40 years together we have been incredibly fortunate to maintain our deep love for each other. Our two wonderful children, Kris and Brittany, have been a source of great joy and pride. And, we certainly are enjoying our four grandgirls!

"Babe" is a familiar term of endearment shared between us. Not sure where that came from. Perhaps Sonny and Cher had something to do with it emanating from their hit song, 'I've got you Babe.'

"Let them say we are wrong. I don't care, with you I can't go wrong.

But with our love like yours and mine, there ain't no hill or mountain we can't climb...

I got you to kiss goodnight,
I got you to hold me tight.
I got you, I won't let go.
I got you to love me so.
Oh, Babe, I got you Babe,
I got you Babe."

Sherry, "I've got you, Babe"! You are an incredible woman—excelling as a wife, mother, "Nana," daughter, sister, Registered Nurse, Realtor. You have helped me to become a better man. I am grateful beyond words to have you as a loving partner as we have faced the various opportunities and challenges of life. We are a helluva team!

I share this happy occasion with you, Respected Reader, for a few reasons. One, I would like to share our marital happiness with you. Two, I invite you to appreciate and celebrate your good marriage. Three, I invite you to see your marriage as your highest priority and to do whatever it takes to make it special. It is worth it!

Knowing When, Why, And How You Will Die

Respected Reader, do you know, or want to know, the answer to these questions? For me, no choice. I pretty much know the answer. In November 2017 I was told by my oncology surgeon, after biopsy, that I had mesothelioma cancer and statistically speaking have six to sixteen months to live. There is no cure for mesothelioma cancer. I will die from this cancer. When hearing this dreadful news, my wife Sherry and I cried and held each other. Our wonderful life together has been rocked.

I am an optimist, but not naïve, as is Sherry. Team Stathas is trying both conventional and unconventional approaches to this invasive monster, searching for life extension.

This November news has been the shock of my life. I have had a wonderful existence on this planet and am grateful for it. My life has been full of adventure, good health, and much love.

I am most grateful that I have had forty wonderful years so far with the love of my life—Sherry. I am grateful that we have two special kids/adults who have had good fortune in health and love. Both are in good marriages with two girls each. What more could a man ask for? Any misfortune going forward I want to happen to me, not them.

I am not angry or depressed. There are moments of sadness, but they are quickly followed up by an awareness that by living one day at a time there are still many special memories that can be created. I have been overwhelmed by the number of people who in various ways have given Sherry and me love and support. Sure are a lot of wonderful people in this world!

As I write this, it is my birthday week. I hope for many more. I am a fighter and will do my best to live the "good life"! I am continuing my practice, my passion, for as long as I am able to present positive therapeutic assistance to people who trust in me.

I share all of this with you, Respected Reader, because many people have inquired, and I want to share the facts and my perspective on this challenge.

Besides sharing this with you, I want to raise your awareness about death. You will die. Perhaps you might want to think about the quality of your health and the factors that affect it. You may want to get a physical exam. And perhaps you could look at getting a mental and relationship evaluation. The earlier you can get information the better the chance that you can stay ahead of any impending challenge to your well-being.

Prayer: Intent, Expectation, And Effect

Prayers have been an interesting topic for me over many years. Since I have five years of theological studies, in addition to the five more for my doctorate in Counseling Psychology, I have a thorough background to look at this topic.

What are the spiritual and psychological effects of prayer? My Socratic gene continues to ask hard questions to evoke enhanced rational thinking and living. I am moved to address this topic because of my current cancer condition and the response of many people who have offered prayers on my behalf. An overwhelming number of prayerful love and support have come my way! Cards, phone calls, emails, and social media have sent the message of "I am praying for you." I am truly humbled and grateful for such solace.

Respected Reader, if you are one of those persons who is praying for someone, what does that mean? Your intent? Certainly it means you care and want the best for that person. Beyond that what is your expectation? Does God need a certain number of prayers for Him to intercede and heal? If God doesn't heal, no "miracle" occurs. Does that mean that God didn't get enough prayers? Or just doesn't care?

While growing up in my Catholic "bubble," I learned that there are two major types of prayer. One is praise, or worship. Does an all-powerful omnipotent God need to be praised? If so, God is not omnipotent. So, why the worship? Trying to get on God's good side?

The prayer of petition is when people ask for—beg—God to intercede and grant the requests. Does your God receive all these petitions and choose to act on some, and not on others? A theological conundrum perhaps.

If your prayer is not answered, are you one of those who says it is not necessary for us mere mortals to understand the ways of

God? "It is all a part of God's divine plan." "Not for us to question." Are children's deaths, tornado wipeouts, ugly diseases causing pain and heartbreak to individuals and families really a part of the God of love's plan?

I write this not from a place of criticism or negativity, rather of wonderment. Basically, what I am asking you, Respected Reader, is what you mean when you say, "I am praying for you?" What is your expectation—belief?

It feels good to say to someone, "I am praying for you." Best wishes offered. And, it feels good to be thought of and prayed for. People care. Value in this. All in all I am grateful for your prayers as well as those who express their support in different words such as "sending healing energy," "sending positive vibes your way," or the simple "I love you!" Keep 'em comin'!

Chapter Two: Personal Growth And Awareness

"The Unexamined Life Is Not Worth Living": So, Let's Examine!

"The unexamined life is not worth living" is a phrase that I often use. I do that for a couple of reasons. One, I believe it. Second, it is a reminder to myself to continually assess the quality of my life. And thirdly, I want to encourage you, Respected Reader, to do the same for optimal living while on Earth's journey.

Before the "examination" I would like to share something about one of my mentors, Socrates, a Greek philosopher in ancient Greece. Socrates believed that philosophy—the love of wisdom—was the most important pursuit above all else. For many, he exemplifies more than anyone else in history the pursuit of wisdom through questioning and logical argument, by examining and by thinking. His "examination" of life in this way spilled out into the lives of others, such that they began their own "examination" of life, but he knew he would die one day and thus said that "a life without philosophy—an "unexamined life—was not worth living.

Being of Greek heritage, and continually in the quest for a personal life with meaning, I write articles that I hope inspire you, Respected Reader, to think about your life and how you choose to live it in the various facets of your life. I truly believe that seeking wisdom by questioning "sacred cows" (an idea, custom, belief, practice, or institution held, especially unreasonably, to be above criticism) and using logic a better understanding of authentic living will prevail.

So, if you have muddled through my prologue, are you ready to "examine" your life within the following subjects? To bring some kind of evaluation to the process, give yourself a score between 0–100 for each category. (I recognize that this is a subjective evaluation. For added validity you may want someone you trust to do the same for you. Good luck with that!)

- **Health:** What is your health these days? Physical and mental (two scores). Do you exercise regularly to the extent that you are able? Do you challenge your brain to keep it firing at its optimal potential? Do you eat healthily? Do you get regular checkups?
- **Personality:** As you may define it. Do you have "good one"? Or are you kind of a "slug"? (Look it up)
- **Spirituality:** Again, as you define it. Some call it being religious, some church going, others have a broader, more expansive, understanding of it.
- **Communication Skills:** How well do you communicate with others in various contexts and relationships? Are you assertive? Do you listen well? Do you compliment others? Are you respectful in dialogue?
- **Humor:** Do you have a sense of humor? Are you a joke teller, quipper, sarcastic in attempting to be humorous? Or is it not in your repertoire?
- **Recreation:** Do you consistently find recreational outlets that you enjoy?

- **Friending:** Are you a good friend? Do you have any or many? Or are you mostly a loner? Can you be counted on when needed?
- **Childing:** Are you a good child to your parent(s)—if they are still living?
- **Parenting:** If you are a parent, regardless of the age of your kids, do you parent well and appropriate for their and your age? Ask them.
- **Partnering:** If you are in a relationship, do you do the things that make your partner feel loved, valued, nurtured, safe, etc.?
- **Time Management:** Do you use time efficiently, based on priorities, values and needed outcomes?
- **Intelligence:** Do you have some smarts and do you use them well? How do you pursue intellectual pursuits? Or is your brain stagnating?
- **Values:** Are you clear about what your values are? Are you living them with consistency?
- **Body Image:** Are you comfortable with your body image given your age and overall health? Are you vain? Are you critical of your body?
- **Accomplishments:** At this stage of your life do you feel satisfied with what you have accomplished, and are currently accomplishing, given the type of life that you have chosen? Do you feel you could be doing more in this area?
- **Your Sexuality:** It is an integral part of your life's energy. Are you finding a useful and satisfying manner to express it?
- **Do you think you are open-minded?** Are you open to new ideas, understandings, beliefs? Or have you developed "hardening of the categories," thinking you have all the

answers? You don't want to be disturbed by new facts or research.

I guess that is enough categories for now to digest and evaluate. Or perhaps, you have other categories that you use to determine the quality of your life. I hope you find this "examination" of your life at this time to be worthy of your consideration. If not, why not? (Note the Socratic question!) May you continue to examine the quality of your life on a regular basis. I do and find it a worthy endeavor.

Your Number One Love Relationship—With Yourself

Of all the relationships in the world that exist, the one that is the most important for you is the one with yourself.

You are brought into this world to become all that you can be, to develop every ounce of your potential. Your caretakers hopefully have given you a solid core on which to build, but it is the task of every adult to be responsible for full development—physically, emotionally, intellectually, spiritually, and socially. No one is here to take care of you; no one owes you anything. This is not an argument for extreme rugged individualism. There is no question that we can reach our full potential only while connected to other supportive people in our life.

If you do not love yourself, you have nothing to give to others. Each of us has the Spirit of Love within us that empowers us to value ourselves, have high self-esteem, and grow into a loving, contributing human being. (God did not create junk in His image.) Personal self-love is a prerequisite before we can develop a healthy friendship or a romantic relationship. Self-love is not to be equated with being solipsistic, selfish, and self-absorbed. For these people, they are the be all and end all. A truly loving person loves him/herself and shares that love with others.

How do you know if you love yourself? You are not in good balance if you have the following characteristics:

1. Eating disorders
2. Drug and alcohol misuse
3. Smoking
4. Consistent difficulty with relationships
5. Depression or frenetic activity

6. Excessive spending
7. Limited productivity or excessive workaholism
8. Judgmental and critical of others
9. Not forgiving of self or others

People that love themselves act out from their inner core, their loving spirit or intuition. They are free to be themselves. Their motto is "What you think of me is none of my business." They do not need the approval of others to feel adequate. They enjoy acceptance like anyone else, but they do not bend and contort themselves in every conceivable shape to get the praise of the crowd. They are not excessive "pleasers."

An exercise in developing genuine self-love is to write on a piece of paper all the things that you like or value about yourself. Share this list with someone who cares and ask him or her to do the same. You will experience a flow of positive energy/feelings that move you forward to a greater ability to connect with yourself and with others.

Self-awareness of what is "right" and good in you is the first step in positive self-love.

Who Are You?

One's personal identity is a fascinating reality, evolving and changing over time. At each stage of existence a person can be described from a variety of perspectives. The object of this essay is to invite you to explore your identity. This personal perspective will result from answering the following questions. From this basis of knowing, you can take a more proactive role in determining who you want to become.

- **Where did you come from?** An important starting point is to construct a genogram, a family tree. These family members have been very influential in determining much of your physical, emotional, intellectual and spiritual components. Who were your parents, and their parents? What did they look like? What did they believe? How did they act, especially toward you? What did you learn from them? These factors influenced much of your past and present identity.
- **Who are family now?** Are you married? Kids? Who do you live with? These people, too, have shaped, and continue to shape, your being.
- **Where have you lived?** Where you have lived has been instrumental in who you are. Have you moved very often? At what age? Who were your teachers, friends, associates over the years. List the significant ones and rate their influence on you, positively and negatively. Where do you live now? Why? Who are the significant people present to your life and what is their impact?
- **Quality of life?** How have you lived in the past? What has been your lifestyle, jobs, interests, sources of fun? How have

these factors changed over the years? Describe your present way of being. What is important as you live day to day?

- **Belief system?** What has been your belief system and reason for living as you have? Your current raison d'etre? Have you devoted much energy to conscious reflective living or are you on autopilot, just going through the motions?

- **Career choices?** What jobs and careers have you had? How have they affected your life and those closest to you? Are you pleased with your present career? What's next?

- **Accomplishments?** What have you accomplished in your life? Are you proud of them? Any significant poor decisions that have impacted your life? What are your future goals? Any major changes ahead?

- **Unfinished Business?** If you died today, is there unfinished business? What is your legacy? What would people say about you? What would you hope that they would say? If you could do it all over, what would you do differently?

Descartes wrote, "The unexamined life is not worth living?" Hopefully, these Socratic questions will help you know who you are and where you want to go. "If you don't know where you are going, any road will take you there!"

Which of the above factors are most important to you? What are your priorities? If you do not have priorities and goals, you have no direction. Look at your calendar and it will tell you much about your priorities. Where you spend your time and your money says a lot about you.

To what extent is your happiness based on what you GET or on what you GIVE? For many narcissistic (solipsistic, self-absorbed) people, happiness is what they receive. The richest source of happiness, however, is in giving love to people that are special to you. "Tis better to give than receive."

Were You Abused As A Child?

That is a difficult question to answer for many many many reasons.

- You may be uncertain as to what "abuse" is.
- You may use, or have used, the defense mechanisms of denial ("it didn't happen"), minimization (it wasn't that bad"), or rationalization("he was under a lot of stress").
- You may feel guilty for talking about it.
- You are trying to forget, and maybe forgive.
- You feel alone and ashamed regarding it.
- You don't want to get anyone else hurt or in trouble.

I have heard all of the above explanations often in my work with people over the years. In our society, often so cynical and cruel relative to this area, the word "abuse" is often misunderstood, and sometimes ridiculed. Let's try to narrow "abuse" down to six areas for sake of understanding in this article. May the meek and macho keep an open mind on this subject.

Types of Abuse:

- **Physical:** Were you hit, pushed, whipped, bitten, punched, slapped or burned?
- **Sexual:** Were you touched inappropriately? Were you forced, threatened, or coerced into any kind of sexual exposure or contact with another person?
- **Neglect:** Were basic necessities of safety, shelter, food, clothing and medical care kept from you at any time?
- **Emotional Neglect:** Were your caretakers disinterested, fail to hold and hug you, or emotionally unavailable to you?

- **Cruelty:** Did you suffer from extreme punishment or hurtful activities?
- **Mental Suffering:** Were you called names, belittled, or abandoned at times?

Depending on the degree and type of your emotional development at the time of abuse, and now, your responses to this abuse may be a personality loaded with:

- Fear
- Anxiety
- Insecurity
- Shame
- Embarrassment
- Feeling Defective Anger
- Rage

These negative feelings can lead to:

- Difficulties with trust. You do not want to be vulnerable to anyone—especially in a romantic and committed relation-ship.
- Excessive self-protection, physically and emotionally.
- Self-esteem challenges of feeling unlovable and unworthy.
- Achievement challenges. You tend to overachieve, be driven, in order to compensate or you give up and underachieve.
- Difficulties in fitting in with other people in various situations.
- Becoming an abuser also.

Behaviorally speaking, people who have been abused often become:

- **Caretakers—Rescuers:** They find needy "wounded birds" to take care of, so they can feel good about themselves.
- **Hiders:** They try not to be noticed by being too thin, too fat, non-descript, or just stay home. They stay "safe."
- **Easy Marks:** They become easy, are taken advantage of. They give whatever others want from them.
- **Tough Guys:** Nothing hurts them, but they can hurt you.
- **Lost Souls:** They just float around with no direction.
- **Religious Nuts:** They try to "save" everybody in hopes that they may be exalted in others' eyes.
- **Addictors:** They try to kill their pain with drugs, alcohol, food, shopping, sex, gambling. They are out of balance and go to extremes to get a short-lived adrenalin rush.
- **Whiners and Sickies:** They always have something wrong with them so that someone will take care of them and give them attention.

If you were abused, I hope you will own it and deal appropriately with that "hole in your soul." Healing can take place. RELIEF will result, with a new burst of energy enabling you to move forward. You will then gain power and feel better about yourself!

Do You Have High Self Esteem? Genuinely Like Yourself?

It is a fact that the way we view ourselves has a lot to do with our behavior, both personally and professionally. It is very difficult to accurately assess how we see ourselves, because it is a very subjective process, using two different parts of the brain, the cerebral cortex(cognitive) and the limbic (emotional). Add our various defense mechanisms, such as denial and rationalization, and the analysis gets even more complicated.

How about giving it a shot? I have devised an evaluative instrument as a starting point of self-assessment. Give yourself a grade for each category, based on how you perceive yourself. (Use a scale of 1-100.)

Category	Grades
Body	
Personality	
Intelligence	
Emotionality	
Health	
Sexuality	
Capacity to Work Productively	
Capacity to Have Fun	
Exercise	
Relationship with Significant Other	
Relationship with Your Parent(S)	
Relationship with Your Kid(S)	
Relationship with Friends	
Relationship with Co-Workers	
Communication Skills – Personal	

Category	Grades
Communication Skills – Professional	
Living Your Values	
Spirituality	
Coping Ability under Stress	
Sense of Humor	
Financial Condition	
Eating Habits	
Job Satisfaction	
Marital Satisfaction	
Life Accomplishments	

There may be other categories by which you assess yourself. Use them.

Any surprises? Any conclusions or challenges that are derived from this exercise?

Checkpoint Areas To Evaluate Your Degree Of Happiness And Well-Being

I remember a British fellow in therapy with me back in 1987 making these comments: "John, this is how I posit the data" and "I didn't know what I didn't know." He was gaining insight into himself and was feeling grateful and empowered. The reason these two statements have stayed with me is the profound depth they communicate.

Each of us "posits the data," meaning we process events in a certain way; we choose to think about stuff in our own unique way—what makes sense to us. Yet, there is so much that we do not realize that we really do not know. Defensive blinders stifle greater awareness. Follow all that?

Since the Socratic method, and the statement of "the unexamined life is not worth living" is my mantra, I offer the following areas for you to peruse and see if any of these descriptors offer insight into areas that you may need to "know" more about.

- **Relationship Issues:** communication issues, marriage evaluation, dating success/failure, premarital or separation/divorce, parenting assistance, affairs/infidelity, family/in-law concerns, co-dependency.
- **Anxiety:** stress, panic attacks, social anxiety, obsessive behavior, concentration difficulties, irritability, feeling on edge, constant worry, anger management issues, mood swings, loss of control, isolation.
- **Depression:** sadness, loss of interest, sleep challenges, tearfulness, fatigue, indecision, low self-esteem, melancholy.

- **Life Transitions:** relationship break up, job change/loss, retirement, moving, divorce, loss of a loved one, child birth, empty nest syndrome, financial distress, illness, legal issues.
- **Excess Issues:** alcohol, illicit drugs, food intake, tobacco use, gambling, shopping.
- **Sexual Concerns:** quality and quantity, arousal/functionality concerns, pornography, emotional closeness lack.

The above categorizations are not meant to be exhaustive in your self-assessment, rather as a starting point to look at yourself honestly and objectively. Perhaps the way you "posit the data" is distorted and there may be something here that may need to be known and addressed for your movement forward into becoming your best self. You deserve to "be all that you can be!"

It Is Important To Know, Challenge, and Evaluate Your Premises And Enculturation. Your Life Has Been Shaped By Them!

One of the most eye opening and enlightening experiences that changed the way I look at things took place many years ago. It changed the way I think and operate. It changed the way I look at and interpret alleged "facts." Unless you have had a similar learning experience you might wonder why it was, and is, so impactful for me.

The event of which I reference took place when I was twenty-three years old and in my second year of studying theology in the seminary. I had graduated with a degree in Economics from the University of Wisconsin. Economics? What was I thinking? It was a major that I chose without a hint of knowing myself. Upon graduation I realized that I did not want a vocation related to this field of study so I went back to my "default" position based on my enculturation of twelve years of Catholic education. This enculturation was one of priests and nuns telling me that I was "called by God" to be a priest. I bought the validating premise. So I did.

In the seminary I studied the Scriptures for five years. In my very first Scripture class the professor said something that has stuck with me and altered the way I think and operate. The professor began the class by saying, "Gentlemen, the first book we will be studying is *A History of Israel*. Note, it is titled A History of Israel, not THE history of Israel." Lesson learned. I was inclined to believe this WAS Israel's history instead of understanding that this book was presenting Israel's history from the author's perception, understanding and desired impact. From then on I have always tried to look at the premise of something to see what has been presented as fact. This led to a deeper study of the Scriptures, using a process called exegesis, moral theology, the history of God and Christianity, and the development of doctrine. I've done this because what I believe, and why, determines much of who I am and how I behave.

It is important to know how you were enculturated, some would call it brain washed, based on certain premises, and, thus, determined your worldview and consequent behavior. You are a product of your environment. What you were taught and what you experienced, along with your genetics, has created the person you have become to be.

Since I started this "enlightenment" break through about religion, let me give you a couple of examples to illustrate the above paragraph. When I was a young chap going through puberty I was taught that masturbation was evil, a mortal sin, and that if I did that and did not go to confession to a priest to get absolved that I would go to Hell forever should I die. How's that for scary! I believed that until I went to the seminary and learned about moral theology and Church history, which enlightened me as to when this insidious teaching infected the Catholic Church. Carrying around all that guilt was not fun. I got to know the confessional priest very well! Are you laughing, Baptists? You have your own issues relative to behaviors like dancing and alcohol consumption. Do you really believe that Jesus at the wedding at Cana answered his mother's request and turned water into grape juice?

Lest you think this challenging premise writing is just about religion, it is not. It is also, about beliefs/premises about race, gender, age, politics, etc. List any belief/opinion that you have about anything and ask where the starting point was for that. That is your premise and subsequent thoughts, feelings, and actions flow from it.

Two definitions of "premise":

1. "A previous statement or proposition from which another is inferred or follows as a conclusion."
2. "A statement or idea that is accepted as being true and is used as the basis of an argument." In other words, if X exists then Y must follow. My point here is to check out X. It may not be true!

My message in this writing, Respected Reader, is to search and understand your enculturation and the premises from which it has come. Have you looked at the premises and enculturation of your life? Unfortunately, few do. Thus, you live your life based on that which was foisted on you early on. Some of that may be wonderful, applicable, and helpful for you to lead a full and meaningful life. Some may be harmful, retarding, and stifling for you to be the best of what you are capable. For many this "starting from scratch," looking at your formative premises, may be too scary. You may have to move from the land of certitude to the land of doubt and continual seeking for your truth. It takes courage to question your enculturation and the premises you imbibed. May you have such courage!

Knowing Where You Come From Explains Many Things

Some people enjoy the quest for self-knowledge. If you are one of them, the following questions and answers may lead to further enlightenment. I invite you to plunge in for further self-revelation.

- Are you male or female?
- What race are you?
- Are you an only child?
- Do you have siblings?
- Do your siblings have the same biological father and mother?
- Where do you fit in the sibling order?
- Did your parents have a good marriage when you were a child?
- Did your parents nurture you?
- Were your parents "there" for you?
- Was there any physical, emotional or sexual abuse in your family?
- Did your parents divorce? What age were you?
- Did either of your parents abuse alcohol or use drugs?
- Was your father gone a lot due to his job?
- Did you move a lot as a child?
- How did religion affect you?
- What was the culture like in which you were raised?
- If you had a stepparent, what was she/he like?
- Were your teenage years difficult?
- Was school challenging for you?
- Have you felt that you "fit in" in most social situations?
- What kind of relationship did you have with your grand-parents?

- What was your family economic/social status?
- Did you have any serious physical ailments?
- Was there a serious illness or death in your family while growing up?

The above factors, plus genetics, significantly effect and affect your personality, marriage success, parenting style and career. Most people do not pay enough attention to these influences. If people would only do their homework, they could avoid many painful and costly mistakes.

In most cases you probably are quite different from your sibling (s). Think about it. A few stereotypical examples follow, based only on birth order.

- First borns usually are the most left brained, logical, responsible, and successful career wise. They tend to be more emotionally restrained.
- If the first born does mostly the right things, the second borns will tend to have a "rebellious "or "out there" side. They often are more right brained, creative, and emotional.
- If the first born is a "screw up," the second one is usually more successful.
- If the second child is a middle kid, she/he oftentimes will have problems. The "squeezed" child usually feels short-changed and presents challenges.
- The only child, or the last child, tends to be self-centered and self-absorbed. Often they are "spoiled," so they think they are the center of the universe.

Remember, these are stereotypes. There are exceptions because there are so many other idiosyncratic variables involved in the developing brain/personality. There are plusses and minuses to each personality type. One type is not particularly better than another. Each of us is unique!

Knowing where you came from, what developed you, is critical to knowing yourself.

Your Beliefs Create Your Destiny! Where Do They Come From?

Allow my Socratic philosopher side to address you for a few minutes. One of the insights of my life is how our brain is wired and how it affects our life. Part of brain wiring is how we think. How we think affects how we feel. These two then direct us to behave in certain ways. Our thoughts are a developmental process based on how we experienced life and, thus, formed our belief system.

You are a combination product of your birthed genes, which have epigenetically been altered by the life you have lived. Your experienced life has mostly been impacted by your parents and other effective "teachers," which include people and garnered information. They created your beliefs, which you may or may not have changed over time due to newer experiences created by impactful people and your own research.

You tend to think your belief system is "right" because that is how you have experienced life. Others, coming from other cultures and experiences say they are "right" because that is their brain wiring. These life experiences and developed beliefs are deep in our marrow and usually difficult to change, if so warranted.

Let me offer a few examples from the sublime to the superficial to illustrate my point.

- **God:** What is your belief? Where did it come from? Has it changed from your childhood education or later "born again" conversion? How does this belief affect your life in various ways? Are you more or less religious or have you switched to a more scientific/humanist belief orientation?
- **Spouse:** What is your belief in who she/he is? Has your belief in this person changed over the years? For better or worse?

How does your current belief about him/her affect the way you act toward him/her?

- **Kids:** Has your belief/understanding of them changed over the years? What is your current belief and how does it affect the way you interact with them?
- **Career(s):** As you have grown older has your belief about your career changed—in retrospect or currently?
- **Lifestyle:** What has been your belief as to what is important in this area? Have you modified this belief and consequent behavior over the years?
- **Health:** Have you made any adjustments to your beliefs regarding your health and what you do to live healthier?
- **Politics:** Has your belief in party and policy changed over the years? If so, why? What are the implications for this current belief?

I could go on and on with different areas of your life related to your past and present beliefs. Please, Respected Reader, spend some time thinking about how you came to believe what you believe, how some have changed, current beliefs, and what beliefs still are due for a closer examination.

Personally speaking, I continue to examine my beliefs. I find it to be both rewarding and challenging! It has made me keenly aware of how my brain was wired early on and how those brain wirings/"brain washings" have changed over the reflected years.

"So as you think so shall you live." - Bruce Lee

Emotional Boundaries—Who Gets In?

People vary as to who gets close to their heart. Some people are naive, their boundaries porous, and they get emotionally hurt often. They get used and discarded. Others have rigid boundaries protecting their heart and no one gets in. They are candidates for the line in the song 'Desperado': "Your prison is walking through this life all alone." Neither extreme is healthy.

A question to you is who has entered your emotional sanctuary? Has your heart been broken often or rarely? Who have been the people who have come close to your heart? List these people. After you have done that, give a rating from one to ten as to how close you feel toward them now (one = "yuk! ten = heavenly bliss).

What is your current situation relative to emotional closeness? I invite you to do an exercise that graphically illustrates your current emotional boundaries and evaluate how close individuals are to your heart. Draw a series of concentric circles, with a big dot in the middle. The big dot represents the most personal, vulnerable part of your being. Each circle is a boundary representing distance away from your open heart. Plot the people in your life on this grid as to how close they are to you. What you are looking for is who are the people closest to you and how close they actually are.

As you evaluate this heart grid, what do you see? Are there few or many in your circles? Do you like the position of each of these people, or do some of them need to be moved closer or further from your heart? Again I recommend that you grade each of the people on your grid from one to ten for clarification as to positioning.

As part of my doctoral program I wrote a paper called "Love: the Quintessence of Being." In that paper, based on a derived eclectic personality theory, I stated that: "In my personal life I would not allow anyone close to me that was negative, lazy, bigoted, angry or unforgiving." It has provided a valuable guideline for people choices in my life. I am grateful for the positive, energetic, open, loving, and forgiving people that embrace my heart. They invite me into degrees of intimacy and motivate me to give a life of love my best shot.

Your heart circle is based on love. Healthy people have good boundaries and actively control the gate as to who comes in and how close they are allowed to become. Lovers, parents, children, friends, colleagues, acquaintances, neighbors, etc. may have a place in your heart. Evaluate and choose carefully.

Your heart deserves the best!

"Toxic People": Any Of These Types In Your Life?

Your interaction with other people affects you significantly in many ways. A healthy relationship is additive to your well-being. It would include mutual caring, respect, humor, compassion, and support. You feel good around such a person—comfortable, secure, and enhanced. You are a better person because of such a relationship.

A "toxic relationship," on the other hand, does not feel good. You are not a better person as a result of being with such a person. Brett Blumenthal has written an insightful description of some "toxic" people. See if you have any of these folks in your social milieu.

1. **Manipulative Mary/Marvin:** These individuals are experts at manipulative tactics. They figure out what your "buttons" are and push them until they get what they want.

2. **Narcissistic Nancy/Ned:** These people have an extreme sense of self-importance and believe that the world revolves around them. They drain the energy right out of you.

3. **Debbie/Dan Downers:** These people can't appreciate the positive in life. Negative describes them.

4. Judgmental Janice/Jim: They are critical people who act superior as they judge from their righteous rooftop.

5. **Dream Killing Kathy/Keith:** You have an idea and these people tell you why you can't do it. They are the proverbial "wet blanket" type.

6. **Insincere Irene/Iggy:** You never feel these people are real. They lack depth of connection. Who is that person behind the mask?

7. **Disrespectful Diane/Dave:** These people will say or do things at the most inappropriate times and in the most

inappropriate ways. They are demeaning in their interactions with you.

8. **Never enough Nelly/Nathan:** These people are never satisfied with what you do. They always want more.

There are other related "toxic" types. You might recognize:

1. **Takers Theresa/Terry:** These people take and rarely give. They are selfish. They are related to narcissistic Nancy and Ned.

2. **Complaining Cora/Carl:** These people are whiners. They complain about just about everything.

3. **Gossiping Gertrude/Gus:** They like to talk about other people, usually in a negative manner. Don't turn your back on these folks.

4. **Putting down Patty/Patrick:** These people like to put others down. They see and say the negative. Again, watch your back.

5. **Guiltifying Greta/Gene:** They try to make people feel guilty as a way of manipulating or controlling them.

Sometimes "toxic" people are not very obvious. You can recognize them better if you are attuned to how you feel when you are around them or after being with them. A few signs might be that you feel tense around them or feel worse about yourself. Or perhaps you see them being mean to others and nice to you— beware, you may be next. You worry that they may embarrass you. You start losing respect for them. You start to fear them in some way and don't look forward to the next get together.

You are less of a person when you spend much time with "toxic" people. You become uncomfortably vulnerable and more depleted. You start becoming more negative yourself. You've heard the old saying, "Tell me who you hang around with and I'll tell you who you are."

I encourage you to list the people you interact with on a regular basis. After each name put a number as to how close you feel to them on a scale of one to ten, with ten being the most positive. Trust your gut. After you have done that and evaluated the results, you may want to make some changes with respect to the people with whom you spend your time. There are so many wonderful positive people around that there is no need to waste your time, and diminish your well-being, with "toxic" people. Choose well!

Forgiveness Frees The Heart: Some Tips

Over the course of life's trek there are many situations where you may feel hurt or angry in reaction to another's behavior. Someone may do something to you, or someone you care about, that in your mind was inappropriate and uncalled for. Negative feelings and thoughts about that person may be challenging and difficult to put aside. So, what would be a good thing to do? Retaliate? The urge is strong—the decision wrong.

Forgiveness is a better choice. Forgiveness is a healthy psychological and spiritual alternative. Here are a few tips to think about as you explore this option:

1. Know exactly how you feel about what happened and know the reasons why such behavior upset you.

2. Decide what you need to do to feel better. Perhaps you need to address the particular concern or incident with the offending party.

3. Forgiveness does not mean that you condone that person's behavior nor does it mean that you want some type of reconciliation with that person. A boundary here may well need to be established.

4. When you have negative feelings developing about this person, "change the channel" to some other thought. You do not want negative energy to continue to reside in your brain. It is not particularly easy to forget, but by not allowing these thoughts and feelings to linger you gradually extinguish them.

5. Give up naïve expectations about how things "should be" or how such persons "should" behave. "Stuff happens." Be the "bigger" person.

6. The act of forgiveness is for you, nobody else. It is for your own internal calm and peace.
7. "Just do it!"

Further encouraging words:

"The weak can never forgive. Forgiveness is an attribute of the strong." - Gandhi

"To forgive is to set a prisoner free and discover the prisoner was you." - Unknown

"To err is human; to forgive, divine." - Alexander Pope

12 Ways To Forgive Your Parents For Doing Such A Crummy Job Of Raising You!

Love the internet! It's amazing what all I can find there. One of this week's finds was a blog by Ken Wert. His blog is the title of this article. I will list his twelve "ways" and add my own commentary on this topic. Parenting has an enormous effect on you as you evolve your personhood. Some parents do a good job, some suck. Yours? If you are a parent, are you doing a good job? Better than your parents?

Mr. Wert asks, "Have you been holding onto childhood pain? Do you harbor deep-seeded resentment for the way your parents raised you? Do you blame them for the circumstances of your life today?" He says, and I agree, that unless you find ways to let go and move on you will be "condemned to a life plagued by the energy-sapping, happiness-stunting emotions of deep-seeded anger and resentment."

I would add another element to this by including adult children who are blaming their parents for their current misery based on something the parent has done in more recent times. I continually come across adult children who are mad at one of the parents for decisions the parent does in his or her life. Example: an adult child who will not forgive a parent for divorcing the other parent.

The 12 ways to let go and move on:

1. **Redefine Your Relationship:** Who are your parents today? Have they changed? Allow them to change. They may be worth having in your life now if you can get over the past. Most "kids" want to be connected with their parents; not to be connected leaves a void in their lives, no matter what age they may be.

2. **Be Grateful For The Blueprint Of What Not To Do Raising Your Kids:** Examine what parental practices that they exhibited and the effects on you. Some of this blueprint needs improvement in your version.

3. **Forgive Them For Being The Only Thing They Knew How To Be:** Your parents may well have been limited in their capacity to be good parents. Do you ever wonder how they were raised and, therefore, why they parented as they did? Few parents get up in the morning and look for ways that they could hurt their kids.

4. **Recognize They Are Likely Products Of Their Own Parents' Mistakes And Flaws:** Moms and Dads are products of their own parents' strengths and weaknesses. In many cases they perpetuated what they received.

5. **Write It Down:** Sometimes we bury our painful feelings where they fester and decay and then infect our lives in other negative ways. Writing your experiences and feelings can be clarifying and cleansing, thus enabling the door to letting go to swing open. Perhaps after reviewing the painful events you could light it afire and let it disappear into nothingness.

6. **Learn From Parental Strengths And Weaknesses:** Since you saw them up close you have had many opportunities to see very clearly what some of their positives and negatives were. With that upfront and personal knowledge you can define and live a better model.

7. **Read The Book, *A Child Called It*, Then Be Grateful:** The book allegedly helps you see the relativity of your experience. Some have had it much worse. Your parents had some redeeming qualities, didn't they?

8. **Let The Work You Do In Your Own Home Be The Salve That Heals The Wounds In Your Heart:** In other words, parent yourself vicariously through parenting your own children. Extend to them what your parents failed to extend to you and allow the love flowing from you to your children to heal the wounds from the lack of love flowing to you as a child.

9. **Take Responsibility For Your Own Life:** "I am who I choose to be." Learn how to be healthier as a person and better as a parent.

10. **Talk To Them:** Try to be calm and dispassionate, but clear. Ask them their perspective, try to understand, then let go. See if a healthy relationship can be developed with clear expectations and boundaries.

11. **Stop Putting So Much Stock In How You Were Raised:** The past is over. Work on overcoming emotional obstacles and other personal obstructions and get on with living well.

12. **Assume Good Intent:** When we assume good motives behind misguided practices and weak wills, it is often easier to overlook and forgive their failures.

Well, what do you think? Are you ready, willing, and able to forgive your parents and move on? What steps may need to be taken to make that happen? Enlightened communication? And know, in spite of the "crummy" job your parents did in raising you, you turned out to be pretty special, did you not?

Understanding The "Controller" Personality

Personalities are described by various theories and nomenclature. An interesting descriptive paradigm is the "Pleaser-Controller" continuum.

Pleasers and controllers usually end up together, resulting in polarization, tolerable compromise, or synergistic union. Pleasers are reactive personalities, avoiding conflict, and usually are emotionally retentive. Controllers mostly are energetically expressive, go-getters, often with anger overtones.

It can be helpful to know if you are a Controller—or married to one. Controllers are both male and female. The following controller inventory by Dr. Deepak Chopra is taken from his book, *Ageless Body, Timeless Mind.* The following inventory should be helpful to determine if you are a controller or if someone important in your life is one.

Give yourself a point for each one of which you can answer with "frequently," "most of the time," or "almost always."

1. I like to be in control of work situations and am much happier working alone than with others.
2. When I'm under pressure, the easiest emotion for me to show is anger or irritability.
3. I rarely tell anyone that I need them.
4. I tend to harbor old hurts. Rather than telling someone that she/he hurt me, I would rather fantasize about getting even.
5. I have quite a few resentments about the way my brothers and sisters relate to me.
6. The more money I spend on someone, the more that means that I love them.
7. I keep to myself how unfairly others treat me.

8. If a relationship starts to go bad, I secretly wish I could take back everything I bought that person.
9. If it's my house, the people in it should follow my rules.
10. I find it hard to admit being vulnerable. I don't often say "I'm wrong" and mean it.
11. It's better to nurse my wounds than to show someone that I'm weak.
12. I'm a better talker than listener.
13. What I have to say usually is important.
14. I secretly think others don't take my opinions as seriously as they should.
15. I have a pretty good sense of what's good for people.
16. At least once in my life I got caught opening someone else's mail.
17. People have called me cynical or negative.
18. I have high standards, which others sometimes mistake for criticism.
19. I tend to be a perfectionist. It bothers me to let a sloppy job go out.
20. I feel uncomfortable if someone gets too close to me emotionally.
21. After a relationship breaks up, I look back and think I was mostly in the right.
22. I'm neat and orderly. I like my way of doing things and find it hard to live with someone who is sloppy.
23. I'm good at scheduling my day and put a high value on punctuality.
24. I'm good at caring for other people's needs, but then I get disappointed when they don't think as much about mine.
25. I have a logical explanation for the way I act, even if others can't always accept it.

26. I don't care that much if other people don't like me.
27. In my opinion, most people don't usually express their true motives for the way they behave.
28. I'm not good at handling noisy or rambunctious children.
29. I still blame my parents for a lot of my problems, but I haven't told them so.
30. When I get into an argument with my spouse or lover, I can't resist bringing up old grievances.

Total score_____

Evaluating your score:

0-10 points. Your personality isn't dominated by an excessive need to be in control. You are likely to be comfortable with your feelings and tolerant of other people.

10-20 points. Being in control is a frequent issue with you. You have more fears and hurt feelings than you let on, but you don't work hard to resolve these feelings.

Over 20 points. You are a controlling person. You feel that control is necessary because people hurt your feelings a lot, and your memory of this goes back into your painful childhood.

This inventory can be a meaningful instrument to heighten personal awareness and can serve as a valuable tool for dialogue with your significant other. Control is an important dynamic in all relationships.

The Importance Of Being Open Minded In Searching For Personal Beliefs

The journey in search of meaningful truths that affect and guide your personal life can be arduous and challenging. For sake of discussion I would like to present three types of mindsets. Each is represented by a certain type of person; one may be you!

- **Simplistic Sam/Samantha:** This person has bought into a particular worldview in his/her youth and has never modified it. She/he knows what is "right" and refuses to be open-minded. She/he had an early case of "hardening of the categories." Don't confuse this person with the facts! She/he wants everyone to believe what she/he believes. This person can be very irritating and invasive.

- **Rigid Roger/Regina:** This person over-reacted to early life teachings by parents-teachers-preachers, and has become very closed-minded and is threatened by alternative ideas. She/he doesn't like what was taught early on and has "thrown out the baby with the bath." She/he is often bitter, antagonistic, and feels threatened by different viewpoints. She/he is quite defensive, and often "shoots the messenger." This person often leads a self-destructive lifestyle.

- **Evolving Earl/Urlina:** This person continually examines beliefs, theories, and scientific findings. She/he is able to modify, change, or enrich previous ideas. This person looks at new discoveries and viewpoints to see if they can be additive. She/he is open-minded, without necessarily grabbing on to the latest fad of the times. This person welcomes debate, but doesn't need to "win." The sharing is a valuable exchange.

In which category do you think you fall? Have you changed or modified central tenets or beliefs of your earlier, perhaps naïve, life? What about other people in your life, in which category are they?

There is a need in our society for opportunities to discuss important ideas in a civilized, respectful and challenging manner. Religious, political, educational, moral beliefs and practices should continually be able to be discussed and evaluated as new knowledge and findings become available.

Personally, I am amazed at what I have learned and how I have changed since my parochial upbringing in Green Bay. An undergraduate Liberal Arts degree, seminary theological studies, doctoral psychology training, travel, and significant personal experiences have opened up rewarding vistas of knowledge as I seek my personal truths.

Where are you on your journey? Or have you not yet begun to walk down that path, staying "safe" in your Simple or Rigid world? (If you feel threatened or irritated by the previous sentence, the shoe may fit.) Do you know what you do not know? Are you willing to seek, to move on, to evolve? The questioning philosopher, Socrates, said, "The unexamined life is not worth living." I believe him, do you?

"Shoot The Messenger" Is A Defense Mechanism

If you don't like the message, "shoot the messenger." Have you ever shot the messenger? Been shot for delivering the message?

There are many types of defense mechanisms. They protect us from hurt; they also stop us from healing, growth, and, ultimately, love. . The defense mechanism of "shoot the messenger" emanates from the rationale that "the best defense is a strong offense." When the threat (message) hits too close to home, turn the tables on the person generating your defensiveness. You then are emotionally untouchable.

Effective change takes place when you are able to let down your defenses, hear the message, and have the courage to act on it if it has merit. The relationship is important here. Hopefully, the messenger has some credibility and trust to optimize your openness to the message. If the "messenger" is not a person who is trusted, the message probably will not be heard. There are some people who do take "pot shots" at another because of ulterior motives.

Some people "can't handle the truth." They would rather stay in a shallow safe oasis than risk opening up to truths and behaviors that could afford a richer and deeper connection with life and certain significant others. Denial and anger are two typical responses when it gets too close to "home." These people run away, often "shooting the messenger" for bringing up these uncomfort-table feelings and challenges.

The messenger, too, must have courage. It is not easy to "rock the boat" and say to someone things that make him or her defensive. You need to genuinely care for the person and/or have the responsibility to do so.

As a therapist I have had my share of "shootings" and runaways. Some have come back and said that they wish they had listened and dealt with the message. Others say they were not able then, but now are capable and ready to challenge the defenses that are blocking the next step in personal or relational growth.

In therapy I build trust so that people can hear the message and, hopefully, change what is not working. Some people stay in counseling as long as the focus is on someone else in their life who is making them miserable or that the communication stays superficial. These people want a "rent a friend" therapist who listens and supports. The problem with this type of therapist client/patient relationship is that very little change takes place – only feel good understanding for fifty minutes.

Are you open to hearing or giving the "message"? Do you get angry and "shoot the messenger"? Or are you in a run away, excuse making, denial mode? It takes openness and courage to give or receive one's "message."

May the messenger not be shot!

Everyone Has A Story: What's Yours? Willing To Share?

One of the privileges I have with my profession is to know the heart and soul of individuals through the telling of the stories of their lives. I am honored to be trusted for people to share the story of where they have come from, what their current situation is, and hopes for the future. As a confidante I listen with empathy and objectivity, without judgment. Each story is fascinating and stimulating. To be a trusted ally in helping a person, couple, or family make greater sense out of life is a meaningful way to contribute to society. I am grateful for the opportunity.

I would like to enlist your help. People need to talk in depth to another person and be heard and supported. I wish you would reflect more on your "story" and share it with people who are interested and will listen.

What do I mean when I ask you to reflect on your "story"? I mean the tale of your life. You are an interesting person and have much to share.

- Who were your parents? What were they like? Grandparents? Current status?
- Do you have siblings? What kind of relationship have you had? Currently?
- Where did you grow up? Moved where? Why?
- What schooling and training do you have? Good choices? Did you do well? Enjoyed?
- What have been your career choices? Accomplishments? Disappointments?
- Are you married? Happily? Previously? What happened?

- Do you have kids? What is the quality of your relationship with them?
- Who have been your friends? Lovers? (Be selective in sharing that!)
- Who has been there for you? Let you down?
- How have you changed over the years—physically, emotionally, spiritually?
- Who are the special people in your life currently?
- Regrets? Hopes?
- What do you worry about?
- What are you grateful for?
- What is your next challenge?
- What is one sentence that could describe how you want to be remembered?
- Are there other elements of your life, past and present, which are significant for you?

All of us need to create an environment where people can feel freer to share their "story," and where people ask others to talk about their life. Too many conversations are superficial and lame, leaving a void, an emptiness. People want and need to connect—in depth—with others. Tell your story; invite others to share theirs. Good things happen when one person lets another person know the depth of his or her life!

Carl Rogers, the father of Humanistic Psychology, had a wonderful quote: "That which is most personal, is most universal." Sharing the depths of our humanity helps all of us break down the barriers and prejudices that divide us and brings us closer to a uniting communion.

The Psychological Umbilical Cord From Your Parents Needs To Be Severed!

There are three "cords" in life that one needs to cut to attain human fulfillment:

1. The physical umbilical cord from your mother.
2. The psychological cord from each of your parents.
3. "You must cut the rope and be free," says Zorba the Greek

Examples of opportunities to cut the Number 2 "cord" are:

A. "My Dad is trying to talk me into joining him in his business, but I really don't want to. I'm afraid he's going to be mad if I don't."
B. "My mother expects me to call her every day. I feel guilty for not wanting to."
C. "I wish my parents would ask us what is a good time to visit us, rather than just telling us when they are coming, or just dropping in unannounced."
D. "We can't celebrate Christmas in our home, your parents expect us to go to Pittsburgh every year with the kids. I'd like to have our own Christmas in our home."
E. "My mother is constantly criticizing me the way I am raising my child."
F. "I want to go to the University of Georgia, but my Dad wants me to go to Georgia Tech because he went there."

The list could go on and on. Add your own. For those of you who are married, here is an inventory from *Couples in Healthy Families*: Respond to each statement on a scale of 1-5: 1 definitely false, 2 often false, 3 not false or true, 4 usually true, 5 definitely true.

1. My parents are supportive of my choice of partner.

2. My parents respect my right to make decisions on my own.

3. The time I spend with my family of origin is usually spent because I want to, not out of a sense of guilt or obligation.

4. I am very happy with the way my parents treat us as a couple.

5. I am very happy with the way my parents treat my partner.

6. I am very happy with the way my parents treat me.

7. My parents expect me to care for them in ways and amounts that I consider inappropriate.

8. If faced with having to choose on some issue or circumstance, I am more my spouse's partner than my parent's child.

9. I can comfortably invite my parents to our home.

10. I talk freely with my mother about things she does that make me angry.

11. I talk freely with my father about things he does that make me angry.

12. I express to my mother my love for her.

13. I express to my father my love for him.

14. I like the way my partner treats my parents.

15. My mother keeps a good balance between being available to help me and expecting me to run my own life.

16. I can count on my mother to say no to me if I ask too much of her.

17. My father keeps a good balance between being available to help me and expecting me to run my own life.

18. I can count on my father to say no to me if I ask too much of him.

19. My father makes no attempts to undermine my life with my spouse.

20. My mother makes no attempts to undermine my life with my spouse.

21. I spend satisfying one-on-one time with my mother.

22. I spend satisfying one-on-one time with my father.
23. My partner enjoys my family.
24. My partner feels welcomed and respected by my family.
25. I am waiting for my parents to change so my life with them will be better.

Can you relate to any of these situations? What kinds of emotions are felt with regard to your relationship with your parents? The emphasis here is that too many adults, young and senior, still FEEL—and ACT—like emotionally weak children with regard to their parents. They are afraid to confront their parent(s) and express what they really feel and want.

Often this timidity is the result of a two-pronged problem: a parent talks down to, orders, criticizes, the adult child. The adult child blindly obeys, excessively pleases, or cowers so as to not receive a parent's displeasure or rebuke.

Each person in these kinds of situations needs to throw this psychological albatross off his/her back—in a respectful manner. It is particularly necessary for a married couple to do this. I have encountered many examples where a wife feels second to her husband's mother or a husband feels his wife's mother is too involved in their marriage.

The psychological beginnings of independence are meant to begin during adolescence when a teenager starts to create his/her identity. If this is excessively stifled by parents, the adolescent will either meekly obey or rebel in some form or fashion. It is not easy to make this transition, but if it is not made the consequences for your personal and marital life are substantial.

In summary, the goal here is to grow up emotionally, become independent and switch your loyalty from being your parent's child to being your spouse's partner. Hope you have done it or are gearing up for the challenge to accomplish this growth stage. Cut the cord and dance free!

Rejection Hurts: Bounce Back With Rejuvenation

Have you heard the song 'I Don't' by Danielle Peck? There is a repeated refrain that says:

You say I should stay with you
that Jesus forgives you.
You pray that I will, but I won't.
The difference is
Jesus loves you, I don't

Blunt verbiage. This woman was over it with this guy. No more excuses and repeated apologies. Move on cowboy. Apparently this man deserved rejection based on his repeated transgressions.

Rejections happen, deserved or not. Some rejections are more gentle. The Seinfeld way that emphasizes "it's not you, it's me" would be an example (and if you believe that I would like to sell you some waterfront property in the Negev desert!). There are many forms of rejections, verbal and non-verbal. Perhaps you have received or delivered a few yourself. There is pain in rejection. What do you do with it? When rejected, some people cry, go to self-pity, get PO'ed, blame someone else, socially withdraw, eat or drink too much, or go out and "prove" how good she/he is by becoming promiscuous.

Rejection can shake your confidence. It can also serve as a wake-up call to change some behaviors that are not in your best interest. Here are a few steps to help you, or someone you care about, benefit from, and bounce back from rejection and begin a process of rejuvenation.

1. **Introspection:** Evaluate yourself with some objectivity. Perhaps someone else, who knows you well or is trained to perform this function, can assist you in this self-knowledge

endeavor. I will never forget the time when a man in therapy with me said, "Thanks, John, I didn't know what I didn't know." This person was open to knowing things about himself that he was not conscious of. We all have some blind spots. It is important to know what are our strengths and weaknesses. If you are open to seeing your faults you have a good shot at changing them. Awareness is the first step.

2. **Inner Resourcefulness:** Some people need constant OUTSIDE reinforcement as to their value as a human being. These affirmation needs may be in the way of continual compliments, being liked by everybody under the sun, empty sexual conquests, being the center of attention always at a gathering, etc. The goal is to feel better from the inside out, to realize your inner core is spiritual, therefore, good. Find and keep faith, where it serves you well. "Jesus loves you…" Remember the words of another song, "This little light of mine, I'm going to let it shine…" That is the task of each of us, to realize our unique gifts, the light we bring to others. That doesn't mean that everyone will see our light, appreciate our light, or find it the right color, so there still may be some rejection in store. But being rejected will not be so painful because you will not interpret it as being that you are not good.

3. **Support:** Find good people to hang around with, people that care about you, who will be there for you with support and needed guidance when asked for. There are so many good people in the world. Let them get to know you!

Second Chance "Do-Overs": Do What Differently?

Want to take a walk down memory lane—with the power to change some of your experiences along the way? This "walk" entails a look at significant people, events, and choices made by you or on your behalf. The "do-over" power gives you the opportunity to change or correct past events. Given your current insight, or lack of it, what would be different using your "do-over" power?

1. Let's start at the beginning—your parents. Would you choose the same ones? What would you have them do differently regarding the manner in which they got along with each other and raised you? How has this family experience affected you?

2. Would you change where you lived or how often you moved? If so, where would you move to?

3. What about your siblings and the interaction that you had with them? Pleasant memories?

4. Would you choose the same friends? What would you have them, or you, do differently?

5. Go to the same elementary and high school?

6. After high school would you make the same choice in regard to further education and/or experience?

7. Would you make different choices in regard to sex, alcohol, cigarettes, drugs, eating, stealing, fighting, etc.?

8. Would you choose the same career path? Modify any of it? Worked more? Less?

9. Would you live in the same locations as an adult? If not, where?

10. Would you live with the same people that you did along the line?

11. Would you choose again to marry the same person(s)? (Hint: say "yes, dear" to the spouse reading this with you!)

12. Would you parent your children the same way? What might you have done differently?

13. How have you chosen to continue a relationship with your parents, kids, exes, siblings, relatives, friends, etc.? Change any facet?

14. Would you do anything differently in regard to your religious participation?

15. Would you do anything differently in regard to your health? (Are you one of those saying, "If I knew I was going to live this long, I would have taken better care of myself!")

16. Would you have added more "fun" to your life? Traveled more?

17. Financially, would you have made different choices in regard to income production and investments?

18. Do you wish you had not said or done something to someone? Perhaps, should have said?

19. Are there other important areas of your life that you would like to have done something differently?

The purpose of this article is not to rue over choices made or even celebrate the wise choices, but rather to examine your life and see it in perspective. Perhaps such awareness arrived at may generate different choices in the future. You may be inclined to share your thoughts with some of the significant people of your past. There may be reunions to be shared, amends to be made.

What "Mask" Do You Show To Other People?

I'll admit it. One of the things I enjoy most about my career is the opportunity to see who a person truly is behind the mask. In almost every case I find that the core person is very special, vulnerable, and real. A profound connection takes place. I am privileged and I welcome the responsibility that goes with such an opportune sharing.

What is the "mask"? It can be described in superficial terms by "façade" or "game face." Or, it can be described psychologically. Carl Jung, prominent theorist, says that the mask reflects the "persona" of an individual. It is the image we present to the world designed to make a particular impression on others, while concealing our true nature.

The bottom line here is, who is the person behind the image presented? There are the smilers, the frowners, the glad handers, the cynical, the gregarious, the shy, the sarcastic, the combative, the hustler, the flirt, the pseudo intellectual, the arrogant, the pretentious, etc. If you had to put a label on your "mask," which one would it be? Have a different one? Some people have a variety of masks. What might someone else say in describing your "mask"(s)?

Many people don't have a clue about what I am talking about here because they don't understand how they present themselves as they amble through life. Some people have many masks as they become whoever is needed in order to be accepted by another. Others have a rigid pseudo image that they can hide behind. In either case you will not get to know the real person. Defenses take many forms. Superficiality is the boring result. Everyone has witnessed cocktail conversation where mask meets mask. Ho hum.

It is the quest of life to establish an identity—to know who you are and present yourself with inner and external congruence. "Be who you are!" Is the image presented reflective of your core self? The challenge is to be authentic while being open and vulnerable to another depending on the relationship and the circumstance.

In good therapy the "mask" is off. It is a very real experience, both for me and the client/patient. Defenses, walls, come down in the safe and nurturing counseling environment. This connection facilitates awareness of the deeper self and helps a person to be comfortable in one's own skin—coming from new-found strength—and relate to another in an authentic fashion.

There are many opportunities for being and sharing with other people. Parties, church functions, family and friend gatherings, and restaurant socializing all give us a chance to relate to others. May you use these occasions to put your best face/mask forward for the maximal benefit for you and the person(s) that you admit into your private world.

Let people know the person behind the "mask." As Stevie Wonder wrote in song: 'To know you is to love you.'

How Much "Baggage" Do You Carry? Lighten The Load!

One of the most rewarding, and painful, aspects of my role in therapeutic healing is helping people find, recognize, and constructively unload "baggage" that inhabits their psychological core being. This "baggage" is a heavy load and inhibits a person's ability to make good choices in life, both personally and professionally.

"Baggage"—what is that? "Baggage" is an accumulation of all the negative hurtful experiences of your life that were painfully inflicted on you by significant others in your life and/or what you did not receive in your life that you needed from these same significant people. Psychological imprints become imbedded in your brain and stifle optimal functioning. This "baggage" usually hides behind your defense mechanisms, especially denial, sometimes so hidden that you are not even consciously aware of it. But, make no mistake, the "baggage" is there! Everybody has some.

The difficult challenge for me and for the client/patient is to accurately identify the "baggage" by cutting through these defenses blocking access. Once the "baggage" is identified intellectually it has to be integrated emotionally. Emotions are the energy that drive your behaviors and affect your relationships. Each part of the process is important and difficult. Many people quit during the process. Oftentimes they can "own it" intellectually, but cannot connect with it emotionally. Usually these people use various forms of self-medication to block the connection.

For the most part the people I work with are intelligent, successful, rather well off. Yet many just don't get it. Thus they carry their baggage on and on as they hide behind self-destructive behaviors with excesses of tobacco, liquor, porn, eating, shopping, etc. Their interaction with significant people in their lives is to be either hypercritical and judgmental or to withdraw and be unavailable. Often these two opposites join together in a relatively dysfunctional manner. They also pass on this "baggage" to the next generation to carry. Surely you have witnessed that in other people.

So, what deters smart people from getting it? Why do they not unload this heavy and destructive "baggage"?

Fear. Fear of the unknown. Contrary to popular belief, most people do not want to know and feel their truth, their past painful experience. Their defenses keep them "safe" from this hurtful re-experiencing of yesterday's pain.

It is my clinical experience that people need to "feel it to heal it." This does not mean dwelling on or wallowing in past pain. No martyrdom necessary. Nor does it involve the "blame game." For the most part your significant others did the best they could. Unfortunately, they oft times did not have the capacity to do what was called for. The necessary catharsis enables a person to "move on" into a healthier and more emancipated life, free from emotional constriction or destruction. Better choices and a healthier lifestyle result. Relationships are safer and more rewarding.

Dumping "baggage" is not easy, but it surely worth the effort. Do you have some to leave behind?

Perseverance: Do You Have It? Encourage It?

You have probably heard and used the quote "Winners never quit. Quitters never win."

It is one of my favorites because it is a continual reminder to me about setting my goals and striving to reach them. (Being a stubborn Taurus helps a bit also!)

Perseverance is a state of mind. Like grit, it is a determination to accomplish one's ambitions, to reach the goal despite inevitable obstacles. It implies the ability to keep doing whatever is necessary to reach the set goal. It is not the same as self-discipline, which is the ability to refrain from doing something. The two are related. If one has to stay on track with perseverance, one needs to be able to have the necessary self-discipline to not waver or wonder off track.

In an interesting study at the University of Pennsylvania researchers found that perseverance, grit, is every bit as important as talent and aptitude in achieving success in schoolwork and other pursuits. Dr. Martin Seligman, director of the University's Positive Psychology Center says, "Unless you're a genius, I don't think you can ever do better than your competitors without a quality like grit."

Just as self-discipline is a related factor in perseverance, so, too, are other personal characteristics. Passion and optimism are wonderful attributes that help one be successful—and joyful in the process.

It is not easy for many people to find their passion. I remember my days at the University of Wisconsin when I needed to choose a major. I did not have a clue. I did not know myself well, never had a mentor, and was too busy partying with my fraternity brothers, including Steve Miller and Boz Scaggs. (That's thrown in for those of you who know their music. We had fun!) I chose economics out of the grab bag. Not a good fit.

It has taken many years, a few detours, reading, and reflection to find my passion, both personally and professionally. Passion lights the fires of successful living.

Optimism is another quality that fuels perseverance. To be able to see the possibilities, the potential for success without being dragged down by pessimism, is exciting and encouraging. Optimism is a necessary ingredient of faith and hope, spiritual qualities facilitating the drive to succeed in all aspects of life.

The title of this article asked you if you have perseverance and if you encourage it. And the answer is?

Besides your personal quest to add, or continue to have, perseverance as a part of your personal make-up, it is important to assist others in developing this attribute. This is particularly true for your children. Perseverance can be taught. One tip with kids, praise their effort, not their ability or outcomes. Recognize ability and outcome to be sure, but emphasize and reinforce the quality effort/perseverance they exhibited. And modeling perseverance is still the best way to teach your children. Kids usually grow into what they see their parents do.

For those of you who finished this article I appreciate your perseverance!

Becoming "Free": Reaching Your Full Potential

Freedom is a cherished word in our society. We live in the "land of the free." Freedom implies various things to diverse peoples. "Freedom" as referred to here is the freedom to be a psychologically, spiritually and behaviorally free person, capable of continually evolving into one's full potential. I have done workshops in the past on this topic in both community and church settings. I would like to share with you this process of becoming free.

The following quotes from two of my "mentors" are inspiration and direction for a person becoming "free."

"The truth shall make you free." - Jesus

"You must cut the rope and be free." - Zorba the Greek

An odd combination you might say, and you would be right, but stay with me.

Truth is "in the eye of the beholder." It ultimately is subjective based on one's perspective. If there was a totally provable "Truth," then everyone would believe the same thing. Each person must find his or her own "Truth" and live it out with integrity. To do this a person may have to "cut the rope" of whatever binds him or her and stifles growthful connection with self and other healthy beings.

The process I suggest includes eleven steps:

1. Understand your background. This means knowing your genetics and your personal experience thus far in life. This will bring you up to speed as to how you got to be the person that you currently are. This is called enculturation.
2. Know, value, and appreciate your many fine qualities and strengths.
3. Examine what fears, hurts, angers, and guilts that you may harbor.

4. Examine what negative behaviors you have that hinder your growth and connections with others.

5. "Let go" and quit lamenting yesterday's misfortunes. Live in the moment with an eye to the future.

6. Know your current state in life. What are your roles, responsibilities, and opportunities—personally and pro-fessionally?

7. Be aware of your needs and dreams and those of the people with whom you share life most deeply.

8. Let go of negative, toxic people in your life. You are shaped by the five people closest to you.

9. Design a doable plan for living and loving with more gusto, being all you can be without hindrance. This may involve shedding certain thoughts, traditions and beliefs while embracing new ones.

10. Commit to and energize the plan. Be responsible; make the hard decisions that may be called for. Connect with those who feed your soul and have your back. Seek out any appropriate professional help and possible medications that are needed to reach fulfillment.

11. Celebrate existentially, actualizing your full self, yet not reverting to being selfish. This is a delicate balance to be sure, but reachable for she/he who dares to "cut the rope" and find his or her personal "truth" and path in life—being free!

"Please Notice Me. Please Touch Me. I Need That!"

When I meet with couples and ask them what is missing in their relationship I hear many concerns, needs not met. Two of the more frequent complaints I hear are about being "noticed" and "touched" by the other. A deep sadness is inherent in these messages. What is this all about?

To "notice" your partner is to say, "You are very important to me." "I enjoy being with you." "That outfit really looks good on you." "Thanks for doing that." "How did your meeting go today?" "Would you like to go out Saturday night?" Etc. You are saying to that person that you are attuned to his/her presence, aware of what is going on in his/her life, and want him/her to know how special she/he is to you.

To be "touched" is to put your arm around him/her, hold hands, gentle caress or pat on the fanny, give a massage, gentle or passionate kiss, skin-on-skin cuddling, make love, etc. These acts are intimacy reach-outs—meeting the "touch" needs of your partner.

These are basic human needs, all part of a special connection you have with your partner. Giving this type of attention serves to enrich and deepen the relationship.

If such basic needs are not met, the impoverished spouse will go into some type of defense mode:

1. Dry up and withdraw, and probably become passive aggressive to show the underlying hurt and resentment.
2. Be angry and actively hurtful by word or action.
3. Go elsewhere to meet these basic needs.

As you are reading this, Respected Reader, what are you thinking and feeling? Does this apply to you and your relationship? Could you discuss this with your spouse or would it cause one or both of you discomfort? At this point are you ready to wrap the garbage with this article so it can disappear?

I would not be writing about this topic if I did not hear so much complaining about it in counseling sessions. Yes, this is a topic that is difficult to deal with and discuss with your partner. Yet the absence of being noticed and touched leads to a deep loneliness felt inside when a person allows these oft buried feelings to surface.

What is it in you that has closed you down from giving that special notice and touch to your partner? Have you been irreparably hurt so that you have shut down this capacity? Or is it that you have never learned how to give this gift? It is worth exploring.

Most all human beings have a deep capacity to love and be loved. How is such love best expressed? Watch a grandparent with his/her young grandchild. A pure, open, giving love is shown. Watch a person with his/her new puppy. How often I have heard a spouse saying that she/he wishes that she/he would be treated as well as the dog is by his/her spouse. Am I saying that a spouse should treat his/her partner the way she/he treats a grandchild or dog? Perhaps so. A good start would be to offer genuine welcoming smiles, expressed interest, tender touch, and genuine hugs. Want to try it?

Trust Can Be Rebuilt By Taking These Steps

Trust can be destroyed in many ways by a variety of people in many life situations. When trust is broken the violated one often puts up protective walls and establishes boundaries that say "Do not enter!" Such defenses may be expressed with angry push aways or hurt withdrawals.

Trust can be destroyed in marriages around such issues as money, sex, abuse—and more. Trust can be seriously damaged in families by bad parenting and irresponsible kids—and more. Trust can deteriorate friendships by certain hurtful verbiage or actions—and more. Trust can be violated by dishonest business and financial transactions—and more.

In some cases when trust has been broken the true character of the offender becomes clear. In such cases it may be wise to keep the wall up, the boundary maintained. The same holds true when irreparable damage has been done and the violated person feels that she/he is not willing, or capable, to be open to that individual.

There are many situations, however, where the victim of the trust violation desires to heal the relationship and re-establish trust with the dishonest trust-breaker who also wants to re-establish a healthier relationship.

In such situations where trust is to be renewed and the infractions healed, certain steps may be taken to give the best opportunity for success. A few of these would be:

1. An openness by both parties to re-connect
2. An apology by the trust violator
3. An acceptance of the apology by the violated one
4. Establish good communication that would clarify the process of healing and building trust

When I facilitate or mediate such a trust re-connection, I ask the violated one what she/he needs from the violator to begin the process of healing the wound and opening up again to that person. If the violator can agree to these conditions then the healing process can begin.

Such a re-building process takes time, sometimes a very long time. The desired, and agreed upon, conditions need to take place with consistency over a period of time. If this happens, the violated one can begin to lower the walls and slowly let the other in with some degree of trust.

Depending on the extent and the severity of the trust infraction, it may be wise to use a mediator who could move the process forward with the minimum display of anger, blaming or other negative verbiage and actions that could detour or destroy the process.

When trust has been broken the individuals need to search their souls to see if they really want to attempt the re-building of trust. Is a positive outcome desired? And possible?

In my practice I witness many a tarnished relationship where trust has been broken. I encourage each person to give it a try so that some healing may occur, especially if the situation necessitates some form of continued interaction. In most cases a healed relationship is a better outcome than staying distrustful.

Respected Reader, do you have broken relationships because of trust violations? Were you the victim or the violator? Do you want to work on re-building trust? It may be worth a try!

"Just Do The Next Right Thing": "Suit Up And Show Up"!

These are two of my favorite sayings. My kids have heard them often, along with "fake it 'til you make it"! And they do all three, of which I am proud. I first heard these first two expressions from the "Recovery Community." Do you know what that community is all about?

The "Recovery Community" is a support group for addicts— alcohol, drugs, sex, gambling, etc. Part of my earlier vocation as a priest and later as a psychotherapist has been working in concert with this recovering community. I have had many a heartwarming moment seeing the results of such dedication.

Many years ago I spent a Christmas Eve at an AA meeting. It was my first exposure to this group. I was invited by one of my parishioners who was an active member and wanted me to see firsthand the workings of this group—and add my "spirited" presence. Christmas Eve can be a very lonely night for many people who are not connected and participating with family. Many would be inclined to drink excessively if such an understanding support group was not available.

The "Recovery Community" has been a wonderful source of inspiration, guidance, and support for those who are struggling with some form of addiction. Besides the aforementioned addictions, others that have such groups are those who are addicted to over-spending, cigarettes, hyper-sexuality, and eating. People who suffer with such compelling addictions know that changing this negative habit is a day-to-day challenge. They say, and rightly so, "one day at a time," "just do the next right thing," and "suit up and show up!"

Hoping that you like music with a spiritual bent, I close with these words from the song 'The Next Right Thing':

"Caught myself worrying again today
Seems like it's always something, something I can't change.
I'm either looking back, haunted by regret
Or finding trouble with tomorrow that hasn't even happened yet.
Every day the choices just keep on comin' up
And I know it all comes down to fear, oh Lord.
And I surrender myself to what the future will bring.
Well, I'm just trying to DO THE NEXT RIGHT THING.
I'm just trying to DO THE NEXT RIGHT THING."

May the message be heard and practiced! "By their works you will know them." AMEN.

What Is Your "Achilles Heel"? Know It!

You have probably heard the expression "Achilles heel." Do you know what it means? Where it comes from? Implications for you?

In Homer's *Iliad*, Achilles was a Greek warrior, the best. Some thought him to be immortal. This "immortality" was linked, according to legend, to the fact that his mother, in an attempt to make him immortal, took Achilles to the Styx River and dipped him. She held him by one heel. The area where her fingers held him remained dry. As the heel was not touched by the protecting water, it was the one vulnerable place on Achilles. During the Trojan War, Paris, Prince of the Trojans, shot an arrow in the heel of Achilles. Because the heel was the one spot untouched by immortality, Achilles died. His one area of vulnerability lead to him downfall. (For the pop version of this tale watch the movie *Troy* starring Brad Pitt.)

In popular parlance your "Achilles heel" is your vulnerable spot—where you can be hurt. That vulnerable spot usually brings forth a defense (mechanism) to protect being hurt.

In my profession I continually look for, find, and help heal the psychological wound ("Achilles Heel") of a person. The defense protects—but it also blocks—the capacity to be whole and, therefore, open to connect more deeply with yourself and with a significant other.

A few examples might elucidate:

- Alan was neglected by his father, just didn't have time for him, as in the song, 'Cat's in the Cradle'. That sense of deep-rooted abandonment has resulted in a wound that brought forth a defense that Alan would not let a romantic interest develop for fear that it might lead to another abandonment.

- Barbara was sexually abused by a family member. Sexuality became associated in her mind with something painful and shameful, definitely not with loving. Therefore, she is somewhat disconnected from sex as a defense mechanism. A Pavlovian connection between sex and hurt leads to a shutdown of feelings and, perhaps, capacity.
- Carl had a traumatic experience in the military with a bomb going off nearby. The combination of comrade loss and the noise associated with this has left him vulnerable. He therefore overreacts to a loud noise and does not want to get too close to somebody for fear of another loss.
- Debra had a critical over-bearing mother. Therefore, she has developed a vulnerability in this area and has developed low self-esteem and has compensated (defense mechanism) by being an excessive pleaser who does everything right to make sure she is not vulnerable to criticism. She protects a deeper part of herself from ever being wrong. That protect-ing shell makes it difficult to get close to Debra.

I could go on forever in giving examples of people developing a shield, defense mechanism, from previous hurts to protect their "Achilles heel." Everyone has an "Achilles heel," or two, or three!

And yours, Respected Reader? What are your hurts and consequent vulnerability—your "Achilles Heel"? What defense mechanisms have you developed that impede a closer emotional attunement with yourself and another person? Are you ready to deal with it? Or, are you still in denial (another defense mechanism)?

To Be Happier STOP Doing These 10 Things Now!

You want to be happy, do you not? You try to be happy as much as you are able, do you not? You will welcome more insights on how to be happy, will you not? Okay, here goes. You need to STOP doing these things. These insights of Jeff Haden of *INC. Magazine* were sent to me by a friend. I share them with you, adding my own pithy comments.

1. **Blaming:** The blame game saps your energy and rolls you into negativism. Assume responsibility for what you can manage, make good choices, and avoid those persons that hinder your progress.

2. **Impressing:** Just be yourself. Your trappings of clothes, jewelry, other possessions or titles are just "things." They are not you. "Suit up and show up," without the need to impress.

3. **Clinging:** Do not stay stuck and cling to what you know when facing fears and insecurities. Let go and reach for a further goal. If you are not moving forward, you are falling behind.

4. **Interrupting:** For one thing, it is rude. Also, you are sending the message that you are not really listening to the person; you are just looking for the opportunity to say what you want. Focus on what they are saying and ask questions displaying your interest.

5. **Whining:** When you whine, it actually makes you feel worse. Don't talk about what's wrong. Spend that energy on making things better. Nobody wants to hear your whining. "Would you like some cheese with that whine?"

6. **Controlling:** Get real; the only thing you can control is yourself. If you find yourself trying hard to control other

people, you've decided that you, your goals, your dreams and opinions are more important than theirs.

7. **Criticizing:** It doesn't work! Everyone is different—not better or worse, just different. Appreciate the differences instead of the shortcomings and you'll see people—and yourself—in a better light.

8. **Preaching:** This is related to criticizing. Nobody wants to hear it, except maybe in church. It, too, like criticizing, involves judging. Get out of your pulpit!

9. **Dwelling:** The past is valuable for helping you learn from your mistakes. Learn, let go, and move on to create what is needed in finding a better way. You cannot move forward if your head is turned behind you.

10. **Fearing:** Everyone has fears moving forward. Just don't stay "frozen" in fear. De-thaw and get moving in a positive forward direction for whatever the next goal is on your agenda list.

Respected Reader, you probably do not do many of things, except for an occasional slip, but maybe this reminder will help you stay focused on creating a happier you—and thus, affecting the happiness of those around you!

Thirteen Reasons You're Not As Successful As You Should Be!

Are you as "successful" as you would like to be? Quick, give me a gut reaction without taking the time to analyze it. What comes to mind, and in what order? Is it your business or professional life? Is it your marriages(s)? Your parenting and/or relationship with your kids? Your sporting adventures and performances? A faithful steward in living a life of integrity? Avoiding pitfalls that take you down, physically, emotionally, financially, spiritually? The list could go on and on, but this gives you some starting points to help you evaluate how "successful" you are.

If you are not a superstar in everything you do, perhaps the following list of weaknesses will provide some insight that will enable you to rise to new heights! (This list comes from one compiled by Jim Kukral, with added commentary by yours truly.)

1. **You're lazy.** Face it; you are not giving your all to those areas where you deem you are not successful.
2. **You feel entitled.** Only a few people are a part of the lucky sperm club. Doubt that you are. Quit thinking you are owed something. You're not. Get to work.
3. **You're fearful.** Frozen in fear leads to the road not taken for success. Locate your fears and then slay them so that you can see what awaits you beyond fear.
4. **You are a negative person and/or you are surrounded by negative people.** Populate your life with positive, supportive people who believe in you and offer the support needed.
5. **You think too much.** You've heard the term "paralysis by analysis," have you not? There's a point to get in gear and do what needs to be done to execute success.

6. **You don't formulate appropriate goals.** You are not good at planning. You "play it by ear" and hope that magically something good will be forthcoming. "If you don't know where you are going, any road will take you there."

7. **You blame "they" for stifling your success.** There is no "they" out there that can stop you if you plan and execute wisely. You and you along can make your life successful in ways you desire.

8. **You don't have the "X" factor.** You're not good looking enough, bright enough, healthy enough, personality enough, etc. Jerks, idiots, and boring people can be just as successful as anyone else, in case you happen to fit such a profile!

9. **You're poor at time management.** Time wasters lose. Let me see your calendar and I will know why you are successful—or not. Your calendar should reflect your priorities. Using your time well has a lot to do with being a success.

10. **You spend too much time in media land.** You love social networking. It feels so good, but the reality is that more time needs to be devoted to other areas that pragmatically can lead to success.

11. **You don't see the big picture.** You think small. Successful people can see down the road, plan accordingly, and get it done.

12. **You don't really want to be successful.** You are an impractical dreamer. You talk big and deliver small. You aren't willing to pay the price or success. Change, go forward, make the dream a reality!

13. **You're not a believer.** You never really saw yourself as successful. You think that only "exceptional" people are successful. You should just "settle." Believe in yourself, it's a great starting point!

Well, Respected Reader, any of these points hit home. How many? I hope this reading hits home and helps you make the adjustments needed to realize your full potential and be the "success" you want to be!

21 Habits Of Happy People

"Do you want to be happy for the rest of your life?" There was a song entitled this many years ago. Pretty tacky lyrics but the title represents what most of us strive for. Trouble is, nobody gave us that personalized memo instructing us on how to do that. A number of writers, including me, write about this with some regularity. Most of us need reminders to do some basic things that are in our best interest, so here goes some more tips for you to consider. There is a blogger called mindopenerz (not a typo) that writes some good stuff. I am borrowing his 21 points, while adding my own twist to them. C'mon along and let's explore and/or be reminded of some good habits for becoming a "happy" person!

1. **Appreciate Life:** Be thankful that you are experiencing another day on the planet. Make the most of each day, seeking out beauty and not "sweating the small stuff."
2. **Choose Friends Wisely:** Surround yourself with happy, positive people who share your values and goals. They help you feel good about yourself and can lend a helping hand when called upon.
3. **Be Considerate:** Accept and respect those with whom you come in contact, yet keeping a boundary from those who may be hurtful.
4. **Learn Continuously:** Keep an active mind, seeking information and activities that keep you vital and help you avoid "hardening of the categories" and stiffening of the joints.
5. **Creative Problem Solving:** Don't throw yourself a "pity party" when challenging obstacles occur. Actively seek out answers and solutions that move you forward. A whole new positive opportunity may emerge.

6. **Do What You Love:** Ideally your day can be spent enjoying what you do, both vocationally and personally. See how you can max out both of these areas.

7. **Enjoy Life:** Learn to live life in the present, not bemoaning the past or living in fantasyland for the future.

8. **Laugh:** Don't take life or yourself too seriously. Yes, there are moments to focus on the serious stuff. Look for opportunities to laugh, or at lease ones that put a big ol' smile on your face!

9. **Forgive:** Holding a grudge just stores up negative energy within you. But also keep some physical and emotional distance from those who have, or might, hurt you. Forgive yourself as well. Guilt is debilitating.

10. **Gratitude:** Be appreciative of the good people and experiences in your life. Tell those special people how much they mean to you. Don't wait for the memorial service!

11. **Invest In Relationships:** Nurture and grow quality relationships. Some research says that you are a composite of the five closest persons to you. Choose well!

12. **Keep Your Word:** Integrity is important. Be a trustworthy person whose word means something. "Walk your talk!"

13. **Meditate:** Not just any type of meditation. Learn a type that calms your brain, healthfully affects your body, and results in a clearer creative mind.

14. **Mind Your Own Business:** Do not be a busy body, rumormonger, gossiper, judger, name caller. It diminishes you and invites others to negatively talk about you behind your back!

15. **Optimism:** This is a tough one for a lot of people. Seeing the "glass half full," expecting good things, steering clear of pessimistic negative thoughts, is a better way to life.

16. **Love Unconditionally:** I have a problem with this one. I believe there are conditions that are necessary for you to open your heart unconditionally. Cordiality is fine; love deserves reciprocity. It is naïve to think otherwise. It is a good way to get hurt. One exception is when your children are young.

17. **Persistence:** Do not give up. "Quitters never win and winners never quit." If something is worth doing, do it well, and "finish the drill." Closure has merit. One of my favorite sayings is, "just do the next right thing."

18. **Be Proactive:** This, like optimism is very hard for many. Many people are "wired" to be reactive. Proactive people create, make happen, what they want.

19. **Self-Care:** Take care of your body, your mind, and find a "spirit" that is positive, loving and helps you transcend the mundane.

20. **Self-Confidence:** Be all that you can be. Know your strengths and bring that self-awareness confidence to every situation.

21. **Take Responsibility:** Take responsibility for your life, your moods, attitudes, thoughts, feelings, words and actions.

Another of my favorite sayings is "suit up and show up."

Respected Reader, you CAN create happiness. Perhaps these reminders will help steer you in that direction. Certainly there are other factors to help you "be happy for the rest of your life," but add these to your repertoire for now!

Successful Ways To Create A Miserable Life

Many of my articles focus on creating a happy life, one in which a person can learn certain things, practice some new behaviors, and live more joyfully. I have come to understand, regrettably, that there are some people who choose to be miserable. It is their identity, their brand. Thus, I feel that I should give equal opportunity to those people and assist them to become even more miserable. I am aided in this endeavor by an excellent article by Cloe Madanes in the *Psychotherapy Networker*. I will highlight some of her suggestions and embellish them as best I can to help ensure that misery seekers will be successful in their quest.

1. **Practice Sustained Boredom:** "Cultivate the feeling that everything is predictable, that life holds no excitement, no possibility of adventure, that an inherently fascinating person like yourself has been deposited into a completely tedious and pointless life through no fault of your own. Complain a lot about how bored you are." Such a perspective and commentary will surely turn off most people toward you, thus facilitating a life of misery. Yawn!

2. **Give Yourself A Negative Identity:** "Allow a perceived emotional problem to absorb all other aspects of your self-identification. For example, if you feel depressed, become a "Depressed Person." ... Talk about it to everybody. ... Practice the behaviors most associated with being depressed, particularly when it'll interfere with regular activities and relationships." People then may feel sorry for you which can further enhance your state of misery. Play it to the hilt.

3. **Be Conflictual:** "Find a way to pick fights, especially with those closest to you. Be argumentative, critical, and condescending." Thus, you will be rejected and can feel

content that you have further enabled yourself to be a miserable person.

4. **Attribute Bad Intentions:** "Whenever you can, attribute the worst possible intentions to your partner, friends, and coworkers. Take any innocent remark and turn it into an insult or attempt to humiliate you." Whenever you can try to see how someone is trying to hurt you, screw you over, and reject you. This will help with your misery mission.

5. **Avoid Gratitude:** "Research shows that people who express gratitude are happier than those who don't, so never express gratitude. Counting your blessings is for idiots. What blessings? Life is suffering, and then you die. What's there to be thankful for?"

6. **Blame Your Parents:** "Blaming your parents for your defects, shortcomings, and failures is among the most important steps you can make. After all, your parents made you who you are today; you had nothing to do with it. ... Extend the blame to other people from your past." As long as you can dwell in the past and play the blame game, you can be assured that you will in no way move toward happiness. Misery is sustained.

7. **Don't Enjoy Life's Pleasures:** If you inadvertently find yourself enjoying anything or anyone in your life quickly change your thought to focus on something that is negative, wrong, or depressing.

8. **Ruminate:** "Spend a great deal of time focused on yourself. Worry constantly about the causes of your behavior, analyze your defects, and chew on your problems. This will help you foster a pessimistic view of your life. Don't allow yourself to become distracted by any positive experiences or influence."

Negative self-absorption is one of the keys ways to stay miserable. Cultivate this ability.

9. **Find Something Wrong At Every Opportunity:** Look for and find something wrong as much as possible, and be sure to mention it to anyone and everyone around. Most people will shun you because you are a negative person, a downer. In reality, misery does NOT like company. Enjoy your loneliness, miserable person.

Respected Reader, there are many more ways to develop a life of misery. You may well be an expert on this lifestyle. These, however, are good starting points to ensure that you can develop, practice, and maintain a life of misery.

It is my hope that this master guide will serve as a mirror for you to look into and determine if you have been creating a life of misery—that it is your identity. Or, perhaps, you will recognize that some of the things you are doing need to be changed should you desire to create a life of happiness. May your mirror accurately reflect currently and in the future who you are and assist you in becoming the person you want to be.

I hope you do not want to be a miserable person! (There is so much joy and goodness in the world to be enjoyed. May you add to it!)

Journaling Can Help You See Yourself And Your Life Better!

Journaling helps you live a better life. Why? Because, as one of my mentors, Socrates says, "The unexamined life is not worth living." A person that does not reflect on his or her life stays stuck in life, continuing to have the same thoughts and unfulfilling behaviors. As one of my favorite expression states, "If you don't know where you are going, any road will take you there." Journaling is a wonderful technique for reflection and consequent personal growth.

Ericson Ay Mires has stated five reasons why you should do journal writing.

1. Journal writing helps you have a better connection with your values, emotions, and goals.
2. Journaling improves mental clarity/helps solve problems/ improves overall focus.
3. Journaling improves insight and understanding.
4. Journals track your overall development.
5. Journals facilitate personal growth.

So, if you were to pursue journaling, how would you do it? Well, that depends on who you are. One's gender often reveals different focus, content, and styles. Some people write a lot—mostly women. Others write less, use bullet points—mostly men. Some people do it more religiously; others do it more sporadically.

Journaling is an opportunity to sit down, be with yourself, and reflect on your life—past, present, or future. There is no right or wrong way to journal. Whatever comes to your mind and out your writing instrument is what is right.

I invite my clients as a part of the therapeutic experience to journal. I give a very simple instruction. I ask clients to take some time, as often as they want, to write down what is going on in their mind and in their life. That may mean once a day, or once a week, or whatever. I ask them to write down a number somewhere between one to ten, with one being "the pits" and ten being "heavenly bliss." Once they have written the number then explain why that number reflects how they are feeling at that particular time.

I encourage clients to keep their journals. Over time these writings reflect a moment in their personal history. Often it is interesting to look back and see where they were in a particular moment in time. Has there been progress? Regression?

Give it a try in some fashion or another. I think you will find it additive to your life!

Personal Growth Involves "Shedding And Creating!"

A client of mine in her early twenties is in the process of finding her identity as she moves into the new developmental stage of young adulthood. She is very bright and determined to understand how she has become the young woman she currently is and who she wants to become as she moves forward in life. She has taken to heart a motto that I shared with her: "The unexamined life is not worth living." - Socrates.

Life evolving is about developmental stages—where you are currently in life—chronologically, vocationally, financially, and in your relational life. To evolve is to create. To create is to make choices that move you forward. Such choices involve trade-offs. Trade-offs involve cutting off of options.

To move forward then is to shed certain parts of your being that stifle your momentum. This may involve shifting or modifying some perceptions, beliefs, and practices. It takes courage and commitment to challenge the status quo and seek the next variation of who you could become.

One of my other "mentors," Zorba the Greek, offers this inspiring quote: "You must cut the rope and be free!" Personally speaking, I have cut some binding "ropes" that have held me back. Three in particular come to mind. One is spiritual, another relational, and the third is vocational. Each of these "cuts" have propelled me forward, creating more fulfilling joyous identity components. Each of these cuttings, however, involved facing significant fears to be overcome. "The truth shall set you free." I find it very satisfying when I examine my life, looking at options, facing my fears, making an informed choice, and courageously moving into a promising unknown. I feel free shedding the old me and creating my next step of a life worth living.

Respected Reader, have you continually examined your life, looking at possibilities, facing your fears, creating options, and choosing wisely while shedding yesterday's baggage? If you are doing so then you are creating the best you at this time of your life. You only have one life to live!

I continue to be inspired by clients such as this young lady who make the commitment to spend time and money to move forward into their best self for the developmental stage in which they exist. May you do the same and see what your next step may be!

Thirteen Things Mentally Strong People Don't Do

As a professional in the mental health field, I am continually trying to assist clients to become stronger mentally in order to become more successful in everyday living and in their relationships. Recently I came across a book by Amy Morin with the above quoted title that I thought was terrific and embodies many of the principles that I have tried to convey through my articles. I quote these things and add my own embellishment.

1. **They Don't Waste Time Feeling Sorry For Themselves:** No pity parties for these folks! You never have to say to them, "Would you like some cheese with your whine." Pity parties waste time, create negative energy, hurt your relationships, and stifles moving forward.

2. **They Don't Give Away Their Power:** People that give away their power become impotent and lack physical and emotional boundaries. I encourage people to know their strengths and come from that position going forward. If you don't own your power you stay stuck.

3. **They Don't Shy Away From Change:** To change is to grow and go forward. Morin lists five stages of change: pre-contemplation, contemplation, preparation, action, and maintenance.

4. **They Don't Focus On Things They Can't Control:** Know what you can control and what you cannot. Focus on what is possible and don't waste energy in fruitless efforts to go beyond the limits of your power.

5. **They Don't Worry About Pleasing Everyone:** When your self-esteem is based on how well other people like you, you will continue to be just "blowin' in the wind" of other

people's perspectives. You will not be centered, empowered, and moving in your own proper direction.

6. **They Don't Fear Taking Calculated Risks:** Morin suggests these self-answered questions: What are the potential costs? What are the potential benefits? How will this help me achieve my goal? What are the alternatives? Personally speaking, my two biggest "risks" have turned out to be incredibly successful, satisfying, and empowering. "No guts, no glory"—an old standby motto that still can make sense.

7. **They Don't Dwell On The Past:** This is one of my favorites. I say that you cannot move forward if your head is still turned backwards. You can't change the past, but you can learn something from mistakes made and move forward.

8. **They Don't Make The Same Mistakes Over And Over:** Mentally strong people accept responsibility for a mistake, learn from it, and create a plan to move forward.

9. **They Don't Resent Other People's Success:** Jealousy is a wasted energy, fruitless, and it takes you off course. You need to focus on creating your own path. Compliment those that are successful and perhaps learn from them as to how you may be more successful.

10. **They Don't Give Up After The First Failure:** Persistence, constantly reflecting on a better course, leads to success. A favorite quote of mine is "I don't lose, I learn."

11. **They Don't Fear Alone Time:** Morin states, "Creating time to be alone with your thoughts can be a powerful experience, instrumental in helping you reach your goals." Personally, I crave and utilize productively my solitude time. Beware of those dependent people who need to be with someone all the time.

12. **They Don't Feel The World Owes Them Anything:** Entitlement shackles true creativity and growth. Self-motivated people earn their successes and, thus, feel confident and empowered.

13. **They Don't Expect Immediate Results:** They have a willingness to expect realistic expectations and an understanding that persistence and grinding it out ultimately will bring success to a well-thought-out plan.

Well, Respected Reader, how mentally strong are you based on these benchmarks? Which ones are strengths of yours and which ones need some shoring up? These thirteen deserve to be posted in a conspicuous place for continued reminding!

Top Five: "Living A Life Without (Major) Regrets"— Younger People Take Heed!

One of my favorite mottos from my Socratic mentor is "The unexamined life is not worth living." I challenge myself in this manner and invite other people who want to live the fullest and happiest life possible to do the same. If you examine your life, both backwards and forwards, you probably say to yourself, "I wish I had not done that," whatever "that" may be. Everyone has some of them, hopefully none too catastrophic in impact. And going forward, what are areas to be "examined" that involved life choices that could lead to fulfillment or regret?

Dr. Kari Plummer, Professor of Human Development, at Cornell University has written an intriguing article entitled "Living a life without (major) regrets." Over the past ten years he has surveyed around 2000 older people. He asked these elders this question, "What can younger people do now to avoid having regrets at your age?" The results were interesting and may shed light on how to make life decisions, big and small.

Here are the results—the top five recommendations by these thoughtful elders.

1. **Choose A Mate With Extreme Care:** The elders felt that this was the most important decision a human being makes. They say, "We are not careful enough." They say, "Question the decision, then question it again, or you may be in for deep and serious regrets." Respected Reader, do you have any doubt as to why I chose this topic to write about? I truly believe that your marriage is the most impactful event in your life. Thus "due diligence" is so important. I'll say it again—too many people spend more time and money

researching a car, house, or other significant investment than they do a potential life partner. Incredible!

2. **Always Be Honest:** Elders felt that honesty is an indisputable core value. Dishonesty was mentioned over and over as a source of profound regret. To avoid later life remorse, "Tell the truth and don't cheat anybody."

3. **Travel More:** Do it now as much as you are able. Elders say that when your traveling days are over, you will wish you had taken one more trip.

4. **Worry Less:** Elders deeply regret wasted worrying time about things that never happened. "Worry wastes your life," said one.

5. **Say It Now:** Elders emphasize this lesson either because they were grateful that they spoke their piece while there was still time, or because they profoundly regret not having done so. "Send flowers to the living. The dead never see them!"

Surely there are other possible regrets but these are some of the major ones for most people. May this message heighten your awareness, Respected Reader, of potential regrets that you may have should you leave this planet earlier than you were expecting!

Do You Strive To Be An "Authentic" Person? Know What That Looks Like?

I am fascinated by life changes, the developmental process and choices an individual makes along the journey of life. I take seriously one of my mottos, which is the Socratic dictum of "the unexamined life is not worth living."

Looking back at my developmental history I "woke up" as I was graduating from college. The "real world" was staring me in the face and I was searching for my next step. I became aware that my major in Economics was not a fit for me going forward. So what was? I realized that my life needed to have meaning at a deeper level and that I wanted to connect profoundly with people in a way that would move them forward. I did not understand it at the time but I was searching for my authentic self. What the deuce does that mean?

The Merriam-Webster dictionary defines authenticity as the quality of being real or genuine. The essence or core of your being must be realized and expressed. You are called to be the fullness of your potential being. My circuitous journey has led me through a few detours but I've always landed on my feet going forward to this wonderful time in my life.

In my search to be "authentic" (a work in progress!) I have been guided and motivated by some of the following descriptors of what to do and what not to do. I am taking this occasion to remind myself and invite you to be an authentic person. May the following be helpful.

1. They aren't afraid to express their opinions even if they are different from the majority.

2. They are driven to action by the inner self rather than external societal triggers.

3. They choose a career path that they enjoy.

4. They don't fear taking a path in life that not many travel. They find it exhilarating.

5. They fall in love with themselves before they fall in love with anyone else.

6. They don't need others' affirmations. "What you think of me is none of my business."

7. They want friends and partners who value deep conversations and serious emotional connection.

8. They follow their heart.

9. They don't wish ill will on others. They desire others to be happy.

10. They see the soul, the whole person, not just the outer appearance.

11. They allow their fellow human beings to show their true selves.

12. They are perfectly happy in their own company.

13. They value experiences over things.

14. They make the best out of situations.

15. They don't judge or criticize others.

16. They talk less and listen closely, exploring the depths of others.

17. They don't complain and they take full responsibility for their lives.

18. They have high self-esteem, confident in themselves.

19. They try to support others.

20. They don't dwell on the past.

21. They don't blame others for their mistakes.

22. They don't get jealous of other people's successes.

23. They have an open mind to new discoveries and understandings.
24. They avoid toxic people.
25. They see the unity and connectedness of all life.

Respected Reader, is being authentic important to you? If so, how well are you doing relative to this list? As for me, I've got a ways to go but I'm gaining on it!

It Is Important To Know Two Core Components Of Your Personality

When I work with people doing therapy, coaching, or career evaluation, I try to help a client/patient understand his or her core personality. By this I mean a basic style of interacting with other people, emanating from their core nature. For the sake of this writing I will focus on two components and the variance within each. The two component factors are *Controller-Pleaser* and *Emotional Expression-Retention.* These factors greatly influence how your personality affects your personal relationships and career choices. They are mostly genetically generated with experiential influences.

Do you have a Controller or Pleaser personality component? The Controller personality person has a take-charge style in various facets of his life. The Controller person typically is pro-active toward life, usually "Type A." She/he makes things happen in a way that allows him/her to be safe, not vulnerable, and productive. Like all personality components there are degrees of control manifest in such a person ranging from very aggressive to assured assertiveness. Conflict and confrontation are usual byproducts of this component.

The Pleaser personality is very different. This person, usually "Type B," has more of a reactive style. She/he wants to be accepted and liked. She/he tends to be non-assertive and works hard to avoid conflict or confrontation. She/he tends to get along well with most everybody.

The second personality component factor focused on here is the emotionally *Expressive* and *Retentive* types. The Expressive type usually is present more in the Control personality. This person tends to get his or her emotions out no matter what. The intensity of expression will vary. This person will readily display his or her anger and, occasionally, tears. You know where this person is coming from!

The emotionally Retentive person is vastly different. This person usually is associated with the Pleaser personality. She/he tends to hold in his or her emotions. It is difficult to know the emotions hidden within this person. She/he shies away from anger and is more inclined to shelter feelings of sadness/depression or fears/anxiety.

These factors, Controller-Pleaser, Expressive-Retentive, are not inherently healthy or unhealthy, good or bad. Depending on where they are on the continuum, each person will reveal the productive or destructive elements of each factor. To be in control without being controlling has value. To be pleasing without denying your needs works well. To be expressive without blowing another away is good style. To be able to restrain negative or harmful expressions is wise.

These personality core components are two of the most important and impactful of your being. It is important for you to know them because they significantly influence your relationships, especially romantic, as well as career direction. In one session with you I can explain which ones you are, as well as the implications for your life.

Bottom line, be all you can be. Bring the best out of what your nature has provided. "To thine own self be true!"

To Succeed You Need To Do These Twenty "Hard Things"!

This I believe. Most people want to lead a successful life. Success is defined by each person. Your "success" may not be my "success." However, each life of success involves doing certain things. I try to write about such efforts in various categories in my articles. Today I am sharing a perspective offered by Marc Chernoff. His writing, entitled "20 Hard Things You Need To Do To Be Happy," mentioned the following twenty. I think happiness and success are intertwined, so I am focusing on the perspective of reaching success. And, yes, these things can be hard, but mediocrity is not acceptable. Chernoff says these "hard things" include the things no one else can do for you and that may even frighten you to do. I add my perspective to Chernoff's.

1. **You Need To Take Small Chances Every Day:** With a perspective of taking chances you will peck away at any fear that may inhibit you.
2. **You Need To Worry Less About What Other People Think Of You:** One of my favorite all time expressions is "What you think of me is none of my business." Chameleon personalities that turn whatever color is needed to be liked by another are not authentic and cannot be trusted.
3. **You Need To Ignore What Everyone Else Is Doing And Achieving:** Be your best self, developing your talents to the fullest, and get on with your successes.
4. **You Need To Invest In Yourself Even When No One Else Is:** Prioritize your needs, develop a daily to-do list, and vote for yourself (without being selfish).

5. **You Need To Walk The Talk:** Talk is cheap. Take responsibility for making your goals a top priority. Do the grunt work.

6. **You Need To Put Your Heart Into Your Work:** Find your passion where possible and let that passion fuel your drive to success.

7. **You Need To Deliver Results, Even When Making Excuses Is Easier:** Bottom line is "git 'er done!" Crybabies and blamers do not succeed—not your style.

8. **You Need To Make Mistakes And Look Like A Fool Sometimes:** I'm not very comfortable with this one. Yes, you will make mistakes and sometimes look like a fool, but I'm not sure you "need" to do this or that it always happens. Here, I like this phrase, "I don't lose, I learn." Mistakes are just a part of the learning curve.

9. **You Need To Let Go Of Yesterday's Struggles:** With your head turned backward it is hard to move forward, especially loaded down with that negative energy. Turn the page and create a new and successful chapter.

10. **You Need To Refrain From Feeling Sorry For Yourself:** Pity parties serve no purpose. Mourn, let go, move on. Get the support and advice where needed to do so.

11. **You Need To Toughen Up:** Evolution is all about survival of the fittest. The weak fall apart and away. That can't be you.

12. **You Need To Fight Hard For What You Believe In:** If your goal is worthwhile you need to put that extra effort into attaining in. Be sure you know what you believe in and then develop the passion to go for it.

13. **You Need To Be Patient:** Sometimes you can't push your goal ahead if the time is not right. Readiness is a necessary component for moving forward. Thus, patience is needed.

14. **You Need To Take Control Of Your Thoughts Before They Take Control Of You:** This is one of my favorites. I practice and teach this. You can do much to control your thoughts which affect your feeling which affect your behavior.

15. **You Need To Be Positive:** Stay away from negative thoughts and people. Being positive and optimistic greatly raises the probability of success.

16. **You Need To Spend More Time With The Right People:** Some research states that you are a composite of the five people closest to you. Choose wisely.

17. **You Need To Stand Up For Yourself:** Be assertive without being aggressive. Learn how to "vote for yourself" without being selfish. Shrinking violets fade away and lose.

18. **You Need To Forgive Everyone Who Has Wronged You:** Carrying around the negative energy of resentment just depletes you, but also develop a boundary from such people so that they may not do it again.

19. **You Need To Reach Out And Help People:** Being cared for and caring for others go hand in hand. Activate your heart and reach out and touch.

20. **You Need To Be Present Enough To Enjoy Your Journey:** Being present, focused, and attuned lead to greater connection within yourself and a deeper union with others.

Respected Reader, what is your reaction to these mandates? Why don't you give yourself a score between one to ten (ten being the highest) and rate yourself on each. Perhaps even ask someone who knows you well to give their opinion.

12 Lessons You Learn Or Regret Forever

I bring a particular philosophical perspective to life. It begins with the challenge to be the best person I can be, to develop my talents to their fullest extent. I want to experience all that life can possibly present. I want to give back. I want to live in such a way that I have no regrets. To live this life I try to continually learn about what it takes to "max out" on the short journey that I have in this world. I truly believe the Socratic statement that "the unexamined life is not worth living."

That said, I recently read an article that fit nicely into the perspective above. The article is entitled "12 Lessons You Learn Or Regret Forever." It was written by Dr. Travis Bradberry. You can understand why the title caught my attention, and, hopefully, catches yours, Respected Reader. The intent of the article is to assist the reader to be successful. The "Lessons" follow, with added commentary by this writer.

1. **Confidence Must Come First:** It takes confidence to reach new challenges. People who are fearful or insecure tend to stay within their comfort zones. But comfort zones do not expand on their own. Self-doubt stifles.

2. **You're Living The Life You Created:** You are not a victim of circumstance. Don't play the victim card. You can create the future you want. It is up to you to overcome where you are stuck and any obstacles in your way.

3. **Being Busy Does Not Equal Being Productive:** Success does not come from sheer movement and activity. It comes from focus on goals, time management, and prioritized efforts.

4. **You're Only As Good As Those You Associate With:** This is a big one. You need to associate with those people who inspire

you, people who make you want to be better. Shed those people who drag you down in any shape or form.

5. **Don't Say Yes Unless You Really Want To:** Saying no is a challenge for many people pleasers. Stick to your guns, your plan, your direction. Be able to say no to that which interferes with your goal.

6. **Squash Your Negative Self-Talk:** Negative self-talk is self-defeating. If you are not your own champion you become less capable of bringing out your best to a situation. Pessimists tend to do this to themselves. Optimists are their own cheerleaders. "Go self!"

7. **Avoid Asking "What If?":** "What if" throws fuel on the fire of stress and worry, which are detrimental to reaching your goals. Focus on realistic achievable goals without the detour of "what if."

8. **Schedule Exercise And Sleep:** Productive lives use good time management based on priorities. First, exercise. Exercise lowers stress and gives more energy to reach goals. Doing this regularly leads to more self-confidence and more competence socially, academically, and job performance. Sleep is necessary to get rid of toxic proteins in the brain which impair your ability to think clearly. It helps the brain reconfigure for optimal functioning.

9. **Seek Out Small Victories:** Small victories build new androgen receptors in the areas of the brain responsible for reward and motivation. Thus, confidence increases and eagerness to take on new challenges builds.

10. **Don't Seek Perfection:** Perfection does not exist. If you choose it for a goal you will continually be disappointed and have a sense of failure. Thus, your confidence, and will to go after it, will dwindle. When you miss the mark, say to

yourself one of my favorite sayings, "I don't lose (fail), I learn!"

11. **Focus On Solutions:** Be positive and be pragmatic searching for solutions that work. Doing this creates a sense of personal efficacy that produces positive emotions and better performance.

12. **Forgive Yourself:** When you get down on yourself and don't forgive yourself for mistakes made, you allow negative thinking and emotions to continue to affect your capacity for excellence. Self-esteem and confidence diminish. You owe yourself more. Love yourself and the ability to forgive yourself increases.

I hope the above "lessons" speak to you, remind you, and increase your ability to live them out with some degree of consistency. It is worth the effort!

Successful People Give Up These Things!

Have you ever met anyone who did not want to be successful? Doubt it. Have you ever met anyone who was not successful and did not know how to achieve it? Probably. Personally, I realize that the more I know, the more I know how much I don't know. Thus, I am continually searching for ways to maximize my potential to be all that I can be. I share a perspective presented by educator Zdravko Cvijetic with my added commentary.

Successful people give up:

1. **Unhealthy Lifestyle:** "Take care of your body. It's the only place you have to live." - Jim Rohn. I would add, take care of your brain. Thus, maintain a healthy diet and get a lot of physical and mental exercise.

2. **Short Term Mind Set:** Successful people set long-term goals and then develop short-term habits to help them reach their goals.

3. **Playing Small:** We are all meant to shine. If you never try and take significant opportunities, or let your dreams become realities, you will never unleash your true potential. Think big and get after it!

4. **Your Excuses:** "It's not about the cards you're dealt, but how you play the hand." -Randy Pausch. Successful people know they are responsible for their life, no matter their starting point, weakness, and past failures. Excuses are a cop out and prevent the efforts to succeed.

5. **Fixed Mindset:** Successful people continue to challenge what they know by continuing to acquire new knowledge, learn new skills, and creatively evolve into the fullness of their being. They do not have "hardening of their categories."

6. **Believing In The "Magic Bullet":** There is no easy answer, easy way. Overnight success is a myth. Successful people know that

making small continual improvements every day will be compounded over time and give the desired results.

7. **Perfectionism:** Fear of failure, or perhaps success, often prevents people from taking the risks, making the effort, to reach their goal. They think that they have to get it perfect; thus they don't get after it. Get started with your plan and keep plugging away at it and it will continue to come into fruition.

8. **Multi-Tasking:** "You will never reach your destination if you stop and throw stones at every dog that barks." - Winston Churchill. Successful people are focused on the goal, minimizing distractions. They are fully present and committed to the primary committed task.

9. **Need To Control Everything:** "Some things are up to us, and some things are not up to us." - Epictetus. Detach from the things you cannot control and focus on the ones you can.

10. **Give Up On Saying Yes To Things That Don't Support Your Goals:** Successful people know that to achieve their goal they must be able to say NO to certain tasks, activities, and demands from other people.

11. **Toxic People:** This is a big one. "You are the average of the five people you spend the most time with." - Jim Rohn. People we spend time with, add up to who we become. Move on from those who stifle your growth and connect with those who may well be ahead of you so that you can move forward faster.

12. **Need To Be Liked:** "The only way to avoid pissing off people is to do nothing important." - Oliver Emberton. Remain authentic, committed, improve, and bring value and substance to what you do. "What you think of me in none of my business." is a good motto.

13. **Dependency On Social Media And Television:** "The trouble is, you think you have time." - Jack Kornfield). Time management is

important in order to be successful. Too much social media and TV time can be distracting and slow your progress toward achievement.

This list is not meant to be exhaustive. It is a snapshot, a perspective to think about if SUCCESS is your goal—what that means to you personally. What areas are there for you to focus on in order to be "successful"?

10 Mistakes Smart People Never Make Twice!

Ever made a mistake? Repeated it? Most of you—and me—have done so. Perhaps we just need to get smarter. According to prolific writer, Dr. Travis Bradberry, "smart" people never make a mistake twice. Who are the "smart" people?

Researchers from the Clinical Psychophysiology Lab at Michigan State University found that people fall into two groups when it comes to making mistakes: those who have a "fixed mindset" ("forget this, I'll never be good at it") and those who have a "growth mindset" ("wake up call! Let's see what I did wrong so I won't do it again"). Those with a growth mindset acknowledge their mistakes and use them to get better. They have the commitment and tools in place to learn from their errors. Those with the fixed mindset are bound to repeat their mistakes because they try their best to ignore them. And which type are you, Respected Reader?

Dr. Bradberry's tips on how to not repeat mistakes. If you want to get "smarter" embrace the following directives.

1. **Believing In Someone Or Something That's Too Good To Be True:** Naivety and lack of due diligence can be catastrophic. I remember making a foolish stock investment years ago that turned out to be a dud. A stockbroker near my office was all hyped about it—and I bought in. The stock sunk, as did my trust in him. Did not use him again and have since researched much better my stock choices.

2. **Doing The Same Thing Over And Over And Expecting A Different Result:** Famous Einstein quote. Smart people know that if you want a different result, they need to change their approach, even when it's painful to do so. I see this in my practice when certain people keep dating and marrying the same type of people—and failing.

3. **Failing To Delay Gratification:** This is particularly true during these times of instant news and communication. Smart people know that you have to put in the hard work, whether it be in career or personal relationships, in order to get the reward.

4. **Operating Without A Budget:** Budgets are built on analysis, commitment, and discipline. Such traits are necessary for any worthwhile goal.

5. **Losing Sight Of The Big Picture:** Getting caught up in details, needing instant gratification, not adequately seeing the ultimate goal lead to failure. "Keep your eye on the prize!"

6. **Not Doing Your Homework:** Shortcuts don't work. You must pay the price, do the grunt work, get in the trenches, in order to get the desired result.

7. **Trying To Be Someone Or Something You're Not:** This is a big one. Fake leads to failure. Authenticity and integrity, being real, are the core of who you are. Display with openness and confidence.

8. **Trying To Please Everyone:** It doesn't work. You become a chameleon with no core of essence. You must know who you are and live it out with integrity and consistency.

9. **Playing The Victim:** This is a form of manipulation by a weak person. By trying this tactic you unwittingly give up your power—and that makes no sense.

10. **Trying To Change Someone:** People change only when they want to and have the wherewithal to accomplish it. You cannot "fix" someone. Instead, built your life around genuine, positive people that can synergize with you into moving forward.

I leave you with this favorite quote of mine from Nelson Mandela: "I never lose, I either win or I learn."

Advice From Old People: Listen Up, Young Uns!

Whether you are young or old, the following is sage advice. You might want to read, cogitate, incorporate, and act on them. If you choose not to, perhaps there is a reason—or maybe you are just not old/wise enough! I found this list on the internet offered by "derodave," whoever he is. It is a great compilation. I will add some commentary for your consideration.

1. "The most important person in your life is the person who agreed to share their life with you. Treat them as such." Yes, Respected Reader, this is so true. I have screamed this for years. Put your relationship first. That person will affect your ultimate happiness more than any other person/situation.

2. "You might live a long life or you may live a short one—who knows. But either way, trust me when I say you're going to wish you took better care of yourself in your youth." It is never too late to do your best to be in the best shape you can be at this point in your life.

3. "Stuff is just stuff. Don't hold on to material objects; hold on to time and experiences instead." Experiences, especially shared with people you love, are so much more important, and last forever in your heart and mind.

4. "Jealousy destroys relationships. Trust your significant other because who else are you supposed to trust." If you are jealous of, and cannot trust, your partner, you are in big trouble. Fix or get the hell out!

5. People always say, "Make sure you get a job doing what you love." But that isn't the best advice. The right job is the job you love some days, can tolerate most days, and still pays the bills. Almost nobody has the job they love every day." If you think otherwise you are living in La La land!

6. "If you are being overwhelmed by life, just return to the immediate present moment and savor all that is beautiful and comforting. Take a deep breath. Relax."

7. "Years go by in the blink of an eye. Don't marry young. Live your life. Go places. Do things. If you have the means or not. Pack a bag and go wherever you can afford to go. While you have no dependents, don't buy stuff. Any stuff. See the world. Look through travel magazines and pick a spot. GO!" Yes. When I was 21, I traveled to 13 countries in Europe, sleeping in the back of a VW Beetle! Slept in a graveyard in Israel. No money! Learned a lot about people, different cultures, and about myself!

8. "Don't take life so seriously. Even if things seem dark and helpless, try to laugh at how ridiculous life is." Laughter is the cure for many a perceived problems. Find a way to incorporate it into your lifestyle.

9. "A true friend will come running at 2 A.M. Everyone else is just an acquaintance." True wisdom. "Who loves ya?!

10. "Children grow up way too fast. Make the most of the time you have with them." Wow, how true. Parents, don't miss the message of the song, 'Cats in the cradle,' by Harry Chapin. You will get payback for failing to be the best parent you can be.

11. "Nobody dies wishing they had worked more. Work hard, but don't prioritize work over family, friends, or even yourself." A balanced life is never easy, but priorities are a starting place. Look at your calendar and see how much time is spent on various endeavors.

12. "Eat and exercise like you're a diabetic heart patient with a stroke—so you never actually become one." Good nutrition and exercise are core elements for optimizing a healthy life.

13. "Maybe this one isn't as profound as the others, but I think it is important. Floss regularly; dental problems are awful." All right, all right, I'll keep trying! I know it is good for me.

14. "Don't take anyone else's advice as gospel. You can ask for advice from someone you respect, then take your situation into consideration and make your own decision. Essentially, take your own advice as my advice." Please get a second opinion! Most people think they know more than they do. I like the quote, "I didn't know what I didn't know." Then own it and act.

15. "The joints you damage today will get their revenge later. Even if you think they've recovered completely. **Trust Me!**" I am enjoying my new knee, while trying to keep my elbow and shoulder tears from advancing anymore. It's been worth it, however!

16. "We have one time on this earth. Don't wake up and realize that you are 60 years old and haven't done the things you dreamed about." Listen to Harry Chapin's song, 'As Dreams Go By' as a reminder. Carpe diem!

17. "Appreciate the small things and be present in the moment." To be existentially present to savor all that life presents is a gift. Hope you open it!

18. "Pay your bills and stay the hell out of debt." Do you need a reminder from Dave Ramsey? You know of him—correct?

19. "If you have dreams of being or doing something that seems impossible, do it anyway." Not sure I buy this at face value. If it is truly "impossible," don't do it, but if it just seems "impossible," explore the possibility and you may find a way. Don't be a person who gives up too easily.

20. "When you meet someone for the first time, stop and realize you know nothing about them. You see race, gender, age,

clothes. Forget it all. You know nothing. Those biased assumptions that pop into your head because of the way your brain likes categories are limiting your life and other people's lives." To be open to all people as a starting point is a better way to live. Discover the depth of another by reminding yourself of this Carl Rogers' quote, "That which is most personal is most universal."

Well, Respected Reader, young or old, what do you think of these "pearls of wisdom"?

8 Warning Signs That You Are Emotionally And Mentally Exhausted

Life can get hectic. You are going in a thousand directions, sometimes feeling that you are not really accomplishing anything. It can wear you down. Emotional and mental exhaustion may have taken over. It is worth checking this out. Stephanie Reeds has written a checklist regarding this. I present them to you with my added comments.

1. **You Are Easily Irritated:** Everything seems to get on your nerves. Agitation and anger are more present than what is warranted.

2. **Your Motivation Levels Are Dropping:** You just don't want to do much. Everything is a major chore. Your confidence level drops along with motivation.

3. **You Are Experiencing Anxiety Attacks More Than Usual:** As your confidence dips your stress goes up. This heightened stress can lead to greater and greater anxiety, ultimately leading to anxiety attacks.

4. **You Have Trouble Sleeping:** You may have difficulty in getting to sleep because of your exhausted mental state. Or if depression is present, and it usually is, then you may be sleeping a lot. Sleep can be an unhealthy escape in this situation.

5. **Meaningless Things Upset You:** Smallest interactions and conversations can upset you. You are raw emotionally and tend to take things personally, often catastrophizing such situations. You make things bigger than they actually are.

6. **You Feel Dizzy And Nauseous:** Feelings of dizziness, headaches, nervous beating of the heart, upset stomach all are possible outcomes from built up mental exhaustion.

7. **You Feel Like Crying For No Reason:** All this emotional turmoil wears down your resistance. You just want to sit down and cry from this overload.

8. **You Start To Feel Detached:** This buildup starts to make you feel numb. Your senses are less aware. You just want to isolate. You are not connectable in this state.

Respected Reader, do you have any of these symptoms? Or are you in denial? Ask someone who knows you well for his or her opinion of your well-being. This is serious stuff, and if you are experiencing such emotional and mental exhaustion, address it with a competent psychotherapist. A mental health professional can help you figure out why you are in this state and how to get back to a healthier more emotionally balanced life.

15 Traits Of An Emotionally Mature Person

Maturity, what is it? How defined? You've heard the expressions, "He's so immature" or "He's so mature for his age." This writing seeks to characterize the emotionally mature person. I am guided by the fifteen traits listed by a blog entitled "Conscious Rethink." I will embellish these descriptions with my own thoughts.

1. **Self-Awareness:** Essentially, self-awareness is about building up an understanding of your personality, its strengths and weakness, its potential and limitations, and every little nuance. This means you take the time and develop the means to raise your consciousness to a level to be able to do that. Another trusted person's description of you may assist in developing this capacity.

2. **Self-Control:** Building on self-awareness you are better positioned to exert more self-control. You can better understand urges that build up in you and develop the restraint to behaviors that are self-destructive or damaging to others.

3. **Accountability:** You take a proactive stance in your life. You develop goals and progress toward them, willing to be accountable for your commitment and actions.

4. **Humility:** You don't have the need to put yourself above others. You are not arrogant or boastful. You respect others and treat everyone fairly.

5. **Self-Acceptance:** You own who you are, with your strengths and weaknesses. You do not live in the past or blame the past for your shortcomings. You move forward, challenging yourself to be the best person that you can be.

6. **Gratitude:** You appreciate the good things that exist in your life. You are grateful to be in a position in your life that you can read this and appreciate the blessings in your life and the capacity to continue to create a wonderful life.

7. **Compassion:** When you are grateful you usually also develop the capacity to empathize, have concern for others, and do what you can to help others.

8. **Being Other-Centered:** You recognize your interconnectedness with others. You celebrate their successes and assist where possible with their failings.

9. **Open-Mindedness:** You no longer see things black or white, right or wrong. You are open to endless possibilities, ideas, beliefs, etc. beyond your own enculturation.

10. **A Sense Of Wonder:** You view the universe as an incredible thing as it evolves and see more and more of its wondrous complexity. As a devotee of Einstein, I offer this quote of his: "The most beautiful emotion we can express is the mystical. It is the power of all true art and science. He to whom this emotion is a stranger, who can no longer wonder and stand rapt in awe, is as good as dead. To know that what is impenetrable to us really exists, manifesting itself as the highest wisdom and the most radiant beauty, which our dull faculties can comprehend only in their most primitive forms—this knowledge, this feeling, is at the center of true religiousness. In this sense, and in this sense only, I belong to the rank of devoutly religious men."

11. **Optimism Tinged With Realism:** You understand good things don't always happen but you maintain a positive mindset because you know that the alternative is defeatism and despair.

12. **Flexibility:** You adapt to situations. You are not stubborn or rigid. You are capable of change when the situation or knowledge calls for such. You do not have "hardening of the categories."

13. **Resilience:** Even when things are going badly, you do not give up. You are not overwhelmed. You persevere, continuing to seek solutions for moving forward.

14. **Patience:** You do not overreact to situations. You do not try to do things before the time is right.

15. **Honesty:** You are a person of integrity. You have no need to deceive. You seek and speak truth to the best of your ability. You can be trusted.

Personally, I am impressed with this list of fifteen and will review them periodically to assess to what degree I am an emotionally mature person. I invite you to do the same. Only good things can come out of such an effort!

You Don't Have To Feel That Way!

Do you feel that you have no control over what you feel? If you say "yes," well then, you are wrong. One of the insights of my life is that there is a lot that can be done so that you are not "stuck" in a negative feeling. Kajai Pandey has written a quality article about this subject. He gives seven reasons on why you can manage feelings more effectively. You have more control than you thought you had. I list them here with my added commentary.

1. **No One Can Make You Feel A Certain Way Unless You Give Them Permission:** The key here is to be aware of your thoughts, especially the negative ones that cause you to be afraid, hurt, angry, and guilty. Once you are aware of such thoughts you can change them. You do have that power.

2. **No Matter What, You Can Choose A Better Feeling Thought:** When you have a negative feeling stuck in your brain, think of a thought that makes you feel good.

3. **How You Think Will Determine Your Experience:** I will always remember a gentleman who said to me, "John, this is how I posit the data." What we, in fact, do too often is let negative thoughts stay in our brain to long. "Change the channel" and bring another more positive thought into your brain. A positive thought replacing the negative one changes the way you experience something.

4. **What You Give Power To Has Power Over You:** Again, awareness is key here. You have more power than you think you do. Don't give away your power to a thought that is uncomfortable, unless it is something that needs to be addressed. So, address it, and move to the positive.

5. **How You Feel About Yourself Determines The Relationship You Have With Yourself:** Positive self-esteem, self-love, is

important here. If you do not love yourself your being/thoughts will be permeated with negative energy. Learn to love yourself. It will be the best gift you can ever give yourself!

6. **What You Keep Telling Yourself Daily Will Manifest Itself In Your Life Experiences:** Self-talk is important. Are you overly critical of yourself? When you make a mistake, do you hang on to it and feel bad? Or are you able to say, "lesson learned," won't do that again.

7. **You Feelings Are Always An Indicator Of Your Thinking. If You Change Your Thinking, You Change Your Life.** Again, I emphasize awareness. Know what you are feeling, don't push those feelings down. Once you know them, you can start putting different thoughts into your brain. With different thoughts come different feelings!

Respected Reader, is this making sense to you? Hope so. I find this approach to be very helpful in my life and I find my clients putting this into practice as well. It works!

Chapter Three: Men's Challenges In Relationships

Characteristics Of The Overly Independent Man

Two psychological terms used to describe personality types are independent and dependent. These two types have significant implications for a couple, being the forerunners for interdependent or co-dependent relationships. This article portrays the independent personality, who, more often than not, is male.

Stereotypically most males have been raised, or expected to be very independent. One of their inherent mantras is "big boys don't cry"—suck it up. These boys-to-men generally are successful from a professional point of view. Achievement is their goal, and no feeling, obstacle, or person is to get in the way.

These men, however, pay a price for that shutdown, independent style. They generally struggle in marriage and parenting. They are not emotionally congruent in that mode, and therefore ill-suited for those nurturing roles. I will never forget when a very successful banker came into my office, threw down a *Forbes* magazine, which contained an article on the independent driven male, and said, "John, the very things that have made me a success in my business life have F...U.. (contributed to the failure of) my relationships with my wife and kids."

It is difficult for the independent, achieving, Type A male, who is driven to succeed, to become capable of emotional connection—to himself or another. Part of the formula for success is to not feel, protect yourself with various defenses, so that you are not vulnerable to anyone in any situation. The defenses, however, become a liability. Many of these defenses are unconscious and come from the emotional wiring of childhood.

To paraphrase the song 'Desperado,' "let down your fences, let someone love you." That is a challenge for many. Defensive walls do protect, but they also inhibit "the good stuff," from coming in or going out. Isolation and loneliness become the outcome, "to walk through this world all alone."

Too often, Desperado or Lone Ranger types stay independent, not letting anyone close. They generally marry dependent women whom they can control. Usually, however, later in life these dependent women get their backs up and get angry and/or become independent themselves. Two independents don't work well either, just as two dependents don't. Two independents either fight often or lead separate lives as "roommates" with limited intimacy.

Look at yourself, your mate or potential mate. Look around you at others, what type are they and what kind of relationship do they have?

The goal of a good relationship is for the independent to let his guard down, open up to emotional vulnerability, and let the loved one in. When this happens one is able to form an interdependent relationship with another. Such a union opens up synergistic growth leading to amazing things!

What To Do With The Post Midlife "Grumpy" Male

Movies are made about it. Research articles are increasingly focusing on the phenomenon of the midlife-plus male. Often he is described as "grumpy."

Most people are aware of the acronym IBS. It stands for Irritable Bowel Syndrome. Most people know about it and its symptoms only too well. IMS is a relatively new articulation meaning Irritable Male Syndrome. Sometimes there is a correlation or causality factor involved.

Psychotherapist Jed Diamond wrote the book, *Male Menopause*. He contends that "andropause," the decline of testosterone that accompanies aging, really brings a guy down. In a follow up book, *The Irritable Male Syndrome: Managing the Four Causes of Depression and Aggression*, Diamond tells of hormonal changes that can make men "grumpy."

Grumpy men usually are afflicted with the 3C's. They are Critical, Cynical, and Cranky. Know any males with those characteristics? They are a real joy to be around! They have outlived enthusiasm.

If you are afflicted with IMS, do all you can to minimize the symptoms, because you are a pain in the posterior to others. You are a "downer," as you sap the energy out of any encounter. People talk about you behind your back, wishing you would vacate the premises and go get a more positive view and demeanor.

So, what's 'ol grumpy to do? Suggestions vary:

1. Include more protein and carbohydrates in your diet so that your body develops the neurotransmitter serotonin that elevates mood.
2. Be careful with too much alcohol that temporarily raises serotonin, and then significantly drops it, resulting in a more depressed state.

3. Exercise more to kick in the "feel good" endorphins.

4. Meditate: it blocks stress cortisol, changes brain wave activity and oxygen intake, and results in an elevated mood.

5. Have more orgasms. You may need more education, instruction, and/or pharmacology to maximize Nature's stress reducer and pleasure enhancer.

6. Find greater purpose in your life. Newfound passion and well-being will result.

If there is someone is your immediate environment who is "grumpy" you may:

1. Ask him if he is having a bad day or suffering from IMS

2. Tell, or help, him to "chill"

3. Give him a Tums or laxative. It may be IBS.

4. Establish a "boundary" and get some distance from him.

5. Encourage him to read this article and look into the above-mentioned books.

May we all work to eliminate the "grumpy" in ourselves and in those around us!

Men And "Touchy Feely" Confusion: A Personal Conversation Between A Husband And A Wife:

Marge: I've cut out an article for you to read, Fred.

Fred: It's not one of those "touchy feely" articles, is it?

Marge: I'm not sure what you mean by "touchy feely"? This one is by Dr. Stathas.

Fred: He's "touchy feely"; he writes about relationships, emotions, doing nice things for your wife, snuggling. Why don't you cut out articles about improving your golf game or how to catch bass?

Marge: But, Fred, our relationship is important and I would like you to grow in a few areas. You're a good husband but there's always room for improvement. I swear, you act more like your father every day. Besides, you have emotions. Why, I saw you cry the day Dan Marino was inducted into the Hall of Fame. You even shed a tear when you were watching that *Father of the Bride* movie.

Fred: Well, I was raised that "big boys don't cry." We're not supposed to show our feelings. We need to be strong.

Marge: I like it when you let your guard down, show some emotion. I feel closer to you and still see you as strong—even stronger. Then I see more of the man I love.

Fred: Does that mean more sex?

Marge: Is that all you ever think about?

Fred: Not just that. I'm wondering how to talk you into moving that art piece above the mantle so that I can get that deer head up there.

Marge: You're hopeless. I hope someday that you'll *get it* and learn more about deepening our relationship, communicating better, and parenting better together. If that's "touchy feely," so be it!

Fred: Pass the sports page. I'll read the article later.

Later That Night:

Fred: I read the article by Dr. Stathas. He said you need to let go of the past and quit bringing up stuff that I did years ago. He said forgiveness and moving on were important. Maybe that "touchy feely" stuff isn't so bad after all.

Marge: That wasn't the article I was referring to. You must have gone into my stack of articles that I've cut out. Wouldn't you know that you would bring up one that focuses on what women need to work on.

Fred: Can I get you some wine, honey, before bedtime?

Marge: Sounds good to me. After you bring the wine, would you mind giving me a back massage?

Fred: Sure, darlin', anything you want.

Marge: Tonight could be special. I have hope that you're *getting it*. By the way, I left some more articles on your bed stand.

Fred: I am *getting it.* I guess I've had the wrong idea of what "touchy feely" is. Turn over Darlin'!

Male Thoughtfulness: Toilet Seat An Example?

Ever been in a conversation with a group of people and the topic came up—offered by a female—about the toilet seat being left up? (Men don't bring those kinds of things up in a conversation!) I was recently, thus the starting point for this essay. For some reason the toilet seat issue is a symbol of male thoughtlessness with regard to the person he is living with, or in some cases, visiting.

Men aren't famous for paying attention to the little things that can leave the female appreciative or aggravated. Most men did not see much male thoughtfulness exhibited in the home in which they were raised. John Wayne, Marlon Brando and Hulk Hogan weren't much help either.

Thoughtful or thoughtless behavior can make a significant difference in a relationship. If a man demonstrates thoughtfulness toward his mate/significant other she feels appreciated and valued. Consequently, she opens her heart and other aspects of her being to that man who does things that show he is attuned to her.

I do not pretend to be an expert on what every woman desires in terms of male thoughtfulness, (even though I saw the Mel Gibson movie, *What Women Want*—but I've learned a few things from women over the years by listening to their wishes and concerns.

Ladies, what are some of the little things that you wish your significant other would pay more attention to and put into practice in order to show he is thoughtful? Have you "invited" him to do some of these things?

1. Take out the trash.
2. Bring you flowers because it is Tuesday.
3. Put dirty dishes in the dishwasher. Empty the dishwasher.
4. Dust (don't be silly)
5. Iron (now you're really dreaming)

6. Clean up after dinner

7. Give the kids a bath, and read them a story

8. Offer to go to the grocery store

9. Keep your car clean and in good shape

10. A back massage (without expecting anything in return)

11. Give you some alone time while he covers whatever needs to be done.

12. Compliment you for looking good, working hard, cooking a fine meal, etc.

13. Have good hygiene so that you can desire him more.

14. Certainly you have others…!

The main point of this article is to try and enhance male thoughtfulness toward the important person(s) in his life. A good place to start is to put the darn toilet seat back down!

Gentlemen: Be Careful – Watch What You Say To Your Lady!

In the course of my practice and personal observation, I see and hear of mistakes being made by men as they try to communicate with their spouse. Most men are not famous for good communication as a rule, except when conversing with other men.

Men understand each other pretty well and rarely get their feelings hurt regarding their banter. The usual topics include money, women and sex, cars, and sports. Booze usually helps men have "deeper" conversations about such profound topics. Certainly there are some men that broaden the scope of their interests, but they are in the minority.

A man talking to his spouse is a whole different ball game (note the sports metaphor). I am listing a few of the "caution zone" topics below that men should try to be more aware of, and sensitive to, in any discussion with his beloved.

- Looks: This category includes, but not be limited to, height, weight, hair, breast and derriere size, complexion, etc.
- Meals prepared by spouse, especially that new recipe that she's excited about.
- Apparel chosen to wear.
- Cleanliness of the house.
- Her driving, tennis, or golf style and form.
- Her breath or body odor.
- Money spent on things you think are frivolous.
- Comments you may make about women who you find attractive.
- How her time is spent.
- Her temperament at a given time.

If you are not careful in your communication in these areas you may find yourself sleeping on the couch, or in the guest room, taking matters into your own hands. It is important to be empathic and tactful when speaking with your wife about the above topics. You need to be even more sensitive when your spouse is in the PMS zone! In order to give you some guidelines for effective communication during this vulnerable time, I am sharing the examples below. The author is unknown (or won't admit it).

- **Dangerous:** What's for dinner?
- **Safer:** Can I help you with dinner?
- **Safest:** Where would you like to go for dinner?
- **Ultra-Safe:** Here, have some chocolate.

- **Dangerous:** Are you wearing that?
- **Safer:** Gee, you look good in brown.
- **Safest:** Wow! Look at you!
- **Ultra-Safe:** Here, have some chocolate.

- **Dangerous:** What are you so worked up about?
- **Safer:** What did I do wrong?
- **Safest:** Here's fifty dollars.
- **Ultra-Safe:** Here, have some chocolate.

- **Dangerous:** Should you be eating that?
- **Safer:** You know, there are a lot of apples left.
- **Safest:** Can I get you a glass of wine with that?
- **Ultra-Safe:** Here, have some chocolate.

- **Dangerous:** What did you do all day?
- **Safer:** I hope you didn't overdo it today.
- **Safest:** I've always loved you in that robe!
- **Ultra-Safe:** Here, have some chocolate.

Needless to say, not all men are poor communicators, or women that sensitive, but if the shoe fits... and please, don't shoot the messenger!

Men Don't Get It—Until ....They Might Lose!

Most men are pretty stubborn. I don't think I'll get much disagreement on that statement from the majority of women. Why does such a phenomenon exist?

Men typically come from a competitive posture, where win-lose is the name of the game. Most men with testy testosterone can't stand to be the loser. Another related factor is that men do not like to be vulnerable in any sense of the word. Included in this profile is that most men like to be in control, sitting in the power seat.

This article began with the word *most* for a reason. There are other stereotypical varieties of men that have a different modus operandi. I am profiling a particular type of man who is probably in the majority and who presents some of the more significant obstacles to women. These are the men who have the strongest defenses and go through the ugliest divorces if they don't *get it*.

These men generally are successful professionally. The above characteristics lead to positions of leadership and responsibility where the big bucks beckon. There is a lot of emotional payoff in such recognition. It often is hard for these men to realize that what works in the boardroom strikes out eventually in the bedroom. Oftentimes a woman early on accepts this type of partner because:

a. He is bringing in the big bucks, therefore, a comfy lifestyle.

b. She is a "pleaser" who does not like confrontation.

c. She has young kids who consume her time and energies.

d. She is not in touch with her feelings.

e. She is not aware that she deserves, and can have, a better relationship.

Once a woman deals with the above pertinent factors she is more ready to challenge this type of man to create a different type of relationship. She may start by withdrawing, withholding sex, spending more time with girlfriends, joining organizations, watching more Oprah and Dr. Phil, and reading more articles like this one. She will ask for what she needs. Then, hopefully, with this knowledge and behavior she will be able to assist her man to understand her needs and, thus help him to be more appreciative, thoughtful, and romantic.

If the above doesn't get the desired change then relationship counseling is called for. Getting a good fit with a licensed Marriage and Family Therapist is important. Some therapists and pastors can offer quality advice and cosmetic corrections, but only a trained professional in marriage and family issues can be of real help here. Understanding emotional wiring is critical in this process. Too often when a woman suggests counseling the man balks. If such a situation arises, I encourage the woman to contact a marriage counselor, who usually can find a way to get the man to come in to try counseling.

The very last resort is to see an attorney to help the blind bloke see that he must change or he may lose his wife, accessibility to his kids, half his net worth, and his home. Too often these types of men don't realize what they will lose until it is too late and the judge has issued the final decree. (There is a popular country song that features a man saying, "Who's that man living in my house? Who's that man raising my kids...?")

The song 'Desperado' speaks to this type of man, who hides behind the defenses of power and control, so as to not be vulnerable and let a partner in.

"Desperado, why don't you come to your senses?
   Come down from your fences, open the gate...
   You better let somebody love you, before it's too late."

Thirty-nine years ago that song, sung by Banks & Shane at the Steak and Ale in Tucker, GA hit me between the eyes and helped me let in the one I was with that night. I never let her go, and we are still together—happily. Had some "fences" that needed to come down. How about you?

"I'm Trying To Fix My Wife—Make Her A Better Person."

This statement, or a variant of it, has been spoken by many a man to me over the years. The statement is sincere and comes from a good heart—usually. These men do love their wives and want the best for them, and ultimately, for themselves.

The men who think this way are usually highly successful men who are 'type A' driven men who must succeed, be perfect, so that no blunder or blemish may tarnish their good image. They must look good and their wife must as well—as perceived and judged by them. After all, the wife is an extension of themselves. It is an odd sense of co-dependence by men, who for the most part, are very independent. The very traits that have helped them succeed in the business world—critical analysis, objective judgment, leadership, being right, decision making, frank communication—work against them in a relationship with their wife. The wife tends to feel less good about herself as the "fixer" finds fault—all with *good intention*. Over the years the wife feels more and more resentful. Generally, she pushes down her anger and gradually withdraws, both emotionally and sexually. Occasionally she flares up in anger and the husband is very surprised by it, especially its intensity.

These men have been charged with the responsibility—and they welcome the challenge—to lead, correct, fix, the business domain in their career. This personality type therefore assumes it is their sacred rite to pass on their wisdom to enhance their wives—help them to be better, to do the *right* things.

Au contraire, my friend. It is the husband's job to listen, to empathize, not fix. Advice is not to be offered unless requested. In most cases the wife just wants to be heard—not remodeled. She is competent. Let me say that again, *she is competent*, perhaps different, but not incompetent. Listening, empathy and support actually do much more to help the woman be all she can be, rather than *fixing*.

Did you ever see the movie, *When a Man Loves a Woman* with Meg Ryan and Andy Garcia? It's about a woman who has "issues" and a man who wants to "fix" her, rather than be an empathic listening husband. She becomes more and more depressed and turns to alcohol as a refuge for her emptiness and loneliness. Her husband is unable to be a helpful partner. Ultimately she turns to AA and finds that a supportive group helps her get back on track. One man in the group is particularly helpful. He listens, empathizes, and supports. Voila, a deep connection is made, one that cannot be made with her husband.

This is not to say that a man who feels hurt by his wife cannot offer feedback requesting a change. Two types of message can convey this to his wife. The first goes something like this: "Honey, when you do xyz it really hurts." The other goes like this: "Why do you always do xyz? You need to change that." The first style is not easy for a man because he admits to being vulnerable, capable of being hurt by this woman he loves. Therefore, he often resorts to the second option that comes from judgment and control and puts his wife down.

It is my intent, and hope, that this article helps a caring man to modify his need and behavior that tries to "improve" his wife. Also, may more wives stand up and say, "Please just listen." By taking a stand and feeling good about it, most women then become more powerful, have higher self-esteem, and, thus, "improve" on their own. If a man doesn't hear and empathize, in time he has one angry woman to deal with.

Men, be proactive, as you are in other parts of your life; be attuned to your wife, empathize without judgment or criticism, and you will have back that loving wife that you married.

Men: Are You Married To A "High Maintenance Woman"? Women: Are You One?

I was driving home from Atlanta late the other night, changing stations with my deft never-miss-a-beat male fingers, and one song played three times within an hour. It is called 'High Maintenance Woman.' Since I am always looking for topics that fit under the umbrella of mental health and relationships, I felt that this was a sign from the universe that this topic needed to be addressed. Actually this topic is often discussed in relationship counseling. (Another motivating factor was that many men got really defensive about my article a couple of weeks ago asking men to quit "fixing" or "improving" their wife and, thus, they felt their wives needed to be under the microscope as well.)

In my research I found many descriptors of a "high maintenance woman." Most have common threads. One writer is Madeline Murphy (note I am using a woman commentator here to illustrate my non-sexist bias). To quote Ms. Murphy:

"High maintenance women are like high maintenance sports cars. They're lots of fun when you're out on the town together, but for every hour of showing off, there are another ten spent on upkeep and repair behind the scenes... Broadly defined, high maintenance women are those who need many things (money, material goods, affection) to be happy. These women love dressing up whenever possible, and are obsessed with all aspects of their personal appearance and grooming in general. This almost obsessive attention to detail usually extends beyond their person, to their homes, pets, and even to their men. They tend to be perfectionists."

According to Ms. Murphy there are pros and cons regarding the HMW:

- Pro: She looks like a million bucks. Their fascination with their own looks means that whenever they step out of the house, they look perfect.
- Con: She knows she looks like a million bucks. She's never met a mirror she doesn't like. She may blow huge wads on things like manicures, self-tanning, and keeping up with each and every trend. She also may take herself too seriously.
- Pro: She's a challenge. For men who like to be challenged on a daily basis, the HMW is the perfect choice. She likes attention, compliments, and fancy dinners, and she demands the best of these things. She will keep you on your toes.
- Con: She can't be satisfied. She is like a ravenous beast, always wanting more of everything. She will find fault in all your best efforts.

Clinton Bland, author of *American Epidemic: High Maintenance Women* lists five characteristics of such a breed:

- Hard to please: she's never satisfied.
- Center of attention: she has to have the spotlight at all times.
- Can't distinguish between needs and wants: she's irrationally demanding and confuses what she wants with what she actually needs.
- Won't take responsibility: she never admits to being at fault but is quick to blame. She depends on others to meet her needs.
- Plays hard to get: she prides herself on being a challenge, because it puts her in control. She takes more than she gives.

Bland feels "high maintenance habits stem from a need to fill a void or soothe insecurities."

The emphasis in this article is not to judge, but rather to describe a certain type of woman. My desire in all articles is to raise awareness at to what exists, evaluate the findings, and change whatever may be deemed suitable for optimal functioning and healthy relationships. May the focus of this article on "high maintenance women" help women look at themselves and men assess what they may desire, or not.

What Women Want Men To Know!

"**W**e want men to understand us, to truly grasp why we are the way we are, and why we need the things we do." This is the reason stated by Dr. Barbara De Angelis, author of "love, sex, and relationship" books, on why she has written these books. She has written many books and is usually on the bestseller lists. I would like to share some of her observations for your edification and/or debate from her book, *What Women Want Men to Know.*

One of the first observations Dr. De Angelis makes is "that for most women love is a non-stop reality—a consistent awareness—while for men the experience of love is much more compartmentalized." The "needs" that flow from this reality are such that women need to continually feel safe, connected, valued. It is incumbent for a man to understand the particular ways that his woman wants him to deliver. If these needs are met she will move into a more intimate connection with him.

Men, here's how to make your woman feel SAFE. You are to be:

1. Consistent.
2. Reliable
3. Inclusive.
4. Compassionate
5. Reach out
6. Communicate
7. Confront issues
8. Schedule time and plan
9. Reassure

Men, here's how to make your woman feel CONNECTED. You are to offer:

1. Physical affection

2. Communicate

3. Share information

4. Harmony

5. Inclusion

6. Reaching out

7. Compliments

8. Reassurance

9. Schedule time and plans

Men, here's how to make your woman feel VALUED. You are to:

1. Pay attention to what's going on with her

2. Verbal appreciation

3. Acting like a team

4. Showing her you need her

5. Asking her for input

6. Making her a priority

7. Respecting her time and concerns

8. Showing interest in her life

Dr. De Angelis goes on to offer what she says are the "Seven Myths Men Believe About Women." They are:

1. Women are never satisfied

2. Women are high maintenance

3. Women want to control men

4. Women are jealous and possessive

5. Women are too emotional

6. Women who appear to be strong and competent don't' need to be taken care of

7. Women want to rob men of their freedom

I think Dr. De Angelis may have gone off the deep end on these "myths." Every day I meet up with women, as well as men, who possess some, or many, of these very real characteristics.

Another interesting chapter in this book is Dr. De Angelis describing symptoms of women who may be "love starved." Her signs of women who are "love starved" are:

1. Irritable
2. High strung and nervous
3. Needy
4. Chronically tired
5. Eating poorly or too much
6. Depressed
7. Fanatically busy
8. Sexually turned off and disinterested
9. Emotionally distant
10. Numbing herself with drugs or alcohol

I guess Dr. De Angelis is saying love conquers/heals most all of women's problems. May be some debate issues here!

Dr. De Angelis does encourage women to do these things for men:

1. Be in a better mood
2. Be calmer and less anxious
3. Don't nag or complain
4. Be more fun
5. Think your man is the best there is
6. Have sex more than before

There is much more about relationships, communication, and sexual enhancement in this book but that's enough for now. I'll conclude this article with Dr. De Angelis' comments on how to feed your partner's heart: ATTENTION, AFFECTION, APPRECIATION.

Eight Mistakes Men Make With Women!

Mistakes happen. We all make them. Most of us try to learn from our mistakes so we can be more successful in the particular endeavor/opportunity/relationship at hand. Thus, whenever I come across an article pointing out mistakes, I pay attention to see if I am making that mistake, and if so, how I can correct it. May I presume that you have a similar outlook? This "mistake" article focuses on some of the mistakes men make with women. I will present the view as presented by Stephanie O'Neill (those in quotation marks) with a few comments where I feel differently or embellishment might be appropriate.

The "Mistakes":

1. **Not Listening:** "The number one complaint of women is that men don't listen to them. Women get a dopamine hit (feel good chemical) which build bonds through conversation. Women talk to connect. A man thinks she is talking to tell him something." Men would be wise to get those ears in prime working condition as well as saying things such as "Tell me more," "That's interesting." Might even look at her some!

2. **Not Offering Help:** "Men often are not attuned to seeing what a woman is doing to make the household work or what might be done in that vein." It would be nice to say, "What can I do?" or noticing something that needs to be done and then doing it. Examples: dishwashers usually need to be emptied and dishes put up and trash may need to be taken out.

3. **Thinking Men And Women Are Alike:** "When men "give" it's often based on what they want, not what their partner wants." I don't like this one for its overly stereotyped

statement. Yes, men and women are different (insight of the millennium) and I think most men are very aware of that— sometimes painfully so. I would prefer a statement that says men often are not very attuned to a woman's thinking and/or needs and the consequent behavior required.

4. **Misunderstanding The "Silent Treatment":** "The silent treatment is not meant to punish – it just means she's hurt and can't speak. Silence is not a good sign." Here, men should ask what's wrong. Come with compassion so a woman feels safe enough to express her real emotions. Too often men get defensive and withdraw instead of staying engaged and assisting in working through whatever caused the "silent treatment."

5. **Failing To Communicate:** "Women say men don't tell them what they are thinking. Men save words and don't explain well. Often the wrong message is sent or received." Yes, men need to speak up more and contribute better. However, a fundamental difference between most men and women is that men go into much less detail than women do. I continually say to couples in counseling that men should talk more and listen better and women should give more bullet points, less details and not detour into ancillary subjects.

6. **Thinking That Physically Present Is Enough:** "A man believes if his body is in the house it's a form of intimacy. Women want more." Examples would be more reaching out— physically, emotionally, and mentally. O'Neill suggests the "Three T's": talking, touching, and tuning in. Remember that song, 'Reach out and touch.' Worth trying.

7. **Feeling Hurt By A Woman's Distractions:** "Women multi-task. Men feel hurt or less important and they get their feelings hurt." Not so sure about this one. How many men

really get bent out of shape when a woman is doing something else while communicating with her man?

8. **Not Getting How We Operate:** "A man screens out everything irrelevant to his task. Women multi-task, men are more focused." I think Ms. O'Neill should have quit after Number Seven. This one seems redundant.

I guess the reason for the O'Neill article, as well as this one, is to help men—and women—realize some of the "mistakes" that individuals make in a relationship that deter a closer bond. It never hurts for each person to raise his or her awareness of what "mistakes" are occurring and how he/she may be limiting the relationship. Perhaps some "good communication" dialogue between you and your loved one might uncover a mistake or two in the relationship that could be corrected. If so, this writing will have served its purpose.

10 Mistakes Men Make In Life—Seriously!

Let' start this reading with a quiz. We all make mistakes. That's a given. Some people learn from their mistakes. Some do not. Respected Reader, what mistakes do men in general make? Take a pause and come up with your list. All Pro Dad web site had an article with the above named title. I will list them and add some commentary. See how these ten compare with what you came up with.

1. **The Belief That Denial Is An Effective Relationship Tool:** As long as a man can put blinders on and pretend that a problem doesn't exist, he can believe that it will go away or fix itself.

2. **Thinking Of Themselves First And Others As An Afterthought:** Stereotypically, men have big egos, are often full of themselves, and want to live as large as possible. This can lead toward developing a narcissistic way of life. This focus on self tends to not being very attuned to others.

3. **The Tendency To Believe That, Once Men Explain Themselves, Women Will Automatically Change Their Point Of View:** This one ties into the above mistake that the narcissism that they are "right" and women just need to understand that.

4. **Not Really Listening:** Too often men presume to know what the other is going to say (sometimes true) and they don't really tune into the other person by truly hearing what is said. Or, sometimes, they have the "fix" needed so they interrupt and come up with the "solution." This is not respectful behavior.

5. **Not Really Paying Attention:** Again, attunement is the issue here. To be truly present to another is giving that person a gift. It says you are important to me.

6. **I Don't Need Any Help:** A big one. Men never want to appear as weak. It's unmanly. Therefore, they fumble through some things that would better be served by asking for help.

7. **Wanting To "Fix" Problems Rather Than Understand Them:** Many men see themselves as "fixers." Oftentimes they rush in to "fix" someone or something without fully grasping the situation or context.

8. **I Can Put This Together Without Reading The Directions: This Must Be Built Into Men's DNA!** This one ties into a few of the above mentioned. Men are in a hurry to get it done and often think they can do it without the understanding that the directions offer.

9. **The Irrational Belief That Hiding Feelings And Building A Wall Around Emotions Will Make For A Strong, More Attractive Man:** Actually the opposite is true. Women appreciate, and connect with, a man who is in touch with his feelings and can appropriately share them. He then can present his whole self, not the self that is shut down behind his wall.

10. **Attempting To Impress Other People By Trying To Do Stuff That Send Them To The Hospital:** Here again, the opposite is true. Women are attracted to men that are alive, exhibit sound judgment, and act in ways that suggest a secure future.

Needless to say, this is not an exhaustive look at men's mistakes. You ladies probably could add a few more! But in fairness, many of these mistakes do not belong exclusively to the male gender.

Well, Respected Reader of either gender, what do you think of these ten? Do they apply in the world you live in? Perhaps a conversation about these stereotypes might serve some value for better understanding and communication.

7 Things Husbands Do That Drive Their Wives Crazy!

Is there anybody out there that believes men and women are the same? Well, they are not! Now that this is clear, let me show a few ways, amongst many, that men demonstrate how they drive their wives crazy. B. J. Foster has written a short treatise on this, which is the title of this writing. I will share his seven points and add my commentary.

1. **Inability To Multi-Task:** Have you seen the You Tube that displays Mark Gungor showing how men and women's brains are different? He says women's brains are like a big ball of wires, while men's brains are a collection of boxes. For women, everything is connected through all those wires, but men's brains can only deal with one box at a time. Bottom line, women can handle several subjects at one time. Men can't.

2. **Zone Out:** Gungor points out that men have a "zone-out box" with nothing in it. It is a man's favorite box. Men love to sit and not have to think. Women's brains never stop. Thus, women get frustrated when men go into their "zone-out box." This situation is not conducive to good communication between a man and a woman.

3. **Don't Respond:** Some men still think that when a woman is venting he is supposed to "fix" the problem. More enlightened men are aware that women just want men to listen, not "fix." But in this new non-fixer role, a man does not know how to respond.

4. **Don't Connect Emotionally:** This is not a strength for most men. They do not realize what emotional connection is, and

therefore, do not deliver on that count. This is a big thing for women!

5. **Expect Sex Without Trying To Connect:** 4 comes before 5. Many men do not realize the importance of this, and thus, try to hustle sex because they do not know how to get close emotionally and "make love."

6. **Show No Initiative:** This is problematic for men. If he comes in too hard, he is guilty of trying to "fix" the situation. If he holds back, he is not "responding." Good communication may help him to understand that there is a time when a woman wants a man to show initiative, to be aware and present as to what needs to be done.

7. **Don't Plan:** Women with their "multi-tasking" brain often see better into the future and want to plan. Many a man wants to "live in the now" and doesn't put in the effort to also work with their partner in future planning.

Where do you fit in these gender stereotypes? The reason for this writing is to raise awareness for women and men, to know what irritates, disappoints, and/or frustrates you about how you interact with your significant other. I invite you as a couple to discuss these 7 to see if they are applicable, or if others might be present and worthy of discussion.

Father Needs To Be "Leader Of The Band"

As you encounter Father's Day, if you are a father, what does it mean to you? If you are a child, what does it mean to you? Is the day important? Does it bring forth any particular thoughts and feelings? I hope that it does, for it is important to reflect on the role of father in the family.

As Father's Day approaches this year, a particular song keeps coming to my mind. It is an emotional song for many sons and daughters. It's called 'Leader of the Band,' sung by Dan Fogelberg. Some of the lyrics are:

> The leader of the band is tired
> and his eyes are growing old,
> but his blood runs through my instrument
> and his song is in my soul.
>
> I thank you for the kindness
> and the times when you got tough.
> And, Pap, I don't think
> I said "I love you" near enough.
>
> My life has been a poor attempt
> to imitate the man.
> I'm just a living legacy
> to the leader of the band.

The father sets the tone (or tune) in the family—good or bad. The influence on the family, on kids, is very significant, both through heredity and example. The father's blood runs through us in many influential ways.

What has been the impact of your father on you? Have you wanted to be like your father or have you chosen to modify or do the opposite? Usually "the apple doesn't fall far from the tree." It is important to know who your father was and what his influence has been on you. Even if you did not have a father present, that abandonment by him has deeply impacted you—perhaps in ways that you are not very in touch with.

The message here is to know the influence of your father on you. Perhaps you could reflect on that, get in touch with the related feelings, and, perhaps, even share that with a significant other.

Also, those of you who are currently fathers, what kind are you? Where can improvement be made? Dare you ask your children what kind of father you are or have been? If improvement is called for, rise to the occasion. A father always has some influence.

Make no mistake, you are called to be the "Leader of the Band." Let the "blood run deep." Bring forth a beautiful song of love! HAPPY FATHER'S DAY!

Fathers Need To Be Present To Their Children!

Over the years I have seen many kids who are missing dads in their lives and seeing the ramifications of it—short term and long term over the course of their lives. Recently I saw a young boy who broke down sobbing while talking about how much he was missing his dad. It broke my heart to see him hurting so badly. Kids should not have to feel such pain!

Kids need both parents in their lives—every day, if possible. However, in our society this often is not feasible due to divorce, job demands, military obligation or other factors that pull a dad or a mom away from their kid(s).

Yet, each parent needs to do the very best job possible to be there for their kids. When away, parents sometime need to call and check in. At some stages of a child's life that parent call needs to be every day. Yes, every day.

Parents often are not aware of how much a child is missing one or the other parent. Sometimes kids don't tell, and sometimes their feelings are so pushed down that they are not conscious of this underlying feeling. But I will guarantee you that the absence will affect the child in some significant way along the line.

Recently, I talked to a single parent dad who has primary custody of his child. He told me that he was bringing the snacks to his child's soccer practice. He is an involved dad. It is very important to him. He talks to his child's teachers to get progress reports, helps with homework, spends quality time with his boy. His heart and time are present to his child. Lucky boy. It helps to heal the pain of not having Mom and Dad together parenting him.

If there are any dad's out there who say your dad was not around for you and that it did not affect you, give me one session with you and I will demonstrate how it has impacted your life. In some cases it may actually have helped you become a better dad because you know first-hand the pain of not having your dad present and active in your life. I know I can relate to that.

This article is not meant to judge or guiltify any dad. Each father has created a life and is—hopefully—doing the best he can to be present to his child in the most significant ways possible. I am trying to emphasize the importance of a dad's presence in a child's life. Perhaps there is some dad out there that will welcome this reminder and encouragement. Your child needs his daddy!

Father Role And Impact—Deserve A Recognition Day?

Fathers are a frequent topic of conversation in many of my therapy sessions with individuals. Among the scenarios would be:

1. The person who is angry at his/her father for:
   a) not being there physically and/or emotionally
   b) being an abuser—physically, sexually, emotionally
   c) being a poor role model: as a husband, father, his lifestyle, not taking care of his health
2. The person who is a father and is confused, frustrated, or disgusted with his child, designated as a "problem child" and he seeks assistance in parenting.
3. The person who doesn't know his father and needs to understand and deal with that abandonment and needs a mentor in his life.
4. The father who wants to re-connect with his kids after being absent from their lives.
5. The father who wants to be the best father possible and sees me for educational purposes.

If I had not been in my profession I would never have known the incredible impact that a father has on a child, on a family. My own father was largely absent from my life due to his excessive work demands. So not having a father around was normal for me. I did not know what I needed or what was missing from the father-son connection.

Not having a father model, mentor, or advisor helped lead me to my "Lone Ranger" orientation. I did not need anybody so I took my detoured direction toward vocation, marriage and family, lifestyle fulfillment. A father around probably would have led to less detours along the way, though I am happy the way things have turned out. My profession and wife have had a significant impact on this life journey. I have attempted to be a very different father from the one I rarely knew growing up. I am blessed to have an incredibly wonderful father-child relationship with both of our kids, Kris and Brittany.

Bottom line here, Respected Reader, where does the "father factor" fit in your life—past, present, and future? May you take the time to reflect on your experience with your own father and determine what kind of father you are or aim to be. It will be time well spent, perhaps joyous, perhaps painful.

A father is impactful! Positively or negatively. Happy Father's Day to those of you who deserve it. For those of you who have not earned that positive recognition, may next year be yours to deserve.

Dad: "I've Been Watchin' You": Show Me The Good Stuff!

There's a popular country song entitled 'Watching You' by Rodney Atkins, that tells a story about a dad driving a car with his four-year-old little boy. Suddenly he slams on the brakes and the boy's "happy meal" goes flying. The boy mutters a four-letter word that begins with "s." The Dad is startled and concerned. He asks the boy, "Where did you learn to talk like that?" The boy responds:

"I've been watchin' you Dad, now ain't that cool
I'm your buckaroo, I wanna be like you"
I wanna do everything you do
So I've been watchin' you"

With Father's Day soon to arrive, this article is meant as a reminder to dads everywhere that their sons and daughters are always "watchin' you." Whether near or far away, dads are being watched as to how to live life. Presence, character, values, lifestyle, all are absorbed by children of fathers. Even if the father is not present, his absence negatively impacts his children.

In my many years of practice I have been consistently amazed at the "radar" that kids have regarding their parents. Kids take in what is going on. They may not choose or be able to express it, but they do know. They hear, see, and sense. Never doubt that! Kids and adults often tell me what has gone on in their home and its effect on them.

So, what kind of role model are you, Dad? To help with your awareness, you might want to ask the kids themselves. Or, perhaps, their mother. This feedback could be informative and interesting. Might even lead to some changes in behavior, perhaps an apology or two.

Basic premise: If you are going to father a child, then be there to lead and protect that child. She/he needs your guidance. You need to model behaviors that inspire and encourage your child to be the very best person possible. Without your leadership your child will flounder in some form or fashion. Guaranteed.

Perhaps, Father's Day could be an opportune day to reflect on your father. What kind of man was he when you were "watchin'" him? Was he present? Was he a good dad? If not, did he become one? Your father always impacts you. You are probably very much like him, or for one reason or another, you have chosen to be significantly different.

In recent times in my office I have heard a twelve-year-old girl say, "Daddy, please quit smoking, I'm afraid you are going to die." (The dad threw his pack in the wastebasket and said, "I'm done.") A seventeen-year-old boy told me his dad smoked marijuana with him starting at age twelve. An eight-year-old boy asked me to ask his father to quit yelling at his mother. A fourteen-year-old girl was upset that her father divorced her mother, was drinking a lot in her presence, and rarely wanted to spend time with her. A seventeen-year-old girl said she was shut down, shy, and had low esteem in reaction to her parents fighting all the time. The list could go on and on.

Most of you fathers deserve high praise and deserve to be honored.

Happy father's day!

For those of you who have not been a good dad, there probably is time to make amends and give it your best shot. A child always needs a good role model from Dad no matter what his or her age may be. Remember, your child is always "watchin' you"!

Chapter Four: Women's Challenges

A Quiz For Married Women

I receive much feedback from readers. I welcome it and gain insight as to what topics speak to certain people. Some say that I shouldn't write about lovemaking (mostly women). Some offer topics (usually at a cocktail party when someone has been "over served"). Some like a quiz to check up on how they (or someone else) are doing. So here goes a quiz.

This quiz, complete with scoring and interpretation, is courtesy of author Laura Doyle. I will present it in its entirety. Finish each question with a "rarely," "sometimes," or "frequently." Do you...

1. Feel superior to your husband?
2. Nag your husband?
3. Commiserate with other women about your husband?
4. Hear yourself say, "I told my husband..."?
5. Think that everything would be fine if your husband would do what you tell him to do?
6. Eavesdrop on your husband's conversations?
7. Feel like the only adult in the family?
8. Feel over-burdened in parenting your children?
9. Do things for your husband that he is capable of doing for himself?
10. Have recurring anxiety and depression?
11. Feel exhausted?

12. Find either of you are disinterested in sex?

13. Feel resentful or jealous about your husband's victories in life?

14. Reject or criticize his gifts?

15. Fantasize about divorce or life with a man who would better match you?

16. Discount the reasons you chose your husband in the first place?

17. Feel hopeless about your marriage because your needs have gone unmet for so long?

18. Have a hard time trusting your husband in even small matters?

19. Find yourself trying to control your husband?

20. Get angry with your husband when he makes a poor decision?

Now it is time to total your score and find out what it means. Give yourself 5 points for each "rarely," 3 points for each "sometimes, and 1 point for each "frequently." Add them up and see what's there. In Ms. Doyle's thinking:

If Your Score Is 35 Or Less: You're probably wondering what the heck you ever saw in this guy! But not to worry, the tenderness you seek may just be dormant. If you remember the reasons you agreed to marry him in the first place and start respecting him for those reasons, you can still have the marriage you dreamed was possible. Find the courage to stop controlling your husband today. You won't be sorry. You can transform your marriage starting now.

If Your Score Is 36 To 60: It's hard to tell because you make it look easy, but you're doing too much and you need a break. Start to take better care of yourself and ask for help more often. Your vulnerability will be rewarded if your husband feels respected.

Thank your husband for his contributions and you will be well on your way to igniting passion and achieving intimacy.

If Your Score Is 61 Or Above: Congratulations! Your marriage is very intimate and passionate. You found a man you respect, and the two of you have a positive impact on each other. This union is a healthy mix of individuality and togetherness. You practice good self-care, you're quick to apologize, and he adores you for it.

Well, what do you think, Ladies? Does this inventory tell you anything about yourself or your marriage? Does Ms. Doyle speak to you with her interpretation of the scores? You men who may have joined in, what are your thoughts and feelings? Might the two of you discuss these matters?

Quizzes invite you to think about the question matter. They raise awareness in a particular area of thought. Hopefully, this exploration has had benefit and provoked further discussion and possible change where warranted.

Ten Things Men Want From Their Wives

There are a plethora of articles written about what men want in marriage, as well as what women want in marriage. I think the "wants" overlap in many or most marriages, but for sake of discussion, I will focus on what men want. I'm guided in this by a woman—yes, a woman—speaking about what men want. Sheri Stritof, marriage consultant and co-author of advice book *The Everything Great Marriage Book,* has opined well with her list of ten. I will share them with you, adding my own commentary. I would have a different priority list than what she states, but overall I think she nails important factors.

1. **Affection:** While noting that sex is usually on top of most men's list, Ms. Stritof states than men want more than that. They want emotional romantic expressions and various acts of fondness that help them feel connected with their wife.

2. **Belief In His Capabilities:** Men like to be heroes, including to their wives. To be "the man" is important. Women would be wise to say and do things that make him feel valued and capable.

3. **Understanding:** Men want to know that you "get them." To be known, really known, is a deep need in most people. Good communication, non-judgment, and positive reinforcement help make that understanding happen.

4. **APPRECIATION And AFFIRMATION:** Compliments, recognition of a "job well done" feels good and raises the prospect that more of such behavior will continue. Give him some deserved *attaboys*!

5. **Acceptance:** If you choose to commit to someone, you are buying into the whole package. Do not try to change him; accept him. That is not to say that when certain behaviors

are hurtful that you should shut up. On the contrary, wives need to be strong and stand up for their needs. Due diligence before marriage helps you to know what this "package" is and whether you want to buy into and accept it.

6. **Less Chatter:** Stereotypically, women talk too much with too many details and men don't listen well or talk enough. Men just want your bullet points; give the details to your girlfriend. Men need to do a good job to convey that they are truly listening and value what is being said, or at least not brush it off.

7. **Respect:** This is one of the key bedrocks for a good marriage. Good communication can clarify how best such respect may be shown.

8. **Free Time:** A man needs some alone time. This is an opportunity for him to reflect, re-energize himself, have some fun.

9. **Trust:** This, along with respect, is one of the two basic bedrocks of a loving relationship. Trusting your man sexually, financially, communicatively, etc. will build a solid foundation for a life well lived—together.

10. **Companionship:** Most men want their partners to be their best friend. They want their wives to share various life experiences and create memories with them. Lifestyle that is a fit for both is often underestimated as a core-connecting piece for couples.

Personally, I think that most of these could be written under the headline of "what women want" as well. Perhaps a different order would be reflected. The reason for this article is to raise the question for each of you readers as to what you want/need from your spouse. May it spark some thought and increased communication about this worthy topic.

Women Men Love, Women Men Leave

Previously I showcased and amplified a book written by Dr. Barbara De Angelis which tells men what they need to know about women in order to have successful relationships. Equal opportunity is presented here as two male psychologists write to help women understand men.

In *Women Men Love, Women Men Leave,* Drs. Connell Cowan and Melvyn Kinder unravel "the puzzling patterns of man's needs, fears, and expectations."

These insights are designed to help women understand "what makes a man want to make a commitment to a woman... and stay with—forever."

After an opening chapter discussing why love is puzzling, the need everyone has for love, and how experiences teach us about love, Drs. Cowan and Kinder, profile women that men LEAVE. There are five types presented.

1. **Women Who Unknowing Fear Intimacy.** These are "women who unintentionally block a process that is absolutely necessary for a healthy relationship to endure, the development of intimacy." "Intimacy is a close emotional bond characterized by mutual sharing and understanding. It requires a great deal of trust." If a person is to be open to intimacy one must first love oneself and have confidence. It this exists a person can overcome the fears of rejection, abandonment, and loss of one's identity.

2. **How Innocent Expectations Become Dangerous.** The authors address what would be reasonable expectations in a relationship and those that are unreasonable demands. When a woman has demands it reflects an intense need rather than wishes or preferences.

3. **Women Who Secretly Feel Contempt For Men.** Drs. Cowan and Kinder say these women have developed this contempt for men from family and social influences or internal conflict. Various contemptuous forms would the "the ice queen," the "competitor," the "hot number, and the "ball buster." The authors offer tips to help these women get over their anger.

4. **How The Need To Control Backfires.** According to the authors, the need to control comes from a woman's insecurity. Forms of control include women who try to "restrict" men's behavior or "dictate" how he should act. Over monitoring a man's behavior or excessive caretaking a man are more subtle forms of control.

5. **Women Who Give Too Freely.** These are women "who have learned a pattern of giving and self-sacrifice that invariably serves to deplete their emotional resources and, ironically, results in pushing men away—the very outcome they so deeply fear." These women can be found in the "rescuer," the "Siamese Twin," the "Easy Lover," the "Martyr,"and the "Caretaker."

Now that you, the Reader, know the types of women that men *leave*, let's see who the authors present to us that men *love*. What must a woman do who wants love and commitment from a man?

1. **Giving Up The Prince And Finding The Man.** Cowan and Kinder state that "the most fundamental key to a man's passion and his desire to commit himself is a woman's capacity to understand and accept who he really is. "Who men really are" includes these male forces: "the drive toward autonomy," "the need to be brave," "the need to win," "the need to play," and "the need to be a hero."

2. **Trusting A Man To Love Your Strength.** "Men look to women not only for emotional support but also for inspiration... as well as intelligence and intuition." Strength roles of women would include the Partner, the Achiever, and the Adviser.

3. **Arousing A Man's Passion And Desire.** "Passion encompasses the myriad expressions of aliveness and intensity in a relationship... passion makes us feel more alive and vibrant."

4. "People who are passionate want to live life to the fullest." "Our mates may at times inadvertently suppress our childlike enthusiasm, joy, and passion." Men like a passionate woman who is his "lover" and "seductress." The authors encourage women to "assign prominence and priority to sexuality in your life. You need to enjoy sex and your enjoyment has to be communicated to your partner."

5. **Deepening Love Through Friendship.** "While some people believe the epitome of success in a relationship is reached with passionate and romantic highs, others feel blessed when they find someone who's a friend and companion—and this is particularly true for men." Men feel very fortunate if their mate is their "best friend." Without that bond of friendship there is a sense of loneliness and separateness in a man.

The book concludes with the "rules for staying in love" and some "quizzes" about "styles of loving." Cowan and Kinder have a lot of real life scenarios from their practices that enflesh these concepts and stereotypes. The book is provocative and is capable of inspiring deeper communication, and perhaps debate, between men and women. And there's nothing wrong with that!

Ladies, "He's Just Not That Into You"

*H*e's Just Not That Into You is the title of a best-selling book a couple of years ago by Greg Behrendt and Liz Tuccillo. The topic deserves to be continually discussed by women across the land, both single and married.

It may be surprising to some that a book like this, which purports to help the female sex realize that the male that they are interested in may not be in a reciprocal mode, has been so popular. It is not surprising to me, however. Over the years one of my favorite, although painful, tasks has been to help women see the reality of their relationship with a man who means a lot to them. Women often need some objectivity to know what the man is thinking.

Too many women see what they want to see. If troubled at all they seek advice from their women friends (wrong choice!). These "friends" usually tell the anxious one what she wants to hear under the guise of support. (Men usually are more honest—often brutally).

Many single women waste some of their most "marketable" years hanging on to a relationship that has no future. Over and over these women rue their lack of earlier decision-making while they naively waited for their dream relationship to develop. It did not happen. These women fail to realize that they are "convenient" companions for men while they enjoy "the good life"—not anxious to settle down and marry. Once they do decide to marry, men usually marry someone else, often after a short courtship!

While clinging to a "going no place" relationship, women accept/believe lame excuses and oddball explanations. Meanwhile, time goes by, and women are oblivious and deceived. Many of these women stayed in the wrong relationship too long.

Until men get near forty (mid-life adjustment or crisis) men do not need/want a woman in their life as much as women need/want a man in their life. This all begins during puberty. Girls in our society spend most of their time talking about boys. This begins at twelve or thirteen, at which time they call boys incessantly and often offer to "please" them in ways that are not appropriate. Boys in their teens, on the other hand, do not talk about girls very much except to brag about what they "got off" a girl or what a "ho" someone is. Women's Lib and Feminism have had little impact on the obsessive side of girls.

"He's just not that into you" needs to be recognized sooner rather than later for girls and women so that they will have minimal pain and less "lost" years. Hopefully, neither you nor your daughter is in this situation. Maybe you have a friend who is. Within two sessions I am able to tell a woman/girl whether the relationship is solid or not. I also help them develop strategies, time lines, and expectations to help them assess their relationship. Women need to spend less time in bad relationships and find out sooner rather than later if this chap is a "keeper" or if the relationship can evolve into something beautiful and enduring.

Reasons Why Men Sometime Go Silent On Their Spouses

Does the man you share your life with often or occasionally become uncharacteristically close mouthed? Perhaps you are so detached that you haven't noticed. If so, you have deeper issues than the tape-over-mouth man you are co-existing with.

Sometimes men are saying something without speaking. Ky Henderson, writing in that "scholarly journal," *Cosmopolitan*, quotes three Ph.D. relationship experts, William July, Warren Farrell, and Alon Gratch, who comment on men's silence. Let's look at four scenarios representing typical situations and rationales.

- **"He thinks you can't handle the truth."** Sometimes a man makes a judgment that by opening his mouth he would lose more points than he would gain. An example given by Henderson is the situation where a woman had a disagreement with a co-worker and tells her man about it. The man agrees with the co-worker but won't say that because of previous experience. He knows the woman is looking for emotional support, not rational input.

- **"He's afraid of being emotional."** Along the way men have been taught that "big boys don't cry." As men get older often they let go of that message and become more emotional, but they are not comfortable with showing it. They feel they will appear weak or that the woman will respond with emotion and they will not know how to be comforting. Usually men don't like to cry or have their lady cry. Men avoid such fearful expressions.

- **"He's too ashamed."** Stereotypically men are not as comfortable in sharing their mistakes as women are. "Guys worry that if they don't succeed they'll be seen as a failure," says Farrell. A man doesn't want his partner to lose faith in him or lose respect for him. A man wants to be a "hero" to his lady. A chink in the armor is not for display!

- **"He's pondering some other problem."** Men tend to be linear thinkers with intense focusing. They don't multitask nearly as well as women. They stay stuck on one problem until it is solved. Not that his brain is always stuck on a problem; it may be that he is fixated on something like how many wins will UGA have next season! Also, a man does not hear very well with a remote in his hand!

The author comments on how important it is for a man to feel cared about, decompressed and comfortable if a woman is to get a man to share what he is thinking and feeling below his surface presentation. A wise woman knows the right time and method to get a man to share what is going on inside his head. A wise man knows when to open up and when "silence is golden!"

Warning: Women Stay Away From These Kinds Of Men!

There are some women who are naïve, excessively needy, overly tolerant, reformers, or masochists. They choose, stay with, and get hurt by, "bad guys." Let's look at a few types of men to avoid.

Judith Brown, an experienced therapist, has written an engaging book, *How To Spot A Dangerous Man Before You Get Involved.* Ms. Brown is trying to educate women to be on the lookout for these types of dangerous men. These "bad guys" to be avoided hurt women emotionally, physically, sexually, spiritually, or financially. They are pathologically damaged, with limited probability of healing unless committed to serious therapy. These are Brown's "bad guys" along with my commentary.

- **Permanent Clinger**: This man's needs were not met developmentally. He is a weak man, probably looking for a mother figure. He will suck you dry.
- **Parental Seeker:** This emotional "child" is unable to pay bills, hold a steady job, or make good decisions. Who needs this weak leech?
- **Emotionally Unavailable:** This group is not capable of emotional attachment. They are totally into themselves and usually go for the chase and score, rather than attachment and commitment. You become a numerical conquest, not a person to be loved. Bed and be gone is their motto.
- **Hidden Life:** These guys have "deal killer" secrets: married, closet homosexual, children, police record, etc.
- **Mentally Ill:** You would be surprised at how many men have mental health issues. Be sure to meet with a competent

therapist to help you see the true man that exists beyond the presented façade.

- **Addict:** These men are out of balance and control. Something outside of them dominates. They abuse drugs, sex, pornography, gambling, food, achievement.
- **Abusive Or Violent:** These "bad guys" are physically hurtful, and/or emotionally controlling by shaming, blaming, finances, or sex.
- **Emotional Predator:** These chameleons turn themselves into whatever a woman needs him to be. They have no core values or integrity.

Do you know any of the above types? Date them? Marry them? Stay away; get loose from these "bad guys." They will whittle you down, wear you out, and kill your spirit.

Open your eyes; see what you are inclined not to see. Listen to your wonderful feminine intuition. Get rid of your own neediness or desperation to "have a man in your life." Better to be alone than to be absorbed by toxicity.

Ms. Brown says that too many women are "volunteers for abuse" because they won't address their own emotional issues that lead to this detrimental dating behavior. "A woman should not try to make excuses for intolerable behavior, try to "fix" him, or stay because she does not want to be alone."

Women Beware. Be Wise.

Women Beware: Some Men Are Misogynists

Do you know what a misogynist is? Basically, it is a man who dislikes women. He is not gay. He just doesn't like women. Often they are hard to detect because that deep feeling is cosmetically covered or deeply rooted in his subconscious. In either case the negative behavior that emanates from this dislike is hurtful and destructive in male-female relationships—especially in a marriage.

The roots of misogynism grow deep and have been reflected in policy and behavior over the course of history. The Bible is said by some to foster those roots. St. Paul has been charged with being a misogynist, particularly in his Epistle writings in I Timothy and I Corinthians. In these Epistles he spoke of how women were created second, sinned first, and should keep silent. I Peter 3 says a "woman should be subject to a man." The second creation story in Genesis 3:16 states that God said, "Your yearning shall be for your husband, yet he shall rule over you."

Religious, political, and business practices have often reflected misogynistic leanings. Examples would be that women cannot be Catholic priests; women were not allowed to vote; women were held back from responsible business positions.

At a more personal level, in my practice I frequently come across misogynistic men. One of my first encounters was meeting with a mean spirited, yet superficially charming, misogynist many years ago. My first clue was that he called his mother by her first name when he talked with me about her. This distancing away from the title "Mom" or "Mother" was indicative of the hostility he had for her. Part of the reason for this was that she and her husband sent him off to boarding school at a young age. (I do not believe that kids should go to boarding schools. The academic and discipline gains are usually developed at the expense of emotional growth and capacity for intimacy in relationships. There are exceptions to this rule, rare to be sure.)

This man married twice, divorced twice. He married "pleaser" type women who were beguiled by his charm and take-charge manner. Once the dust had settled on the marriage papers he turned into a mean, angry, and controlling husband. I told him that if he didn't do the necessary therapy to get rid of this misogynistic core he was going to end up as a lonely old man. He didn't like that message and "shot the messenger."

A woman would be wise to do a thorough due diligence to see if there are any misogynistic leanings in a man she aspires to work with or for, befriend, date or marry. What was, and is, his relationship with his mother? How does he speak to and about her? How does he speak about and treat women in general? Misogynistic men are hurtful. Beware!

(P.S. For those who wonder what a woman who dislikes men is called, the answer is misandrist. You don't want to be in the same room when a misogynist and misandrist lock horns!)

7 Things Your Husband Isn't Telling You He Needs

I've written often about what women need from their husbands. Men are telling me that I don't write enough about their needs. Thus, this writing springs forth. Assisting me with this effort is Brittany Wong, who wrote an article after doing her research on this topic, with the above listed headline. I will add my thoughts to her efforts.

- **Men Want Their Wives To Say "I Love You."** Don't assume your husband knows how much you love him. You do, do you not? Express daily you love in words and actions.

- **Men Want Their Space, Especially After An Argument.** A man usually needs more breaks from coupledom than a woman does. He needs to cool down, shut his mouth, process things before trying to again address the issue. But, he may not stay distanced for very long in pout mode.

- **Men Want Their Wives To Initiate Sex.** Men want to feel wanted and sex is a special way of feeling wanted! Men are sensitive to being turned down because usually men want sex more often than women do. If the wife initiates, the husband doesn't have to deal with the angry/hurt feelings of rejection.

- **Men Want To Be Heard.** Women generally process and verbalize faster than men. While a man may be silent while reflecting on an issue, the wife should remain quiet and give the man time to offer his thoughts. Men often feel that their wives don't really care what they have to say or talk on over them.

- **Men Want To Be Praised, Appreciated And Validated.** Men want their "attaboys" from a cheerleading wife for their efforts on behalf of her and the family, or just from an individual accomplishment. Look for things to praise and thank him for doing.

- **Men Want To Be Touched:** Short casual touches, pecks on the lips, a quick hug, all help a man feel desired and connected to his wife. They say, "I care about you."
- **Men Want To Be Respected.** They want to be respected for who they are and how they act. They want their wife to be proud of them.

Certainly there are more things that particular husbands desire from their wives that Ms. Wong does not mention. A big one is trust. Trust at multiple levels. And there are others. Men feel free to jump in here and read this article to your wife if she is failing in any of these. And feel free to add to the list!

Okay, I have given men their due. After reading this I am again reminded of how in most cases that men and women want similar things. They may vary among people and at certain ages, but a good marriage needs to contain the above factors. Why? Because they are basic human needs, building blocks for two people to continue to grow in love.

I hope your marriage contains these elements. If not, work to develop them so that a good marriage continues and deepens. It's worth it!

Options To Keep Your Husband Alive Longer!

The presumption here is that you do want to continue sharing your blissful life with him for many more years. Thus, here is some solid scientifically based information for you. If you really do not want to continue this union, come see me, not a hit man!

Fact, based on a number of research studies: married men are healthier than man who are single, divorced, or widowed. The "marriage benefit" both protects men's health and also prolongs their lives. Three factors are listed as the main reasons for such an outcome.

- **Touch:** Holding hands, hugging, embracing, and cuddling warm the heart and lower stress. Dr. James Coan showed in his research that such touch actually reduced agitation in the hypothalamus area of the brain, which controls the release of stress hormones. These stress hormones turn off our immune function, thus leading to a weakened immune system. A weakened immune system invites poor health.

- **Emotional Support:** Men tend to be inattentive to, and deny, their physical symptoms. Attentive loving spouses pay attention to their husbands and nudge and nurse them toward better health. Studies show that husbands with loving supportive wives get sick less often and, when ill, recover faster than husbands who did not have such a caring companion.

- **Sex Matters:** A man who has a secure marriage and continues to be sexually active succumbs to illness less often and heals from wounds and surgery faster. According to Dr. Harry Lodge, the emotional brain circuit sits next to, and is connected to, the brain circuits that control heart rate, blood pressure, and how much adrenaline one secretes.

In a decade long longitudinal study done at Queen's University, it was found that men who had sex three or more times a week had a 50% reduced risk of heart attacks or stroke. And those men who reported the most orgasms had a death rate of one-half that of the less sexually active men. The research did not indicate how many of those orgasms involved intercourse. (A woman's heart is also protected by sensual affection because of the release of the hormone oxytocin and the resulting lower blood pressure.)

In summary, scientific studies show that long-married men, in marriages with the above present elements, live up to five years longer than their contemporaries. Such men have, to quote Dr. Lodge, "a luminescence to them—a deep, calm, subtle glow."

I am aware that this article will be brought to the attention of some women by their "ailing" men, hidden by some reluctant women, and on the pillow of men with sensually deprived wives. I present these facts in hopes that most wives want to do all they can to assure that they have a long life with a healthy man who appreciates such a loving spouse!

The Downside Of Women's Memory

Women have many amazing attributes. One of them is their memory. Women do not forget! It is their gift and their cross. Contrast this ability with man's inability to remember yesterday—except for the fish he caught, the golf score he had, or how great he was in everything in high school (distortions)!

One of the biggest challenges in marriage counseling is helping the woman to let go of all the bad things her husband has done to her over the years they have been together. This is not to say that these hurts and misbehaviors were insignificant. The point here is that they took place in the past and should not be used in the present as a club to emotionally bludgeon the poor bloke over and over. This presumes that the husband has admitted the wrongdoing and has apologized. (Love means saying you're sorry!)

Most women have difficulty in forgiving and forgetting. Forgetting is not easy because women generally are more emotionally sensitive and their brain is larger in the area of emotional memory storage. Forgiveness is a different but related area. Forgiveness is a spiritual act.

Some of the conscious (or unconscious) reasons women do not let go are:

1. What he did was very painful.
2. As long as I stay angry I won't be vulnerable to be hurt again by him.
3. I want the SOB to pay for it —again and again.
4. Why let him off easy; let him continue to feel my pain and anger.
5. I'm a masochist and like to stay in this hurting position.
6. As long as I keep this issue alive I don't have to have sex with him.

Realistically, forgetting is hard; but one can remember without having to keep bringing it up. Every thought and feeling does not have to be spoken. Keeping the issue alive is like continually re-opening a cut. No healing takes place. Bad memories do fade. Pain does ease.

I ask couples to observe the "24 Hour Rule." If you have been hurt by your mate, bring the issue up within twenty-four hours, deal with it, and let it go, never to mention it again. This assertive communication facilitates the reconnection needed for a couple to move on—together.

If the injuring spouse is basically a good guy, he will be remorseful, make his apology, and will do his best to not do it again. If he is not willing or capable of "getting it," you have other options to consider. Abuse is not to be tolerated!

Women who hold on to and repeatedly bring up yesterday's ouches also hurt themselves by staying within a negative framework. A life sated with those negative feelings permeates all feelings and actions. And negative energy does kill brain cells! They also, obviously, hurt their relationship by not allowing a remorseful husband to come back and work on healing the hurt and expressing the love that, hopefully, is still present. Fresh starts can be very uplifting!

Why Many Stay At Home Moms Get Depressed And Lose Self-Esteem

Being a mother is challenging. One of the many challenges is the decision to be a stay at home mom (SAHM) or go back to work, full or part time. Sometimes there is no decision to be made. The only choice is one or the other. This writing focuses on the stay at home mom and why so often she becomes depressed and loses her self-esteem. To be clear here, there are many moms who thrive being a stay at home mom. They feel very fortunate to be able to stay home with their children and find many ways to remain happy and feel good about themselves. Our daughter, Brittany, is thriving in this SAHM role and is excited to begin home schooling her oldest, who is closing in on six years old.

Quality research published by the American Psychological Association, citing various studies, found that working mothers reported better health and fewer symptoms of depression than stay at home moms. There are many variables involved in such studies, i.e. age, economic status, number of children, age of children, husband presence/support, etc.

A University of Washington study by Katrina Leupp stated that stay at home moms showed signs of depression more than working moms. These stay at home moms shared these symptoms: withdrawal from people, work, pleasures and activities; spurts of restlessness; sighing, crying, moaning; difficultly getting out of bed; lower activity and energy levels; lack of motivation; weight gain or loss. Their thinking patterns were inability to make decisions; lack of concentration or focus; self-criticism, self-blame, self-loathing; pessimism; preoccupation with problems and failures; thoughts of self-harm and suicide; sleep deprivation.

Leupp further states that "the root of the problem could be low self-esteem ... sometimes staying at home with children isn't valued as much as other professions." Rosenquist, another researcher, echoed this belief by saying our "culture doesn't value that particular activity. ... It doesn't feel important. It's pretty boring, and it's pretty demanding and the tasks are pretty repetitive. ... The lack of adult interaction and feelings of isolation can lead to feeling unappreciated." Rosenquist continues by saying that, "when someone has a baby in our culture ... they can lose status, income, friends, and the life they knew and were used to."

Dr. Elizabeth Lombardo, a psychologist and mother of two, talks about the importance of overcoming the social isolation that can lead to feeling sad and resentful. There is a need for adult interaction as "having conversations with children only over the course of the day can be isolating."

Various suggestions are offered by the researchers. Some would include talking with your partner about your feelings and hopefully getting back valid appreciation for a job well done; having personal alone time; join a gym/club/organization; forming friendships with other stay at home moms; play groups with others; finding an interest/hobby that you can enjoy while still taking care of the kids.

May this article help focus on the many challenges of being a mom, whether it be the stay at home or working mother. May she get the recognition and support needed to accomplish the goal that every mom (and dad) wants for their children – to be safe, healthy, feel loved, happy, and have the opportunity to grow into their full potential. They deserve that opportunity!

Women Often Turn Into Their Mothers

Surprisingly often in the course of counseling with women I hear them say, "I can't believe it; I am turning into my mother!" More often than not they are not pleased with that deductive conclusion. Such a realization oftentimes helps them look more closely at their behaviors, where they have come from, and be more motivated to change some of them. In some cases women are pleased to be becoming more like the mother they cherish. Your situation would be?

It would seem only natural that this similarity between mother and daughter would emerge since "the acorn does not fall far from the tree." Genetics play a big part here. Often, a woman's genetics would be a reflection of the mother. However, if there are two children, odds are that one would genetically reflect the mother; the other would see some father genetic factors. Examples would be body type, emotionality, and overall personality style.

In addition, there is the role model factor presented by the mother. You have probably heard the expression, "Monkey see, monkey do." It is a way of expressing that what you observe, especially from a significant person in your life, you probably will emulate those behaviors in your life. A mother is a pretty significant person in one's life, as a blessing or a curse as the case may be.

Sandra Reishus, a California therapist, has written a book called *Oh No! I've Become My Mother!* She speaks of the "mom gene" that gets passed on to daughters. She says that there are five negative role model mom types that women need to be aware of and not emulate. They are:

- **Intrusive:** They come into their children's life uninvited and in ways not welcomed by them. Physical presence or advice not asked for would be examples.

- **No Show:** They are, or were, not present in their children's life, either physically or emotionally.
- **Critical:** They point out what is wrong with their children and/or their behavior.
- **Helpless:** They are weak and suck the life out of their children with their neediness.
- **Drama Queen:** They are hysterics with exaggerated life situations.

I invite you ladies to ask the question of yourself as to what degree you are like your mother. Is the answer, whatever it may be, one that pleases you? It may even be that you are not like her, but would like to be. What is stopping you?

Men, be careful here! You certainly have your opinion on this and it may or may not be welcomed by your wife/significant other, depending on what that observation is. For your part, do you wish that your wife was more, or less, like her mother—or, perhaps like your mother? Your mother has been significant in "wiring" you emotionally and affects how you relate to your wife. Also, the same basic question to you—to what extent are you like your father? Is the answer good or bad news?

Parents obviously play a big role in who you become. Heredity and family conditioning are the most influential factors in shaping your identity. But, you are malleable. With heightened awareness, and a direction chosen, you have the capacity for a healthier adaptive change into who you want to become. A newly emerging self can be more satisfying to you, and perhaps to the person who is trying to love you.

Bottom line. Ladies, is your mother your ideal role model to be imitated? Or an example of what to avoid, or at least modify?

Women And The Various Types Of Friendship

The word "friend" is commonly used, perhaps, too commonly. It is one of those words that says everything and can say nothing. I've heard people call someone a "friend" when they just met that person the day before. Also, I've heard someone who a person has been sleeping with for six years described as a "friend." So what describes a genuine friend? True friendships are important for your mental health.

Men and women have different kinds of friendships for the most part. The following is a look at women's friendships as portrayed by Susan Shapiro Barash in the book *Toxic Friends: The Antidote For Women Stuck In Complicated Friendships.* Ms. Shapiro Barash purports to assist women in describing what kind of friends they have and which ones are worth keeping. She says that some types come at too high a price. A sampling of her types and the descriptors follow.

1. **Leader of the pack: It's all on her terms.** Does this friend feel more powerful to you than other friends? Would you go to extremes to stay in her good graces? Do you depend on her plans for your social life? Have you always been attracted to friends who call all the shots?

2. **Doormat: She pays the price.** Does your friend soothe you when you are down? Does she avoid any drama or tension? Does she seem to have little identity or her own? Do you wonder if she ever tires of her "poor me" mode? Does she sympathize with your problems and always take your side?

3. **Sacrificer:** Does she make herself available when no one else would? Is she unable to face it when a friend is contentious?

4. **User:** Is she overly interested in your lifestyle or status? Does she work the crowd attaching herself to your friends? Does

she slide herself into your life? Is she nosy and intrusive? Do you feel slightly uncomfortable confiding in her for fear it might come back and haunt you.

5.   Other types listed are **Misery Lover** (she wants to feel your pain); **Frenemy** (she is after something); **Trophy** (what can she gain from you).

6. **Authentic:** Does she empathize? Can you count on her in any circumstance? Does she know her bounds?

Ladies (and men who are minding their lady's business), have you recognized more clearly your types of friends? Do you need to do any weeding out or distancing? Further efforts needed to develop a better friend? Are you fortunate to have, and to be, an authentic friend?

May I suggest this exercise as a way of clarifying how close each "friend" is to you. Draw a series of concentric circles, starting with a small one in the middle. Each circle is a boundary moving out from the small one. The small one represents a vulnerable you. Put your best friend closest to the small circle, and then put in other friends going outward based on how close they are to you emotionally. "A picture is worth a thousand words."

I hope this examination illuminates better for you who your friends are and give you further direction for the enhancement of healthy friendships.

A final thought: "If you make friends with yourself you will never be alone." - Maxwell Maltz

"Born To Be A Mom"! Your Destiny?

Awoman once said these words to me: "I was born to be a mom!" She was describing her desire and hoped-for destiny. The words came from deep in her being. She has been a nanny and now is hoping to find the right man, get married, and fulfill her dream life of being a mom.

Another woman in my practice once said the same thing. She was thirty and hoping that her current relationship was the one that would lead into marriage and parenthood. She, too, felt that she was "born to be a mom."

Our daughter, Brittany, is a SAHM (stay at home mom) and loves it—most days. She also has a "cottage business" income stream from her consulting and blogging in the areas of nutrition, exercise, and overall wellness, including family life tips. Being a mom is her "calling."

The young nanny got me to thinking. She was the nanny for three kids for five years. The parents proclaimed that their life's satisfaction came from their work. The nanny wondered why they chose to have these kids if they were not going to be around them to nurture and mentor them, and give them that security that only a present loving parent can give.

The question I raise to women is this, were you "born to be a mom"? Is this your primary purpose in life, or is it ancillary to what you were really meant to be? Or, perhaps you have a limited maternal instinct and motherhood is not your desire? Or, perhaps a combination or motherhood and career bring the most satisfaction?

These questions of clarification are not meant to critique, judge, or prescribe what any woman should do or be. What I am asking is what is your primary purpose in life? Where does having children fit into your picture? Or not?

As for you men, I also suggest you know who and what you want in your mate. Do you want to be a father? If so, make sure that you do your "due diligence" in choosing a mate. And if fatherhood is not your desire, make sure that you are clear about that with any potential marriage partner.

When I wrote my desired list of qualities that I wanted in a wife, being a "good and devoted mother" was in the top three. And I got her—and more! My wife Sherry has been a terrific mother, as has our daughter, Brittany. And our son, Kris, did his due diligence well. He married Cara, who is a terrific mom to their daughter. Our family is fortunate that these three women knew who they were and in this case each was "born to be a Mom!"

P.S. I wonder if there are some genetics involved here, as my mother, Sherry's mother, and Cara's mother were stay home moms who did a terrific job!

May you, Respected Reader, know what is right for you and be able to fulfill that destiny.

For those of you who have chosen to be a mom, and are doing the best job that you are capable of, you deserve love and appreciation. HAPPY MOTHER'S DAY!

Motherhood: A Body And Soul Journey

This week culminates with the celebration of Mother's Day—a day to honor deserving mothers. My mother Betty is living. My wife Sherry is a mother. Our daughter Brittany is a mother. Some thoughts on being a mother from a grateful son, husband, and father—and therapist!

I am fascinated with life's unfolding of a human being, including the stages reached and the adjustments made over the course of a lifetime. No person goes through more physical, emotional, and spiritual changes than a mother.

Perhaps the journey begins with "Oh my god, I'm late—missed my period!" Is that good or bad news? Depends on the readiness state and stage of the girl/woman involved.

Conception has happened. Her whole being is stirred up. The body expands—breasts and belly—getting ready to welcome and nurture the child. Emotions run the gamut as hormones and life situations play out. The spiritual element of being a co-creator of a baby can be exhilarating. The miracle of life!

The bittersweet, painful and joyous birth is deeply experienced, hopefully accompanied by a loving mate and eager-to-be father. Together a loving couple welcomes their child into the universe. This is the ideal, I know, but the ideal is always the goal.

As the child grows, develops, and tastes the varied menu of what life serves up, a mother is "with" the child like no other. The child came from her body where she nurtured him/her with a healthy lifestyle and a loving welcoming heart.

Infancy, nursing, the during the night "get ups," the "terrible twos," playtime, day care, going off to kindergarten, middle school, puberty with all its upheaval, high school drama, and "where did the time go" empty nest"—and all the varied events and emotions therein—significantly impact a mother. And mothering is not finished here, even as the adult child moves on through life. Mothering continues forever.

Highs and lows, fear, anger, sadness, sacrifices, incredible joy—wrapped in love—are a mother's journey. Hopefully, the trail has been one mostly of happiness and overcome sorrows, and the child has matured into a loving, responsible, happy, and grateful adult. Hopefully, the child/adult is appreciative of what his/her mother has put into her job of parenting. Hopefully, the child's father is grateful for what the mother has given the child, and him, through her efforts.

And, hopefully, sons, daughters, and mates will join me in a well-deserved HAPPY MOTHER'S DAY!

Thank you, Mom and Sherry for your nurturing motherly gifts! I have benefitted!

P.S. If you are a mother who has not done a good job of mothering yet, please turn it around and be the wonderful mother you are capable of being and receive the commendations worthy of your efforts.

Chapter Five: Romantic Relationships

Every Relationship Is A "Power Exchange": Tips For A Good One!

One of the insights of my life is that every human interaction is both an energy and power exchange. In my practice, working with couples, I evaluate interactions in part by listening to the perceptions of the people involved, remembering that each person's perception is his or her reality. No video available! If a person feels overpowered and de-energized by the actions of the other, that person feels hurt and insignificant. As a result, he or she will probably react in some negative and hurtful manner. Thus, the power exchange is worthy of discussion.

Hara Estroff Marano, a gifted writer, has recently penned a stimulating article about power in relationships. She states that power is "a basic force in every social interaction. Power defines the way we relate to each other. It dictates whether you get listened to. It determines whether your needs take priority or get any attention at all."

She continues, "The problem for romantic partners is that power as normally exercised is a barrier to intimacy. It blunts sensitivity to a partner and precludes emotional connectivity. Yet this connection is what human beings all crave, and need. It satisfies deeply. But there's only one path to intimacy. It runs straight through shared power in relationships. … It determines whether you'll be satisfied or have days (and nights) spiked with resentment and depression."

Carmen Knudson-Martin adds, "The ability of couples to withstand stress, respond to change, and enhance each other's health and well-being depends on their having a relatively equal power balance."

Noted psychologist, Harriet Lerner, opines, "Intimacy rests on two people who have the capacity to both listen and speak up, who have the courage to bring more and more of their full selves into the relationship. Both need equal power in defining what they want and what they really think and believe. … If you truly believe you can't survive without a relationship, you have no power to really be yourself within it."

Practically speaking, power exchanges are involved in communication and decision making. Mutual respect and trust are foundational elements to build on as such issues as income production, division of labor, parenting, sexual expression, and others are decided upon.

An important goal here is to affirm identity and worth so that partners can open themselves up and feel safe, so that they can reveal their innermost thoughts, express concerns, even admit weakness, uncertainty, or mistakes in a partner's presence. Mutual vulnerability becomes a "high-water mark of bringing one's whole self into a relationship," according to Estroff Marano.

The author offers the following components necessary for a bountiful power exchange for a couple.

1. **Attention:** Both partners are emotionally attuned to and supportive of each other. They listen to each other. And both feel invested in the relationship.

2. **Influence:** Partners are responsive to each other's needs and each other's bids for attention, conversation, and

connection. Each has the ability to engage and emotionally affect the other.

3. **Accommodation:** Both partners influence the relationship and make pertinent decisions jointly.

4. **Respect:** Each partner sees the other as admirable, worthy of kindness in a considerate and collaborative relationship.

5. **Selfhood:** Each partner retains a viable self, capable of functioning without the relationship if necessary, able to be his or her own person with inviolable boundaries that reflect core values.

6. **Status:** Both partners enjoy the same freedom to directly define and assert what is important and put forth what is the agenda for the relationship. Both feel entitled to have and express their needs and goals and bring their full self into the relationship.

7. **Vulnerability:** Each partner is willing to admit weakness, uncertainty, and mistakes.

8. **Fairness:** Both partners feel that chores and responsibilities are divided in ways that support individual and collective well-being.

9. **Repair:** Partners make deliberate efforts to de-escalate conflict by calming down, apologizing for harshness, becoming less defensive and listening better to the other's position.

10. **Well-Being:** Each partner fosters the well-being of the other physically, emotionally, and financially.

Well, Respected Reader, how are you doing in your current power exchange and/or capacity to effectuate a healthy power exchange? If done well it leads to interdependence, intimate closeness, and a desirable synergy moving forward.

Thinking About Dating? Some Tips

M ost people want to be in a loving relationship. Some people have one at the present time. Others may not and are looking for ways to find and connect with someone who could be a romantic partner. So if you, or someone you care about, want some sage advice about how to go about it, read on. If married, stop right here. Fix your marriage if it is unsatisfying or get out, and then read and apply these tips!

These tips are mainly focused on adults, particularly those over the age of twenty-five and under the age of ninety-nine! On to the tips.

1. Know who you are. Write down all the positive qualities about yourself. If there are not very many, then get yourself together. You may want to see a therapist to help you do that. Quality attracts quality.

2. Know what you want in a partner. Write down the qualities you want in a partner, preferably in priority order.

3. Figure out the strategies you will use to find this special person. Certain people or activities could put you in situations to meet that person. If you know the type you are interested in then find ways to be in the company of such a person.

4. Once you have exhausted friends and potential meeting places/events, you may want to do what most people these days are doing—internet dating. There are a jillion web sites out to offering different possibilities and prices.

5. Once you meet a prospective romantic partner, follow the following guidelines.

- Be safe. Initial meeting should take place at some public site. Shared coffee is a good way to start. Bar and restaurants could follow once you are quite sure of the quality of the person you want to see more of. If you imbibe, limit it! There are many reasons for such.

- When you are in the process of getting to know and sharing your "story", be wise. Don't say too much about your past, focus on who you are now. Minimize the negative, especially about past romantic relationships.

- Take it slow. Too many people rush into relationships, go too fast, and burn out with significant scars.

- When with a person of interest, look for and state the positives of that person. Make it real, false flattery is not the way to go.

- Before you jump headlong and heart-felt into a relationship, do your "due diligence"! Know a lot about this person. A quality relationship therapist can help you get that pertinent understanding.

- Don't get discouraged. The first, or subsequent, people you date may not be a good fit, but the "right one" is out there. Meanwhile you get in some good practice in exploring a relationship.

- Don't rush sex. You want to have quality love-making and usually involves a certain closeness, intimacy, that includes some level of intimacy.

- Explore lifestyle issues. What do you have in common? What do you do for fun?

There are other tips but these will get you off to a good start. Good luck!

7 Reasons You're Attracting The Wrong People

As a "certified" people watcher, I am continually amazed at the choices people make to find a romantic partner—someone to share life with into eternity. Why do such searches so often end up being the "wrong" choice? Brittany Wong has written an interesting piece on that subject. I quote her here and add my comments.

1. **You're Portraying Yourself On Dating Apps (And Possibly In Person) As Someone You're Not.** Insecure people put on a façade, an image, that they think portrays them in a favorable light. It does not! Authenticity is a starting point to meet another authentic person who may be a good fit for you.

2. **You Build A Fantasy About The Other Person Before You Even Meet Up.** You read certain things about a person or you are told about certain qualities of a person and you get all revved up to meet "the one." Attracting the right partner requires intention as well as dedicating time to get to know the real person, not the one who you made up in your mind. So often in marriage therapy I hear one of both partners say, "She/he's not the person I married." BS, the person was—you were just too naïve, needy, or blind to know who was the real person underneath the image.

3. **You're Telling Yourself That You're Unworthy Of Love, Or Even A First Date.** I don't know how many people actually say that, but I do know many feel that and it comes out in the interplay with another. Dating with confidence starts with embracing and valuing who you are now, at this moment in time. "You can't give (love) what you don't have."

4. **You're Searching For Your Perfect Match.** Good luck with that. By the way, you're not perfect. Nobody is. You must be willing to balance having expectations while also accepting your

partner for who they are. Most people, however, are not looking for the perfect match. They rush into an imperfect match out of neediness.

5. **You Have Baggage To Address.** This is a biggee that too few people recognize and address. Everyone has some baggage that inhibits their ability to connect meaningfully and lovingly with another. Some of it comes from family of origin, other from previous relationships—and on and on. It is important to know and unload in order to move forward.

6. **Your Type Is "Emotionally Unavailable."** Many potential people you may want to date are not capable of connecting. Too often you will be dating a "wounded bird" and you will try to "fix" him or her. It doesn't work that way! It sends a message to your partner that they're not good enough, and it positions the two of you in a parent-child dynamic rather than equals and lovers.

7. **You're Looking For Someone You Need, Not Someone You Want.** This is huge. As alluded to earlier, too many people grab on to a partner out of neediness, weakness. If you come into a relationship based on being needy, you will find no one can help you to feel whole or fulfill all your needs. The relationship will not work. You should be looking for an interesting, equal partner (no "bottom fishing"), not an emotional caretaker to help you fill in the blanks in your life.

Well, Respected Reader, where do you fit in all this? How have you done so far in your relationships? In the past have you been with the "wrong" person? Currently? Doing anything to find and maximize a good relationship. Given up? If you're still in the game these tips may help. Hope so!

10 Signs You've Found "The One!"

This title is from an article by Danielle Stein. I would like to share it with you and point out where I agree or differ to some degree from her offering. I do a lot of relationship counseling in my practice, including plenty of the pre-marriage type. Due diligence usually is in short supply when two people say they are "in love" and are anxious to get married. I take every opportunity I can to help couples slow down and look at their relationship from a number of perspectives so that if/when they commit the relationship can be sound and lasting. Here are Ms. Stein's "10 signs:

1. "Your partner is your best friend." I totally agree with this one. Romance, sexual chemistry, lifestyle, beliefs, etc. are important, but in the long run you want a life partner who you can travel through life with.

2. "Your partner is the one you want in your deepest darkest moments." It is easy to be with someone when life is wonderful, but who is there for you when the going gets tough, when you need that extra empathy and support to take on the presenting challenges.

3. "You're capable of being away from each other, but neither of you like it one bit." I quibble with this one somewhat. Smacks of co-dependency. Each secure person needs and relishes a certain amount of time alone. Then when you come back together you have something to share. Beware of people who need to be with the other person all the time. Smothering neediness ultimately wears out the relationship.

4. "Your partner is your # 1 choice for the person you want with you..." Whether it be a special event or an everyday experience, you would prefer to share it with this person. This goes back to number one—"your best friend."

5. "You two compromise with each other. You don't always get your way." Good relationships have good communication that leads to "win-win" compromises. If you do not have that in your relationship you are doomed to failure.

6. "You care about his or her needs more than your own." I don't believe in this oft-used trite saying. I encourage each person in a relationship to know well his or her needs and present them to his or her partner. Optimally each partner's needs can be met, or at least a solid effort is made to do so. If there is a conflict then number five kicks in.

7. "You both know that throughout life you might change and grow, but you'll always change and grow together. Life is about enjoying the stages with each other." This feels a bit idealistic. Certainly change of many types happen, some good, some bad. The goal of a good partnership is to hang in there together through it all because you are committed to be supportive of each other through the various developmental stages of the relationship.

8. "When something significant happens, good or bad, he or she is always the first person you want to call." Agree, this is a natural outcome of number one. This is the person who is your life partner.

9. "He or she balances you out, and you do the same…" So often "opposites attract," and in good relationships the best of each heals the wounds of the past and creates a synergy bringing out the best in each other. In poor relationships the weakness of each brings down the relationship.

10. "You know that no matter what, he or she will always stand by you and be at your side." That is what a committed solid relationship does. To be able to trust the other to "be there" is a wonderful security.

Certainly there are MANY other factors of importance besides these ten in order to have some confidence that your current partner is "the one," but these ten move you in the right direction. These ten can in many ways be summed up by being sure that "the one" is your best friend.

Tips For Building Healthy And Long-Lasting Relationships!

Most people need either instruction or reminders in order to create and maintain a healthy relationship. Some useful tips have recently been written by Catherine Townsend. I would like to share some of her tips and add my own commentary. Here goes:

1. **Apply Ceo Logic To Your Relationship:** Mega-successful people do not focus on their failures; they treat them as learning opportunities. The key here is to truly learn from mistakes. Too many people continue to do the same dumb things and continue to get the same failing result. This is where a relationship professional can offer some guidance.

2. **Shut The Bathroom Door:** You cannot maintain a sexy mystique while squatting on the toilet!

3. **Say You're Sorry:** Forget about being "right" or "winning." Just say you are sorry for the distance that exists between you and your significant other. Odds are that the other person will say "sorry" as well and a re-connection results.

4. **Go To Your Girlfriends Instead Of Your Man To Vent:** Give your man the "bullet points" of your frustrations and, hopefully, you will receive empathy and helpful solutions if you ask for them. Save the details for your girlfriend.

5. **Snuggle More:** Snuggling is as important as sex. It releases the hormone oxytocin and lowers stress and blood pressure while making the two of you feel connected.

6. **Eat And Work Out Like You're Single:** Keep making the same effort to keep your body in good shape after marriage as you did when you were single.

7. **Talk About Money:** Differences of opinion regarding money matters is one of the chief reasons for arguments and divorces.

8. **Put Your Past Behind You:** Make your relationship a "fresh start." Let go of your emotional baggage of hurts and mistakes and live in the present with an eye to the future.

9. **Have Adventures Together:** Have fun, open up new possibilities for living life more fully.

10. **Mind Your Manners During Arguments:** Do not rage, call names, bring up the past, or argue in front of other people.

11. **Clean Out Your Emotional Life:** Get rid of toxic friends or anyone that gets in the way of your relationship with your significant other. Your relationship needs to be number one.

12. **Schedule Sex:** Make time for "date nights," time that is sensually connecting.

13. **Go To Bed Angry:** Not always but sometimes. There may be times when you are both mad and exhausted so it could well be better to get a good night's sleep and wake up refreshed and able to bring a different perspective that allows a forgiving re-connection. One of my favorite sayings is "begin each day with fresh forgiveness."

14. **Compliment Your Significant Other Often:** Criticism doesn't work, compliments do! Look for opportunities to recognize positive things about your significant other and say it.

Of course there are multitudes of other valuable tips to build and maintain a special loving relationship with another person. Perhaps these will serve as reminders of some that may be of value to you, Respected Reader.

What Qualities Do You Want In Your Special Relationship? What Qualities Do You Bring?

In my offerings I continually emphasize certain themes that I believe are essential for personal growth, quality relationships, and ultimate happiness. Two of these themes are self-awareness and due diligence.

A challenging part of my profession is to witness individual and couple's sadness and heartache when their relationship crumbles. The hurt, anger, guilt, and hopelessness that results is devastating, in addition to the negative effect on the children. That is why I have put a lot of research and clinical experience into devising a program for people to be more self-aware and capable of doing due diligence relative to committing to a person in marriage. It is a four-step process. I will focus here on the "10-Q" part of the program.

The 10-Q part consists of two parts: "Ten Qualities you want in the person that you would like to marry" and "Ten Qualities you bring to a relationship that are special." In both instances I ask the individual to put the items on the list in priority fashion. Which ones are the most important?

To illustrate this challenge I am presenting the work done by one of my clients. She is thirty-one years old. I have her permission to share this with you, Respected Reader. Her words:

What I want in a relationship:
True love! Someone who thinks I'm very, very special to his heart—almost a part of it.

1. Someone who values communication in the relationship and sees the value enough to put work into it. Personal integrity and MUTUAL feelings of respect, honesty, and trust. All things that I think will make for better communication.

2. Someone who acknowledges that I may want to think things through endlessly, sticks around for the ride, puts effort into entering the process, but then ultimately can make a decision for us when necessary. I want to trust that that person can make those decisions for us. I want a thoughtful decision-maker.

3. Sense of security financially—budget conscious, aware of money.

4. Very confident in himself (doesn't need to be an extravert, but self-assured when he has an opinion). Confident under pressure and in a casual environment.

5. Thoughtfulness in acts of service.

6. Someone who ultimately wears the pants, but genuinely values and wants my opinion.

7. Pride. Pride in what our relationship is, means to us. Pride in who the other person is individually. That feeling when you look at the person across the room and love exactly who they are—totally separate from you.

8. Someone who appreciates my brain. I ask a lot of questions. I demand a lot of engagement. I don't want to be bored.

9. Romance and thoughtfulness in small gestures. Someone who listens to a small comment about a hope, wish, desire.

10. Sense of adventure, ability to shake things up (takes advantage of small opportunities for fun, isn't lazy).

11. Intellectually stimulating—always stuff to talk about.

12. I want the feeling of being taken care of (my heart and life).

13. Physical chemistry! I want to kiss!

14. Common travel interests. Someone who sees the value in seeing the world—and if he already has, sees it differently with me.

15. A manly man around the house (If you can't fix it, know who to call that can and get it done).
16. Ability to be a little goofy or at least love to laugh.
17. Genuinely enjoys spending time together—even if that is in the cooking, cleaning, errands, etc.
18. A sense of complete confidence in our family unit, whatever that may be!

What I bring to a relationship:

1. Desire for true love! I'm not just a girl following a timeline—I want the man and the great love to come first.
2. Appreciation and sense of excitement for little things in life—ability to make the best out of situations and create joy in small moments.
3. Genuine curiosity, love to learn. I would welcome taking on an interest or hobby that means something to my husband.
4. Passion.
5. Big dreamer with desire to share in a partnership that works toward and end goal.
6. A great loving and welcoming family: wonderful family unit, role models.
7. Easy going—flexible when I need to be thrown into any work/family/social settings.
8. Independence; I'm not needy.
9. Loving and caring with kids—I love being an aunt (and dog owner).
10. Thoughtful. I genuinely love doing stuff for others.
11. I'm not the jealous type and never have been.
12. Self-confidence.
13. My femininity. I love to be sexy and think that's a positive thing.

This person "cheated!" She did more than ten. She raised self-awareness to a high level. She did this because she is conscientious, saw the value of this exercise, and is committed to making a maximal effort for the most important relationship in her life. Most people do not do as good a job as this person. However, any thought and effort put in is a step forward on the road to self-awareness and the process of due diligence to find a match with someone special that is deeply loving, connecting, and enduring.

I so wish more people would take the time to do this so that fewer people would be hurt in their relationship and, instead, thrive in one!

16 Ways To Ruin Your Relationship!

If you have moved beyond the headline of this writing you must have some interest in developing, maintaining, and thriving in your primary love relationship. It is my intent to offer you both the positive things that you might do to enhance your relationship as well as to present behaviors that ruin your relationship. Psychotherapist Amy Morin has put together fifteen factors. I list them and add my commentary. Plus, I have added another that I feel most people need as a reminder.

1. **Nagging Too Much:** Many studies have indicated that this is very high on the list of grievances that men have with women. Hopefully, your communication and negotiation of what needs to be done by whom at what time can be easily agreed upon and carried out accordingly. Men don't need "Mamas" to nag on them nor do they need to act like a petulant or procrastinating teenage boy when certain things need to be done.

2. **Not Taking Care Of Yourself:** I hear this one a lot in relationship counseling. In good relationships each partner makes a big effort to bring his or her best to the other—in every form and fashion. Your partner deserves your best!

3. **Taking Your Partner For Granted:** Think of the time when you were very consumed with your partner when you were dating. You did little—and big—things to make that person feel special. Time should not erode those continued behaviors. Ramp it up a bit.

4. **Half Listening:** Nodding your head with an occasional "ah hah" doesn't get it. Focus in more and maybe mention a point heard and ask him/her to elaborate.

5. **Avoiding Discussions About Problems:** It is amazing for me in counseling to hear how many problems are "shoved under the rug," not brought up and attended to. The more problems are avoided the more serious they usually become.

6. **Not Being Assertive:** Too often individuals passively assent and do not speak up as to what they are thinking and feeling about a particular issue. It's hard to respect someone who is not assertive with regard to issues of importance.

7. **Testing Your Partner's Loyalty:** Trust is not to be tampered with. Consistent confidence in your partner is important. Earn and maintain it.

8. **Complaining About Your Partner:** This is one of my biggest pet peeves. If you have an issue with your partner talk with him or her about it. By bringing the issue to someone else you damage trust and may damage your partner's reputation in ways that cannot be redeemed.

9. **Not Balancing Friend And Family Time:** Your calendar tells you how you divvy up your time. Hopefully, spouse and kids are your highest priority.

10. **Using The Silent Treatment:** Question for you. Who does this more, men or women? You or your spouse? There is a place for short-term silence, as in cooling your temper down. However, communication is necessary for direction, problem resolution, and re-connection when needed.

11. **Taking Teasing Too Far:** Once you are past your teen years teasing should be kept to a minimum or not done at all. Teasing rarely makes the other person feel good and usually tends to move the person away emotionally. Most people are more sensitive, especially in certain areas, than you may believe they are.

12. **Telling "White Lies":** Any lie whittles away at trust. Better to say nothing than to cop out and offer a "white lie." That is not to say that everything that you think and feel needs to come out of your mouth!

13. **Focusing On Your Happiness Only:** You may think you are important, and you are. However, so is your significant other. Being "all about you" is narcissistic and off-putting. Do your best to make your partner happy in various ways. If you are in a good relationship, this will help and assure that you will get plenty back to make you happy.

14. **Keeping Score:** I despise this one. Score keeping ruins relationships. Do your best to fully participate in the relationship and have confidence that your partner is doing the best she/he is capable as well.

15. **Making A Scene In Public:** This is a classy one! You embarrass yourself and your partner doing this and probably assure yourself that you will not be welcomed back to that place again. Watch your drinking, your temper, and your mouth, especially when you are in public.

16. **Criticism:** It doesn't work. Give it up. A better way is to make a positive statement of what you would like or need. Invite your partner to do something rather than criticize what was not done. I know this is tricky, but language can be learned that avoids criticism and optimizes the possibility of getting done what you want.

Needless to say these are not the only ways to ruin a relationship. There are many more! These are some of the more subtle or common ones that well-meaning individuals do to erode their relationship. May these serve as reminders even to the best of you!

The 9 Biggest Myths About "Happy" Couples

Ubiquitous Dr. Phil fills the airwaves and the bookstores with his perspectives on mental health and relationships. Personally, I think most of his stuff is pretty solid. I'm not big on some of his TV dramas, but his advice is sound. Recently I came across a blog he wrote which has the above-mentioned title. I would like to share these "myths" with you and add my commentary.

1. **"Happy couples can see things through each other's eyes."** Definitely a myth. Each person is unique in every sense of the word, especially in gender. So this is not possible. However, "happy" couples have learned to listen well, empathize, try to understand the other person's perspective, and be open to dialogue and compromise.

2. **"Happy couples have lots of romance."** This one is fuzzier. If "romance" is infatuation, PEA infused, with all the newness that first blush brings, then no, it does not continue. However, a deeper sense of romance that involves loving words, actions, surprises, etc. can continue to flourish and nurture the relationship long term.

3. **"Happy couples can resolve all their disagreements."** Definitely a myth. The key to happy couples is that they can agree to disagree. No one has to "win" and the other "lose." Compromise is a developed asset in their marriage.

4. **"Happy couples need to have common interests."** I think this is another fuzzy one. Couples do not need to be "joined at the hip" with overlapping interests, but I do think they need certain connecting points of interest or each will live in his or her own world, making ongoing shared life a challenge. Each person is an individual and has a right and need to

219

pursue an interesting endeavor, but these should not interfere with the higher priority of the relationship.

5. **"Happy couples don't fight."** I guess this depends on your interpretation of "fight." As stated in number one, couples do not agree on everything. Such disagreement can lead to varying degrees of expression, from polite to vicious. The goal is polite and having as much restraint as possible for the ugly.

6. **"Happy couples vent all their feelings to each other."** This is dangerous territory. Words cannot be taken back. Restraint is warranted. What really needs to be shared? In what manner? What will be the probable outcome of such a sharing? Everything a person thinks and feels does not need to come out of the mouth!

7. **"Being a happy couple has nothing to do with sex."** A good sex life needs to be embedded in a good overall relationship. Sexual sharing is important because it can make you feel closer, more relaxed, more accepted, and more involved with your partner. That being said, sexual expression will vary based on age and capability at a given time in the relationship.

8. **"Happy couples are always in sync sexually."** Not true. If they ever were it soon changed. This is where communication, perhaps negotiation, and compromise need to be a part of this ongoing loving relationship. Often this is one of the toughest challenges.

9. **"Happy couples know the right and wrong way to make their relationships great."** So not true. Each relationship is unique, bringing together two very differently "wired" individuals who must find a way to jointly "wire" together in a way that heals the wounds of the past and maximizes the

best potential of each person. Often a competent therapist early on in the relationship can help a couple understand this and facilitate a "game plan" that leads to a "win-win" relation-ship.

Respected Reader, did the reading of the myths and explanations offered speak to you? Do you have other myths in your brain as to what "happy" couples enjoy? Are you happy in your relationship? Hope so!

10 Habits Of People In The Happiest Relationships

Do you happen to remember the song 'If you want to be happy for the rest of your life'? It says to marry a wife (I won't say what kind the lyrics suggest). People that are the happiest, and live the longest, are married people. A caveat to that would suggest those in a good marriage. Thus, that they are "happy." So if you want to be happy in your marriage you need to do certain things. You create consistent habits that make each other feel loved, trusted, and respected. Author, Kelsey Borresen, surveyed relationship experts asking them what such habits are that lead to "happy relationships." I share them for your edification, along with my own embellishment.

- **They Always Kiss Their Spouse Hello And Goodbye:** Yes, that is right. Consistent pecking, smooching, lustful kissing (depending on timing, intent, etc.) allow for a connection each day—even if briefly. (Try to kiss your spouse when you are angry and disconnected. Good luck with that!)
- **They Are Generous With Compliments:** Everyone needs compliments, especially from their partner. Pay attention and notice something superficial or profound on a consistent basis and offer the positive compliment.
- **They Disagree At Times, But They Fight Fair:** It is normal to disagree but how you do it is the key. You need to respect the difference of opinion and work to find common ground using good communication and conflict resolution skills. Do not talk over each other, swear, call names, etc.
- **They Focus On The Things They Like About Their Partner, Rather Than The Things They Don't:** Nobody is perfect. You aren't. Your spouse isn't. If you have bought into a

relationship, help make it grow by focusing on the good qualities of your partner. By doing this positive thing you will create a deeper bond and perhaps help shed some of the things that you struggle to accept in the other. Good helps cancel out bad.

- **They Engage In A Little PDA:** Overt affection, within the boundaries of good taste, especially in public, is endearing and connecting. Loving touch is a basic human need. Timing and style are important here. (The most well-known love-related chemical is phenylethylamine—or "PEA"—a naturally occurring trace ammine in the brain.)

- **They Don't Expect Their Partner To Read Their Mind; They Ask For What They Need:** Partners are encouraged to know their needs and express them. Also, a loving partner asks the other what his or her needs are, listens well, and does his or her best to see that such a reasonable need is met.

- **They Set Aside Time To Reconnect And Make It A Priority:** Happy couples are able to make the relationship a priority. Good time management of this priority is important because there usually are other important, or perhaps unimportant, factors calling for attention.

- **They Laugh Together—Often:** Laughter is a very important component of couple connection. Find a way to have it infiltrate your relationship.

- **They Discuss Their Finances:** Touchy subject often. Spending and saving styles don't always match up with couples. It is one of the top three factors causing divorces. Regular discussion about income, expenditures, saving for retirement, etc. carried out by respectful communication leads to a financial team going forward united.

- **They Give Each Other The Benefit Of The Doubt:** This is a biggee. Try to assume that your partner is doing the best she/he can day by day. Some days are better than others. Focus on the positive. If you reach a frustration point about something communicate it in a non-critical, non-accusatory manner.

Well, are you, Respected Reader, a partner in a "happy couple" relationship? Rate each of the above within a range of 1-10, with ten being the highest. Need improvement? Share this with your partner and get his or her perspective. No, you won't? Why not? Is that saying something?

"If you want to be happy for the rest of your life!"

6 Things You Should ALWAYS Be Selfish About In Relationships!

Getting in, staying, and developing a healthy significant relationship that has depth is not an easy task. Insight of the week! Individuals often error on one extreme or the other in such a relationship. One person may become passive dependent in the relationship, whereas another individual may become egotistical and controlling. Being able to be your full self in a healthy interdependent relationship is a most worthwhile goal. Here are some tips to assist in that endeavor offered by Laura Brown and embellished by me. Ms. Brown has stated that she was such a giver that she lost her true self. She so wanted the other person to not leave that she gave up the following factors to ensure that the other person would not leave. Mistake, now corrected! Now, never give up these six things in a relationship.

1. **Your Independence:** The best relationships exist when both people are independent, not needy or inclined to be dependent. Based on a mutual understanding toward developing a healthy relationship, two independent people thus form a synergistic interdependent relationship with an equal give and take between them. Many years ago I made up a little saying in this regard: "You come into this world alone. You leave alone. Along the way you hold hands with different people, in various degrees of intimacy, for various periods of time. But you are alone." Embrace your aloneness and independence—your essence!

2. **Your Identity:** The goal of each person is to become the best person she/he can be. Healthy relationships foster this. Each person brings experiences, perspective, opinions, etc. to the

other. An independent person decides which ones to adopt and make a part of his/her identity. You need to be in charge of the identity you create and live.

3. **Your Happiness:** Various people and experiences bring us happiness. One person's happiness may not be another's. Life is expansive enough for each to find separate happinesses, as well as happinesses shared together. Trust and the ability to talk about one's individual happinesses are important here.

4. **Your Dreams And Ambitions:** This one seems somewhat redundant to me. If you have your independence, actively developing your identity, and creating happiness, then certainly your dreams and ambitions are part and parcel of them.

5. **Your Faith:** This is a tricky one, less so in these times than past. Certain religions and believers can make this difficult. However, your faith is your faith, not someone else's. What you believe and practice is your right. If your significant other has a problem with that then that person does not deserve such a designation and role. You must be free to be who you are, including whatever faith/beliefs you may currently be espousing.

6. **Your Right To Be Heard:** I like the way Ms. Hilton comments here: "Your voice is your power. It's how you share your ideas with the world, advocate for something you believe in, and stand up for yourself when necessary. Relationships should be breeding grounds for greater security and confidence in our voice." Healthy relationships help bring out the best in you, build confidence, and enable your voice to be heard.

Relationships certainly are complex. Certainly the ones that have a deeper emotional tie have the most impact in affecting who you are and what you do. Choose wisely, do due diligence, stay aware of the interpersonal dynamic going on, and choose to be all of your best self. May these six reminders add to your ability to do that!

Are You An Expert In "Bottom Fishing" For A Relationship?

While reflecting on what to write for this article I asked myself, "What is the most frustrating/disappointing situation you are presented as a therapist?" A number of situations came to mind. I decided on "bottom fishing." What is that, you may ask?

"Bottom fishing" is my term for people who enter into a relationship with an individual that is clearly beneath what such a person is capable of choosing/catching. The person chosen does not measure up to the higher quality of the chooser. Thus, the relationship is very unsatisfactory. So, why does that happen?

One of the main causal factors as to why people "bottom fish" is low self-esteem. Low self-worth can come from a variety of causes, but the number one reason usually is that she/he comes from a dysfunctional family where his or her basic nurturing, supporting needs were not met. If your parents did not appropriately meet your needs of love, validation, safety, motivation, etc. you often end up feeling "something is wrong with me. It can't be my parents."

The second major reason for low self-esteem relative to mate selection and often related to the first reason, is an abandonment issue. If one of both of your parents, or some other significant person in your life "abandoned" you by not being physically or emotionally present, you have "abandonment" issues. If you are abandoned, you feel worthless, not good enough. Therefore, you have low self-esteem, believing you are not special and not worthy of attracting and keeping someone special. Thus, you "bottom fish" and find someone who is so glad to have someone special like you and in no way would abandon you. That person is feeling really lucky! Meanwhile, you have a false security and unfulfilling life because this person does not have the capacity to bring sustained happiness to you.

A third reason for low esteem which fosters "bottom fishing" is an overprotective "helicopter" parent. Such a parent, with usual good intentions, makes the child growing up feel inadequate and incompetent. The parent tends to "smother love," sheltering, and making decisions for the child that the child needs to start making for him or herself. These children grow up feeling insecure, dependent, and needy with low feelings of self-worth.

A fourth reason for low esteem affecting relationship selection is sexual abuse. Individuals who have been sexually abused usually develop low self-worth. They have been "used" and degraded. Thus, who would want such a person? These people either "bottom fish" or have such high defensive walls that no person may enter into their romantic realm.

What's the answer? If you have low self-esteem, own it. This is difficult. Who looks in the mirror and says, "I have low self-esteem"? Looking at your current and/or past relationships may give you a hint. What kind of people have you chosen to enter your heart? Good choices? Worked out well? A good friend who tells the truth may help enlighten you. Usually, however, it takes a competent therapist to assess and remediate such a condition.

Be heartened. It is possible to understand the reasons for low self-esteem leading to "bottom fishing" and to raise it so that you may more confidently seek and find a partner more befitting of your true worth. You deserve that!

"Due Diligence" Is Important When Choosing Your Potential Spouse!

I see couples regularly who feel like they are "in love" and are thinking about getting married. They are doing their "due diligence." Such a term generally means a voluntary investigation of a person or business which you want to know more about, particularly if you are thinking of acquiring such an entity. The investigation process either reassures the person that this would be a good choice or more thought/action is necessary before the final step of acquisition.

Since not enough couples take advantage of such a process I thought I would give an overview of factors involved with a couple doing "due diligence" with me. For those of you already married, it may be interesting to see what goes into researching factors that affect the probability of a success in a marriage.

When I meet with a couple I begin with them telling me how they have fallen "in love"—how they met, how long they have dated, when they contemplate being married. After that the process begins:

1. What do you really like about your fiancée?
2. How do your 10 Qs match up? (Each person is asked to write the 10 qualities desired in the ideal partner, in priority order; and then write 10 qualities that are special about his/her self, in priority order, that she/he brings to the potential mate.) This is a fascinating exercise that generates a lot of discussion.
3. What are things that bother you about your fiancée—things that you wish were different? Are alcohol, cigarettes, drugs, pornography, betting, eating, shopping a concern?

4. What are some of the typical issues or concerns that have arisen during your dating period?
5. Discuss the family that raised you. Do the FAHG list in depth and discuss it individually with the therapist? What was your Father like? Mother? Stepparent?
6. Did your parents have a good marriage? What were the positives? Negatives? Would each of you want a marriage like your parents? How different?
7. What issues are you particularly sensitive to as a result of growing up in your family of origin? How would you have changed your upbringing? Do you have any particular wounds as a result of your family experience? How close are you to each of your parents, stepparents, siblings?
8. What is your previous dating/marriage history? (discussed individually) Any pattern?
9. How well do you communicate? Any issues there? When there is a thorny issue to discuss, what typically happens? Who is the more aggressive? Who is the more passive?
10. How do you resolve conflict? Do you re-connect well when there has been a major disagreement? Who usually initiates? Who is the slowest to come around?
11. Does either person "fight dirty"? How? Does either person bring up the past?
12. Are either/both of you able to forgive and move on?
13. Have you had in depth discussions about money, sex, children, parenting, spirituality, the kind of wedding you want, life style, career plans? Are there any potential "deal breakers" present that are not being addressed?

This outline gives you a sense of how I assist loving couples do their "due diligence." As a result of this process some couples postpone their wedding, realizing they are not quite ready for the next step. Some couples break up as they recognize certain things about themselves that don't fit well for long-term happiness. Those that break up often bring back their next candidate for a "due diligence" examination.

This is some of the most important work that I do because it is preventative and educational. Hopefully, it stifles a couple from going forward, having a poor marriage, and bringing an innocent child into the world to be emotionally hurt. Also, it educates a couple and helps them grow individually and as a couple, thus more capable of marriage success.

I wish each couple contemplating marriage would do their "due diligence." Hopefully, what is written here will be enlightening and helpful!

Want A Good Relationship? Develop A Plan And Script

Does anyone go into a relationship consciously wishing that it would go bad? Of course not. Yet so many people choose a relationship that is destined to go bad. Have you had any bad relationships? Are you in one now? Or, perhaps, some upgrade is needed in the one you have. Would you welcome a fresh perspective?

If you were to start a business, what would you do? (A reflective pause would be welcomed here) Unless you are naïve and/or stupid, you would:

1. Know yourself and what you might like to do
2. Research on what is available
3. Determine the best fit for you with your given talents, resources, and risk capacity
4. Devise a plan for success
5. Script the plan out in detail with specific responsibilities, directions, and accountability.
6. Buy into it
7. Execute it
8. Periodically evaluate
9. Modify certain approaches to maximize success depending on current conditions

You would most probably use a consultant to help you do these things. To fail at such an endeavor would be very painful, costly, leave scars, and result in a hesitancy to try it again. Are there not significant parallels with creating and sustaining a relationship? For those of you who are single, all the above steps are pertinent. For those of you already in a relationship, determine where you might begin.

When I work with a couple I like to position our team perspective as a "Fresh Start." A new beginning would entail getting a better understanding of how each person is emotionally "wired." This is followed up by understanding the *needs* of each person and what *triggers* exist that set off inappropriate behavior. Given that foundation, we are better able to deal with the *issues* that exist causing frustration and pain. As part of the resolution of issues, there needs to be a *plan of action* developed. The *plan* involves understanding the needs of each and working toward compromises through good and respectful communication. A detailed *script* needs to be developed along with heightened awareness of following the directives stated in the script.

The Plan and Script would include Respect, Trust, Romance, Love-making, Income Production, Financial Management/Budget, Parenting Children, Household Responsibilities, Time Management, Parent Relationships, Pet duties, Fun, etc. Also, as a part of the Script would be Who does What When.

Periodic evaluations are a must. If there is much disagreement, definitely use a consultant, a licensed Marriage and Family Therapist, who can help iron out the differences and create new opportunities for success.

"If you don't know where you are going, any road will take you there!" Have a Plan!

Are You A "Pursuer" Or A "Distancer" In A Relationship?

Psychologists describe people and their behavior. They try to help people understand themselves and become the best that they can be. Part of this process is to describe behavior that is healthy and growthful and that which is painful and destructive. Romantic relationships are complex because you are working with two individuals who have their own personality and style and need to come together in a united synergistic partnership.

One of the better psychologist writers over time has been Dr. Harriet Goldhor Lerner. Her book *The Dance Of Anger* is a classic work. A part of this book describes two basics types of people in a relationship—*Pursuers* and *Distancers*. The following are descriptors of each. I would like to encourage you to read them and determine which one best describes you—and your partner, if you have one.

Pursuers:
1. React to anxiety by seeking greater togetherness in a relationship.
2. Place a high value on talking things out and expressing feelings and believe the other should do the same.
3. Feel rejected and take it personally when the partner wants more time and space alone or away from the relationship.
4. Tend to pursue harder and then coldly withdraw when the partner seeks distance.
5. May be labeled as "too dependent" or "too demanding" in a relationship.
6. Tend to criticize their partner as someone who can't handle feelings or tolerate closeness.

Distancers:

1. Seek emotional distance or physical space when stress is high.
2. Consider themselves to be self-reliant and private persons—more "do-it-yourselfers" than help-seekers.
3. Have difficulty showing their needy, vulnerable, and dependent sides.
4. Receive labels as "emotionally unavailable," "withholding," "unable to deal with feelings," from one's partner.
5. Manage anxiety in personal relationships by intensifying work-related projects.
6. May cut off a relationship entirely when things get intense, rather than hanging in and working it out.
7. Open up most freely when they are not pushed or pursued.

Okay, which one fits you best? You may not fit either one completely, but you probably lean strongly toward one or the other. How about your partner, past partners? Are you with the same type as yourself? Attract the opposite.

For those of you who have read Harville Hendrix's works, his "Fusers" would be the Pursuers and his "Isolators" would be the Distancers. He describes the family situations that tend to develop one or the other. You might want to re-examine your childhood experience in the family to help understand why you are oriented to be one or the other.

Knowing your tendency and that of your partner can go a long way to help you both understand each other's emotional wiring and how it affects your relationship. Communication about this topic will explain a lot of each other's behavior. I hope you explore these aspects of your personality. Only good things will come from such effort!

You thought you were "in love." Nope, You Were Not!

Have you ever heard this "oldie" song by Lloyd Price entitled 'I'm Gonna Get Married'? Some of the lyrics are:

"Johnny, you're too young.
But I'm gonna get married.
You're so young.
My name she'll carry.
You're too young. …
How come my heart deserts me, burning full of love and desire.
How come every time she kisses me it sets my soul on fire …
You're so young"

On the journey through life the "chemistry of love" overwhelms us and takes us to a land of euphoria. Question for you, Respected Reader: how many times have you been "in love"? Did you marry each time? Probably not. If you did, "whew"! I have had a few "in love" moments in life before I found my one true love. I am so grateful that I did not let those few "in love" moments lead to commitment. They never would have lasted, for they were not marriage love. What is going on in these "in love" moments is a complex short-term chemical reaction in the brain.

Let me explain. PEA (phenylethylamine) is the chemical that sets off the "in love" feelings. It releases norepinephrine and dopamine into the brain, giving you those dizzying feelings associated with romantic love. Great feelings. However, these activated chemicals don't last long. Three years max. The relationship needs to evolve through the many factors that make for a long-term marriageable love. If that develops, the enduring chemicals of oxytocin and serotonin will abide. This is the true, feel good enduring "love." (We are chemicals!)

It is because of this knowledge, gained personally and professionally, I like one of the roles I have in my multi-faceted practice—"Dating Coach"! In this role I help people know who they are, what they bring to a relationship, what they need in a relationship, what to be aware of in a potential marriage partner, the do's and don'ts of the dating process, what are "red flags" in the relationship, etc. Many elements go into finding the best fit for a long-term relationship. Too many people take the short cut, side tracked by the PEA impact.

Since I'm using music to help convey the message, allow me to offer some other lyrics to help make my point that love is a process deepened over many years. (Sorry, Bachelor and Bachelorette for your lame attempts to couple up individuals to be "in love.")

The song 'Love Takes Time' by Orleans conveys the message:

"I saw the twinkle in her eye; it lit a fire inside (PEA, my insert).
But it burned so wild and strong, I knew it wouldn't last long (wise person, my insert).
Cause love takes time, and it's hard to find.
You gotta take some time to let love grow.
I saw a shooting star go by. It blazed a path across the sky.
But the beauty did not last, no, some things just happen too fast.
But love takes time, and it's hard to find.
You gotta take some time to let love grow."

Respected Reader, how does the above message resonate with you—your past and present? Has a deep, abiding love been found and nurtured? Are you still "in the hunt"? An enduring committed love must pass through various roads; the first one usually is the PEA road. Don't let it detour you on the way to finding "The One."

Love "Masqueraders" Use These Techniques To Capture Your Heart. Foil Them!

Do you know of anybody who does not want a love companion, one worthy of trust and respect? Sometimes a person wants to find that lover so badly that she/he ignores certain signs that a masquerading suitor presents that are duplicitous in intent. Here are some behaviors to look for that may not be what they portend to be. These behaviors can appear to be desirable upon first impression. But, they will capture and hurt a naïve lover-in-need.

In my practice I often see a "naïve lover-in-need. Often it is my responsibility to help the client to see that she/he has been a victim of an adept "masquerader." This counseling interaction initially leaves the client sorrowful, and somewhat disillusioned. The good news here is that the "masquerader's" manipulation has been discovered. Hopefully, the victim of such deception gets out of this unhealthy relationship. Going forward she/he is more aware to recognize these behaviors should another "masquerader" make an attempt at this out-of-balance type of relationship. The following are five behaviors of the "masquerader":

- **The Protector:** This person seemingly "has your back." She/he is very present, seemingly "there" for you. However, the "masquerader" uses this starting posture to gain your confidence so that you let your guard down. This enables him/her to get in and be possessive. You become a possession, which cripples you in a myriad of ways. Bottom line: you are not free to be yourself in a number of critical areas.
- **The Comforter:** This person also purports to "be there" for you, especially in times where emotional comforting is

desired. When you are in need of emotional comforting, you are vulnerable. The "masquerader" sees this as an opening to your heart. Reassured that you are in need of comforting, and having edged into your love-starved psyche, the comforter turns out to be a controller. She/he will take over your life in ways that you do not want. You will be controlled.

- **The Asserter:** This person comes across as direct, self-reliant, self-confident, and protective. These qualities are appealing at first glance. They invite trust. However, the masquerader only uses these qualities in the beginning of a relationship. These qualities morph into that person becoming aggressive. The aggressive person is hurtful.

- **Passionate:** To be with someone who is passionate about life and love is attractive, especially to someone who tends to not be that way. However, for the masquerader, that lively passion has an underbelly of violence, emotional behavior out of control—and scary for you!

- **Confident:** Confident people tend to breed trust. They appear to have it all together. However, many seemingly confident individuals really are full of themselves. As masqueraders wiggle themselves into your vulnerability, they often add an undesirable quality. They become condescending. This behavior leads to a shrinking in your self-confidence because the condescending person seems so secure in his/her beliefs and style. With this lowered self-confidence you are more susceptible to being manipulated.

If you or someone you love tends to be naïve and/or needy in search of a quality lover, keep your heart and eyes open to a "masquerader" using any of these five styles to touch your heart.

Options Available When Your Relationship Is Struggling

In my practice I come across some couples where their marriage has collapsed and one—or both of them—does not want to work on it. Together over the years they have created a particular lifestyle. This lifestyle includes a partnership that contains certain desirable assets and benefits, i.e. financial, social, shared responsibilities, etc. Sometimes children are still living with them. What to do? There are options:

1. Go ahead and bite the bullet and get divorced anyway. Yes, it involves a diminished lifestyle including the above mentioned factors. This option usually involves selling the house or at least one of you moving out.

2. Become platonic roommates. Depending on your age and sexual desires this may or may not work. You agree on a plan on how to live together. Needless to say, this can be tricky, but it is doable for a select few couples. Such agreements, often best mediated, would include financial responsibilities, chores assigned, socialization/dating understandings and boundaries, and more.

    Surprisingly, this switch to a platonic roommate situation occasionally reduces anger and power struggles that were inherent in killing off the marriage relationship. Occasionally a new respect, trust, and caring develops. And sometimes, Seinfeld "friend sex" occurs.

    Such a switch to a "roommate" relationship need not be shared with any or many people. What goes on behind closed doors of a couple is nobody else's business. Besides, there are plenty of your friends who in fact have a roommate type relationship, but they just haven't formally discussed it with each other.

3. Work on it. There were reasons that you married each other. Perhaps buried beneath the tonnage of mistakes and hurts there are remnants that can be revived and new growth can develop. Too often I see individuals change AFTER divorce as they prepare to seek a new relationship. Such changes involve losing weight, drinking less alcohol, becoming a more positive person, quitting smoking, becoming more sensual, working on anger issues, etc. If these changes had been made while married there might not have been a divorce.

Life is always about options and choices. Divorce is hurtful at many levels. It may not be the right or necessary step for you. What your unique situation with regard to age, finances, intimacy needs, kids, etc. are factors to reflect on as you choose to live your life.

So, Respected Reader, where are you in this regard? Good, bad, or ugly marriage? Improvement warranted? Efforts made? Next step might be? Hopefully you have, or will develop, the capacity to create a loving relationship with a significant other. I hope you are taking the steps to achieve that!

Chapter Six: Marriage Success Strategies

Want A Good Marriage? Try These Pointers!

I am always on the lookout for research and articles that may be of interest and assistance to you, the reader, in dealing with possible concerns in your life. Marriage issues are of primary interest and a significant part of my clinical practice. Recently I ran across this article by Kate Stinchfield. I will share her research article findings.

- **Watch Your Waistline:** Research shows that wedded couples tend to have fatter waistlines. Also, if your spouse is fat, there is a 37% chance that you will become fat. Being a partnering team evaluating what and how much you eat can keep you healthier and more sexually attractive.

- **Have A Financial Plan:** Money is the number one reason that couples fight. It is important to have some basic financial understandings, preferably before you marry. Who pays the bills, how much discretionary spending is reasonable, and record keeping are among the factors that should be agreed upon.

- **Figure Out The Family Rules:** When you become a family, other considerations arise. Each person usually has a sense of how a family should run, based on previous familial experience. There needs to be a "we" in the discussion-negotiation-decisions outcome of who does what and why it is to be in such a manner. "Not your way, not my way, but OUR way."

- **Make Sex A Priority But Not A Chore:** The average couple has sex 58 times a year. Ninety percent of couples experienced a decrease in marital satisfaction after the birth of their first child. The ramifications of family start up are significant. Studies show that couples that have any type of sensual intimacy, from holding hands, massages, or intercourse, have lower levels of hormones that produce stress.

- **Be Flexible:** As a marriage evolves conditions change. Aging, financial situation, children, health, etc. may cause a couple to re-evaluate earlier decisions. Again, respect for the other and compromise "we" decisions are desirable.

- **Stay Active As You Age:** Exercise and other active lifestyle adventures help to keep body and mind healthy and adaptable to various life challenges.

- **Gab (A Little) To A Friend:** Sharing concerns with a trusted friend can be helpful. Expressing inner pain, receiving empathy and caring advice from a confidante can be additive. Confidentiality is vital here.

- **Rediscover Each Other As A Couple, Sans Kids:** The empty nest can be destroying or freeing, depending on the marital satisfaction at the time. If the marriage is not in terrible shape, this period free of children can open up time and adventures that can bring a couple closer together. Common lifestyle choices are tools of deeper connection.

- **Be A Conscious Caregiver:** When serious illness incapacitates one spouse, it is important that the caregiver be lovingly present but also do what is necessary to stay as healthy as possible. The caregiver must continually seek revitalizing experiences so as to have the capacity to be there fully for the spouse that is in need of loving assistance.

The above nine factors make sense. They are important reminders of factors needed to develop and maintain a good marriage. Certainly there are other factors. For each couple one factor may be more pertinent and necessary than another. Each person should review and reflect on them—and shore up where needed. Those that have a wonderful marriage and do what is necessary to keep it alive are fortunate indeed!

Knowing And Doing Certain "Tasks" Can Make A Marriage Thrive!

In any profession or business there are the "good, the bad, and the ugly." I'm sure you know that and do your solid due diligence research before you risk your well-being, health, and/or finances with someone. Dr. Judith Wallerstein is one of the very "good" researchers and writers in the field of marriage and family. Her research on the effects of divorce on children was scholarly and illuminative. A more recent effort focuses on the "tasks" that are necessary for a solid marriage. I will highlight these "tasks," based on excerpts gleaned from the American Psychological Association, and add clarifying comments of my own.

- "Separate emotionally from the family you grew up in; not to the point of estrangement, but enough so that your identity is separate from that of your parents and siblings." I call this "cutting the psychological umbilical cord." One must be independent psychologically in preparation for becoming interdependent in a healthy marriage.
- "Build togetherness based on shared intimacy and identity, while at the same time set boundaries to protect each other's autonomy." You want to be close, but not joined at the hip. Be close, have separateness, come back together and share your new experience.
- "Establish a rich and pleasurable sexual relationship and protect it from the intrusions of the workplace and family obligations." Sensual sharing appropriate to age and capacity is important and needs to be prioritized in a couple's time management.

- "For couples with children, embrace the daunting roles of parenthood and absorb the impact of a baby's entrance into marriage. Learn to continue the work of protecting the privacy of you and your spouse as a couple." Too many couples become a parent-centered marriage with children and thus do not nurture the marriage center needed. Too often, later when the kids leave, the marriage ends.

- "Confront and master the inevitable crises of life." Every marriage has significant challenges that threaten the core stability needed to endure and thrive. Partnership, good communication and joint decision-making, and teamwork help a couple make it through the down times.

- "Maintain the strength of the marital bond in the face of adversity. The marriage should be a safe haven in which partners are able to express their differences, anger, and conflict." I can't emphasize this one enough. Your marriage, your home, needs to be a safe sanctuary that enables each person to be vulnerable to the other without risk of hurt or loss.

- "Use humor and laughter to keep things in perspective and to avoid boredom and isolation." Sometimes people "catastrophize," worry too much, and blow things out of proportion. Laughter lowers stress and connects a couple.

- "Nurture and comfort each other, satisfying each partner's needs for dependency and offering continuing encouragement and support." It is so important to be able to have someone on which to depend, one who believes in you and what you can do.

- "Keep alive the early romantic idealized images of falling in love, while facing the sober realities of the changes wrought by time." More and more research is saying that you can truly keep the young idealized love present over time. The bio-chemicals may change from amphetamines to endorphins, but you still feel loving and close to your partner.

Relationships have their ups and downs. You can minimize downturns by continuing to be aware of, and work at, the tasks highlighted above. Be continually aware of what is so very important to you—having a great marriage!

Marriage Can Get Better Over Time!

Marriages exist in many forms. Each marriage is unique yet has similarities with many others. It is the responsibility of researchers to assess some of the common denominators and report them to interested parties. The focus in this article are marriages that last and some of the factors as to why they do, as seen by the following writers.

Are you familiar with the U-shaped curve in marriage? Maggie Scarf, in her book *September Songs,* writes, "Studies have shown that a couple's contentment is at its highest in the earliest phase of marriage. Then you get to know the other person's foibles and faults. Kids come along and you lose sleep and you want the person to do more than they are doing. Then you are negotiating on a daily basis with your adolescents, and your sense of contentment and well-being goes down during that time. But as the nest begins to empty, your sense of well-being, contentment, and time for intimacy go up. The U-curve begins to rise. You rediscover the person you knew early on... There is pleasure in each other's company. They say to each other, 'I love you more than ever.'"

There is hard science demonstrating that romance between a couple does not need to fade. Psychologist Arthur Aron and others, using MRI brain scans, demonstrated that long-term relationships can be just as passionate and romantic as new love. In some cases the closeness is even better, as the brain scans show increased calm and attachment. The brain no longer shows the obsession and anxiety that often goes with new love. Chemically speaking endorphins kick in and replace the intense chemical PEA associated with new love. (A love-related chemical, phenylethylamine—or "PEA"—is a naturally occurring trace ammine in the brain.)

One of the key factors that showed up for couples who still had a special relationship after many years was that the couple "played" together well. These couples made sure that fun was a part of their life on a regular basis. Dr. Howard Markman, co-director of the Center for Marital and Family Studies at the University of Denver, says: "The more you invest in fun and friendship and being there for your partner, the happier the relationship will get over time... The correlation between fun and marital happiness is high, and significant."

In summary I would like to emphasize these points.

- Too many people prematurely give up on their relationship during the tough times. Certainly there are couples who never should have married and those that have no chance for marriage resuscitation. I do wish more people would have the ability to work through the tough times at the bottom of the U-curve and give an opportunity for it to rise.

- Some people "age" too fast and don't do the things that can keep the romance and intimacy alive in their relationship. It can be done!

- Fun is an important variable in keeping a marriage alive and vibrant. In marriage counseling I sometimes assign this task. Each person has the responsibility to find out some fun things that might be available. She/he is to present them to the other and they discuss which one they will do that week. The next week it is the responsibility of the other person to find some fun things to do. They then alternate weeks finding pleasurable opportunities to share together. Want to try it?

It is heartwarming to know that during the aging process when so many debilitating things happen, romance and a loving marriage can thrive!

The 10 Most Deadly Phrases In A Relationship

In my practice I spend a lot of time in relationship counseling discussing communication. In an intimate relationship where both individuals are vulnerable and defensive (in most cases), the words that are shared have an awesome effect on the relationship. Brittany Wong recently wrote an article capturing some of the most deadly phrases not to use in communicating with that special someone in your life. I list them and add my commentary.

1. **"You never do the dishes. You always just leave them there."** There are two mistakes here. One is the use of "never" and "always." Don't use those words. Be specific and situational. Second, this criticism sets up a prosecutor-defendant relationship that usually escalates a negative encounter. I could go on and on as to how to best deal with this issue and those similar to it.

2. **"You sound exactly like your mother."** Boy, there's one that works—not! Do not introduce others into your particular issue, especially Momma. Stick with the concern at hand and not add fuel to the fire by such additions.

3. **"You think you're better than everyone else!"** Mind reading is a no no. Do not pretend that you know what the other is thinking or feeling. Instead, address the issue, or issues, that lead you to that conclusion.

4. **"Do I look like I've put on weight?"** Don't go there with this grenade. What is the asked spouse to say in this situation? The person knows she/he has put on weight and is looking for a confirmation that all is well. The only safe response here is, "You look great to me"—and then go wash out your mouth with soap!

5. **"Have you put on a few pounds?"** Note that here again weight is a point of discussion. This usually is a dangerous topic between lovers. This unconstructive criticism is hurtful and only makes the recipient of such a comment feel bad and defensive and will probably lead to an emotional withdrawal.

6. **"You're a horrible parent, breadwinner, lover..."** This may be the worst. You are going for the jugular here. Such cruel sweeping generalizations serve no purpose except speeding up the exit road to divorce court. If you have a specific issue with one of these areas, or others, address the particular concern in a kind manner and work to resolve this negative perception.

7. **"Ugh, I hate when you do that."** (Said in front of family and friends.) This passive aggressive put-down of your spouse is despicable. If you have a concern about something your spouse does, say it respectfully and privately. Also, when you do it in front of others, you are making a fool of yourself and will be negatively talked about behind your back.

8. **"I barely know him—he's just someone I work with."** I disagree on this one. If you have a short-term crush on someone, you do not need to speak about it to your spouse. Don't downplay it or own it. Just get over it and focus on continuing to build a solid trusting relationship with your spouse.

9. **"You shouldn't feel this way."** This is one of my favorite phrases to eliminate. Never *"should"* on another, especially telling someone what to feel. Feelings just arrive. You don't choose to feel something.

10. **"Don't wait up for me."** This should be a rare exception. Sharing the last minutes of your day in bed with your spouse is a wonderful bonding way to end your day.

Well, Respected Reader, do you agree that these are the most "deadly phrases" not to use in a relationship? If not, what would you add or delete? I would add name-calling and a few others to the list.

Think before you speak. Everything you think and feel does not need to come out of your mouth. Be respectful. Relationships thrive better that way!

Spouse: You Do Not Have To Tell Your Parents Everything!

This article is inspired by something I read in a newspaper. A woman asked for advice from a freelance writer/columnist (yes, that certainly is the person one should write for marriage advice!) Her dilemma was that she and her husband of a year were having marriage problems. She left him for a few months and went back to Mama and Papa. While living there she badmouthed her husband. Later, she and her husband worked it out. BUT, now her parents refuse to talk to the husband or come over to visit. This lass is torn between her parents and her husband.

This problem, in some form or another, is presented to me on a regular basis. The good news here is that a spouse has a good relationship with her parents. The bad news is that she polluted the family waters with her negative comments about her spouse. "Family blood" is impactful here. The talked about spouse becomes the enemy forever more.

Lest any of you think that it is only women who talk to their parents about marriage travails, you are wrong. A surprising number of men do the same. The adage TMI (Too Much Information) is pertinent in these situations.

Certainly in marriage, mistakes—sometimes grievous—are made. Marriages go through challenging times. Many adult children are close to their parents and routinely seek advice from them. Most parents care and want to be helpful.

However, in regard to marriage details, do not share them with your parents. To say, "we are having a rough time" is fair enough to share. Do not give details or badmouth your spouse. Just ask for loving support. Beyond that only danger lurks.

So you're dying inside from your troubled marriage. Who can you talk to? My advice here is simple. If you must talk, share with one friend confidante, one who will listen, support, and not tell anyone else. You know, of course, that this person, hearing only your version of the story, will take your side. The support feels nice, but the advice will be biased—and perhaps wrong. There is danger here as well. If you do patch it up with your spouse your friend may have difficulty accepting your spouse as before, based on the info you have shared.

The damage of such sharing with parents is most often significant and irreparable. Many people do not understand the impact of words spoken. They are damaging and cannot be taken back. The results continue to linger and fester.

Back to the lady who is having trouble choosing between her parents and her spouse. The right choice is simple. You choose your spouse, your life partner. In time, hopefully, her parents will see that the bedeviled spouse is now making a good effort and that their daughter is happier. They will forgive the spouse and perhaps even know that they heard a one-sided version of what was going on in the marriage.

Other people do not need to know the private intimate details of your marriage. A confidante support, okay; the world knowing your marriage problems, not okay. Such blabbing comes back and bites you where it hurts—every time.

I salute those of you who have been able to keep your marriage woes private. Those of you who go to your parents with details, please stop. It is in nobody's best interest to do so. As for you parents, do not ask too many questions. None of your business.

If the marriage is finished, every effort to salvage it has failed, then it is most appropriate to speak to your parents and ask for their support. Again, however, don't share too much information, especially if you have children with your divorcing husband.

(Knowing that every rule or norm has exceptions, there may be a particular family and situation where communication between adult child and parent may be appropriate. Just be sure and be careful.)

If you have a problem, seek out a consultation with a Marriage and Family Therapist who can assist you to evaluate the issues and come up with a game plan for marriage success.

8 Dos And Don'ts Of Dealing With A Grumpy Spouse

Is there anyone out there in Readerland who has now, or has had in the past, a "grumpy spouse"? I didn't think so, cuz I sure have not! Yet there are still some of those folks around. I know that because I see them in my office and occasionally run into them socially when my radar detector has not seen them coming!

At any rate I feel compelled to share this topic with you, in part to remind myself to not bring a "grumpy" face to my beloved Sherry. Jessica Dysart wrote an article with the above listed title. I share her eight dos and don'ts, with added thoughts of my own.

1. **Do: Identify The Reason:** It is a question worth asking—delicately. Once you know the reason you can find the appropriate way to handle this uncomfortable situation. If this "grumpy" person persists for a while, it might be wise to see a therapist who can understand and help eradicate such a downer way of life.

2. **Don't: Take It Personally:** Never get caught up in taking things personally from the git-go. When you observe the grumpy demeanor, make a comment like this, "I see that you're in a bad mood. Would you like to talk about it or would you prefer that I leave you alone?" If it turns out that you are the reason for the grumpiness, try not to get defensive. Stay engaged to try and understand the whole situation and then problem solve constructively.

3. **Do: Use Humor:** Sometimes humor can be helpful. Oftentimes it can be harmful and make things worse. Be sure you know what you are doing here. If there is some tried and true humor that has a history of success, go for it. Personally,

I'm not a big fan of this. When I'm in a grumpy mood (rare as it may be ☺), I want to be left alone.

4. **Don't: Put Them Down:** Criticism, put-downs, name-calling, etc. don't work! They just exacerbate the situation. Like I said before, if your spouse's grumpy behavior persists longer than what you can handle, get some professional help.

5. **Do: Talk The Right Way:** Talking about the bad day or current bad mood may help—if the spouse is inclined to talk about it. If not, back off. And, if your spouse does want to talk, find out if you are to just listen or become a co-problem solver. Don't attempt to "fix" the situation unless requested.

6. **Don't: Confront Them** (in the wrong way): Style is important here. Your words, tone of voice and body language can be huge turn offs and make the situation uglier. Come across caring and supportive, not combative or accusatory. Saying, "What's got into you" is a huge no-no!

7. **Don't: Let It Affect You:** A spouse's grumpiness can be infectious and transferable. Keep your emotional cool. Don't make it your problem. Detach emotionally, and perhaps physically, for a short time.

8. **Do: Know What Works:** Over time spouses get to know each other and determine the best way to deal with certain behaviors of the other. Once you have found a formula that works with some consistency, stay with it. Each individual relationship is unique and the appropriate successful style needs to be repeated. Hopefully, the grumpy spouse goes there less and less in part because his/her loving spouse has read these tips and implements them, along with loving hugs of appreciation for the non-grumpy days!

Telling Your Spouse What To Do Is Not A Good Idea!

I am always looking for ideas to present that touch on the way people live. My hope is that my articles might entice you the reader to be more aware of certain aspects of your life and that you will be able to create a happier life as a result. My daughter, Brittany, loves quotes and lyrics and often passes them on to me for my enlightenment and edification. One of her offerings included the lyrics from the song 'She Don't Tell Me To' by Montgomery Gentry.

These lyrics resonate within me for a number of reasons. First, some of the lyrics:

Every now and then, on my way home
I stop at a spot where the wild flowers grow, an' pick a few,
'Cause she don't tell me to...
Well I got demons and I got pride,
But when I'm wrong, I apologize like she's mine to lose,
'Cause she don't tell me to.
Well, I got dreams in this heart of mine
but nothin' that I wouldn't lay aside if she asked me to.
'Cause she don't tell me to...
Any other woman I know would have tried,
to control me and it would be over.
Plannin' on my goin' on my way attitude.
And all that stubbornness melts away,
when I wake with her head on my shoulder,
An' I know I've got to love her,
until my life is through,...
'Cause she don't tell me to.

In a romantic relationship, two adults try to love each other. How to do that sometimes is unclear, but one thing is for true:

You don't have a right to tell the other person what to do! Not about anything. Ask, yes. Invite, yes. Tell, no. It is a form of talking down to someone. It doesn't feel good for the person being told what to do.

You wouldn't believe how often I hear a person say to me that his/her spouse told them to do this or that. Oftentimes I hear a man tell me that he has to get right home after a tennis or golf match because his wife has her "honey-do" list awaiting him. Ugh. Certainly spouses have responsibilities as partners to share the load of life together, but neither one has a right to tell the other what his/her job is or how to do it. A willingness to do your share, good communication, and, perhaps, negotiation leads to the chore list for each person.

The same goes for giving advice, which is a cousin of telling. If you want to give advice, ask permission. If you desire advice, ask for it. This is basic respect for another.

Certain liberties of communication are sometimes taken with spouses that would not be taken with a friend. Should not a spouse to given the ultimate of respect and consideration?

A Couple's Sex Life: Who, Why, How, When, Where!

Sex is not an easy subject for most people to talk about in any type of intimate sense. Sure, the topic can raucously be thrown around, usually by those who have too much alcohol in them or those that are just crude. But for most couples, discussing their sex life feels like going into the "danger zone"!

The focus of this article is about a couple making love, having a sex life that is satisfying throughout their relationship. Few couples attain a satisfying sex life through the duration of their relationship. Time, and other factors, often erode a good sex life. Sex is one of the main topics that I confront regularly in my office. I will try to break down this audacious topic into five provocative areas: Who, Why, How, When, and Where. Let's see where this goes!

Who: The individuals focused on, for the intent of this writing, are two people who are in love and committed to living together in a trusting monogamous relationship.

Why: The premise is that these couples desire to share their love in a sensuous manner. They want it to be satisfying and enduring. Physical and emotional closeness, sometimes even spiritual, can take a couple to a very special place in their relationship. This bonding connection fuels further an adventurous life through the duration of their time together.

How: A couple's sex life can get more challenging in the "how" portion of their experience. Significant variables emerge once a couple is past the primal early lovemaking that existed early on in their relationship. Physical and psychological issues emerge. These vary in their complexity and their duration. Examples of the physical would include pregnancy factors, ailments, injuries, obesity, medication limitation, position disagreements, aging challenges, alcohol, limping libido, etc. Psychological factors include anger, embarrassment, infidelity, guilt, performance anxiety, lost feelings, stress, etc.

When: Over time the complexities of life can make it difficult to find the time to make love. Kids and their activities, job exhaustion, various commitments, too much TV time, differing priorities, etc. all can impact the frequency of lovemaking.

Where: When younger, the "where" could be anywhere and everywhere. Many couples have some wild tales as to when they "did it" in some unique places and venues. Over time, for most couples, the daring places become less frequent, if at all. Simple routines emerge, which is fine for many, boring for a few.

Respected Reader, I offer the above overview to encourage you to look at your sex life and see if it is satisfactory relative to the five factors listed, or perhaps some other reason that you may be able to identify. I have been able to help many couples to develop an enhanced sex life. In some cases I work in concert with other medical professional to address those factors that are stifling. The health benefits, both physical and psychological, are too numerous to mention for those who partake in a satisfying sex life. Hope you are not missing out!

10 Sex Issues Couples Complain About To Marriage Therapists

The sex life of couples is complex. Insight of millennium! It changes over time and situations, and is usually difficult for most couples to communicate about. It is a frequent issue in marriage counseling. Brittany Wong, Huffington Post divorce editor, has chosen ten sexual topics that marriage therapists frequently hear during a counseling session. I will list them and add my commentary.

1. **Neither Partner Will Make Time For Sex:** Example: He liked evenings for making love. She preferred mornings. Thus, nada. It happens. Also, when a couple is disconnected emotionally, or just plain worn out, time is not allotted for it.

2. **Fetishes Are Laughed Off Or Totally Disregarded:** Some people have some rather different desires for a sexual encounter. Some are really weird (my bias). Generally, those that ask for fetishes are looking for an exciting (to them) romp, but it usually isn't about making love.

3. **There's A Breakdown In Intimacy After An Affair:** Usually the non-affairee, especially if it is a woman, will use sex as a weapon, usually cutting it off.

4. **The Marital Bed Becomes The Family Bed:** When children sleep with their parents there usually isn't time or place for couple sex. Personally, I believe kids need to sleep in their own beds, with some family cuddling the morning after.

5. **The Dog Is In The Bedroom All The Time:** I hear this one often and I cringe! Fido does not need to be in the bedroom.

6. **Less Effort Is Put Into Looking Sexy:** I'm not so sure that one needs to look "sexy" for good sexual relations to happen.

However, keeping reasonably in shape and having good hygiene, including brushing teeth, make the invitation more persuasive.

7. **Couples Aren't Upfront About Their Sexual Preferences:** Who is on top? Bottom? Sideways? Around? How much foreplay? What is desired for orgasm? Anybody blushing?

8. **Sexual Signals Are Misinterpreted:** Example: "Honey, I'm going to bed." The person headed to bed meant that as an invitation for she/her partner to follow. The partner felt the other was just tired and ready to crash. The invitation needs to be a bit clearer. However, You'd be surprised how some overly direct vulgar invitations are spit out. Use your imagination on this one.

9. **Exhaustion Or Busy Schedules Get In The Way:** "I'm too tired." "I've got too much to do." I believe that time management and energy availability reflect priorities.

10. **Sex Becomes Perfunctory Or Too *By The Book*:** Enthusiasm and variety can make the sexual encounter more enjoyable and desirable.

Well, these are the ones listed by Ms. Wong. I could fill many more articles with what I have heard from couples with regard to their sex life. Maybe another time. Sex, money, and kids are the usual biggest conflict areas for couples. Any of the ten fit your situation?

A Couple's Sleep Pattern May Reflect Intimacy Reality

The word "sleeping with" is an interesting verb in our society. It denotes rest and it denotes sexual activity. They often go together. Let me be more explicit.

The National Sleep Foundation in 2001 found out that 12% of married couples slept alone. In 2005 that number jumped to 23%. And today, what is the new number? I suspect that it is continuing to climb. The National Association of Homebuilders says that there has been a steady increase of requests for "two master bedroom" homes to be built.

What is this information indicating? I presume that there are varieties of explanations for this trend. Health, stress, and romance come to mind.

Our society is aging; many citizens are overweight and drink too much. Sleep apnea, snoring, and leg twitching appear to be more prevalent, or, at best, are not as tolerated by spouses as in previous times. Restful sleep can be a challenge is such situations.

Stress is high in most households, due to jobs, income, financial markets, family problems, etc. Stress affects health, sleep, and romance. A good night's sleep is most needed during such times.

Romance may or may not be present in a relationship for a variety of reasons. A partner's snoring, sleep apnea, or leg twitching may be a convenient "excuse" to leave the bedroom and sleep someplace else to avoid intimacy.

Over the years I have heard every explanation possible as to why a couple is not sleeping together, as well as not snuggling or having sex together. Operative word here is "together." Solo sex still thrives in most cases. Different biological "clocks," television, computer, the kids, work demands, snoring, etc. are reasons offered for not going to bed together.

I encourage couples to end their day together on most nights—with their love partner—by spending at least ten to twenty minutes snuggling, preferably without having your boxers, jammies, or nightgown on. Then if one person is not tired or wants to get up for whatever reason, at least the couple has ended the day together with some degree of closeness. This activity helps to maintain a connection so as to not just be living together under the same roof. Just being "roommates" is not enough for a couple who profess to love one another.

I invite you to look at your sleep patterns and why they are what they are. Do your sleep habits say much about what kind of spousal sensual relationship you have? May the need for a good night's sleep not be an excuse for not sharing emotional and physical closeness with your partner. Loving touch is a basic human need for survival.

"Sleep" well—together if at all possible.

"Walking On Egg Shells" In Your Relationship? This Quiz May Help!

Certainly you have heard the expression "walking on egg shells." Have you used it? Lived it? Currently living it? I hear this phrase said in many couples' therapy sessions. Neil Rosenthal, a licensed Marriage and Family Therapist, has written a quality article on the subject, including a questionnaire to help you determine if that is your reality. The answers may help you determine if you are living in such a way, perhaps even with a borderline personality companion. Take the quiz.

Answer each question with a 0 – not a problem; 1 – sometimes a problem; 2 – a problem half the time; 3 – a frequent concern; 4 – an ongoing problem of great concern.

1. Do you find yourself hiding thoughts or feelings because it is easier than dealing with your partner's overreactions—or because talking about problems simply make them worse?

2. After you try to explain yourself to the other person, does she/he use your own words and contort them to prove his/her own point? Does your mate blame you or all the problems in his/her life, and your relationship, and refuse to acknowledge that his/her actions cause problems?

3. Is his/her temper so unpredictable that you're constantly on your toes, adrenaline pumping, waiting for the next verbal attack? Is it difficult to enjoy the good times because you've learned never to let your guard down?

4. When you come home from work each day, do you wonder whether Dr. Jekyll or Mr. Hyde will greet you at the door?

5. Do you feel manipulated, controlled or even lied to sometimes in an attempt for your partner to get what she/he wants?

6. Does your mate seem to demand constant attention? Is everything always about him/her?

7. Are you afraid to ask for things in the relationship because you'll be told you're selfish and demanding? Does she/he imply or show by example that your needs are not as important as his/her needs?

8. Do you feel that your partner's expectations of you are constantly changing so that you can never do anything right?

9. Are you accused of doing things you never did and saying things you never said? Do you feel misunderstood? When you try to explain, do you find that your partner doesn't believe you?

10. Do other people remark that your partner is verbally or emotionally abusive? Do they encourage you to leave the relationship?

11. If and when you try to leave, does your partner prevent you from departing?

12. Do you have a hard time planning social engagements, vacations, and other activities because the other person's moodiness, impulsiveness or unpredictability may destroy your plans at the last minute?

Okay, what did you come up with? According to Dr. Rosenthal:

- A score of 20 or more indicates that your partner probably has a Borderline Personality Disorder.

- A score of 11-20 indicates a relationship with a borderline-borderline: someone who may have borderline personality leanings but who can keep them somewhat in check.

- A score of 11 or below probably means that the person in your life does not have a Borderline Personality Disorder.

Let me stress that this questionnaire is not a diagnostic tool per se. Dr. Rosenthal is putting it out there to help you reflect on your relationship. Are you "walking on egg shells"? Does your partner have possible Borderline Personality Disorder traits? If the answers are pointing out these negatives, please see a qualified Marriage and Family Therapist pronto!

Discuss Responsibilities In Your Marriage And Family

Many couples argue over who does what in regard to mutual responsibilities. What is a fair agreement as to the contribution of each person? Oftentimes one person feels that the other person is not carrying his or her part of the load.

Responsibilities may vary and change over time depending on a number of factors:

1. Do both work outside of the home?
2. Does one person stay home?
3. Are there kids at home? What age(s)?
4. Family income status.
5. Strengths and weaknesses of each person in regard to required tasks.
6. Is there agreement as to what needs to be done?
7. Does either one travel?
8. What is the strength of the marriage?
9. How well does the couple communicate their needs and wants?
10. How good is the couple at compromising?
11. Is either person "retired"?
12. How old and/or infirmed is each person?
13. Is someone "lazy"?
14. Is there a procrastinator present?
15. Is there a "neat freak" or "slob" present?

The list could go on and on. What are your particular issues related to division of labor? Do you agree as to what needs to be done by whom and when? If not, how do you respond? Do you get angry or play the "martyr" role? Is either one of you judgmental and critical? Do you "keep score"? If you do, something is wrong.

Some mates fail to empathize and sense what is going on with his or her partner. Many men do not appreciate what the wife goes through as a working or stay home mom. Some women do not appreciate what the man labors through in his job. Sometimes it is the reverse situation where the woman is the chief breadwinner and the man does more of the home duties.

Each couple has unique expectations and needs. What is important is that they communicate well on what needs to be done and who does the agreed upon responsibilities. Often couples cannot agree and I serve as the mediator as each person argues his or her case as to what is "fair."

May this article serve as a catalyst for you and your spouse to discuss how you take care of the things that are important to you.

"Space" Is An Important Factor In A Relationship

The word "space" is used often in relationships. It is a loaded word. "I need space" is a sentence that elicits strong reactions from the receiver of the message. "What are you saying?" is the usual retort. Clarification is usually needed.

Space or distance is a tricky variable in relationships—from the dating stage to the "it's been a lot of years together, honey" stage. People have different needs in a relationship relative to how emotionally close and/or how much time one needs with or separate from the other. Space is about both physical and emotional closeness. Also, that need for space may change over the years for a number of reasons.

In the early dating period of a developing relationship, when one person says "I need some space," she/he may well be saying I'm on my way out of this relationship. Translated, it usually means "she/he just isn't that much into you." Take the hint and move on. If the person really did not mean that, she/he will rush in to clarify.

Some people are "clingy" and want the other person to be physically and emotionally present an awfully lot. These people are, or are perceived to be, very needy, with a lot of affirmation required. They can wear you out.

Other people prefer to spend much of their time alone, with limited emotional closeness. They appear to be very self-sufficient. Sometimes that aloneness hides one's fear of letting anyone in too close.

Where do you fit in on this continuum? Which type comes closest to describing you? There is no right or wrong here, just personal style and preference. There are reasons for each orientation and preferred styles. What matters here is the match.

Two excessive "clingers" will drive each other nuts. Two "loners" will end up being pretty lonely—when they allow themselves to feel.

The most important fact here is to have a compatibility of styles that can co-exist and be additive to the relationship and can adjust appropriately over time. Most people don't change their "clingy" or "loner" orientation very much. The tendency, however, is for men over time to get more "clingy" and women to develop more of "loner" style, at least in relationship to the marriage.

In summary, how much time a couple spends together, and how emotionally close they are, is an important reference point determining the quality of the relationship. How do you handle your "space" issue? Talk with your significant other about it; it could be enlightening!

Do You Know What the 11 Most Important Phrases A Successful Couple Share?

Communication in a couple's relationship is critically important. I dare say it probably is the number one factor as to whether a couple has a successful relationship or not. Certain phrases a couple uses are critical for developing, maintaining, and restoring a damaged relationship. Kelsey Borresen has done a good job in highlighting an elite eleven critical phrases that are basic for enhancing a relationship. She came up with this list by interviewing relationship experts. I share them with you with my added commentary.

1. **"I am so lucky I married you."** Two basic needs in a loving relationship are affirmation and appreciation. A spouse wants to know that the other continues to feel fortunate that she/he is in this ongoing relationship. Thus, a wise, attuned, and honest spouse will periodically blurt out this complimentary phrase. It's a bigee!

2. **"How can I help you?"** When you offer this phrase it shows you are attuned to the other and willing to assist with any situation that may occur. The spoken-to-spouse feels heard and valued. Team effort.

3. **"I want you."** To be wanted by the person who probably knows you better than anyone, including your flaws, is meaningful and connecting. "I want you" says that the spouse wants and accepts all of you. This includes sexual contact, but only in the larger context of acceptance.

4. **"What do you think?"** By reaching out to the other for an opinion you are saying that you value that person and what

she/he has to say. This opens the door to open dialogue, resulting in good, shared decision making.

5. **"What would I do without you!"** You are stating how very important your spouse is to you. She/he is a critically important part of your life and happiness. Such a wonderful compliment! There is a certain vulnerability in this statement that invites a deeper emotional connection.

6. **"You are so beautiful/handsome."** Looks are not the be all and end all in a marriage—especially as time goes by and the body ages. However, hopefully your spouse stays attractive to you in your own mind. You see the whole person—and that looks good!

7. **"I'm sorry."** It is important in a marriage to be humble enough to say "I'm sorry." Many people struggle with this one. Nobody likes to be wrong or make obvious mistakes. Important to own it and apologize. Again, another way of honoring and showing love to your spouse.

8. **"Tell me about it."** People want to be heard. It is a part of being respected and valued. Showing interest in something that your spouse wants to share with you is important. Regarding sharing of information, I tell this to my clients: Women, please don't give your man too many details. Men can't stay with you that long. Share the details with your woman friend. Men, listen longer and share more. If it is an important topic, shut off the TV and be fully present.

9. **"I was wrong, you were right."** Another toughee, but important. This is related to number seven but somewhat different. If you've got to be "right" all the time, you shove your partner away. Who wants to be "wrong" all the time? Oftentimes, the old expression, "we can agree to disagree" is a nice way to leave disputed issues.

10. **"I accept you as you are."** Too often in my office I hear one spouse trying to "fix" or change the other. Doesn't work. Important to accept the person you chose as your partner. However, you do have the right to say this or that behavior is hurtful to you. Then the offending partner can decide if she/he wants to change. But you are not the change agent!

11. **"I forgive you."** One of the most important phrases! Everyone does things that hurt another. Hopefully the person that offends is able to say "I'm sorry" and the offended one is able to say "I forgive you." Forgive, yes— forget is another issue, depending on the infraction. One of my favorite expressions is "Begin each day with fresh forgiveness." A good way to live!

Respected Reader, how many of these phrases do you say, and how often? Any of them particularly hard to say? Why? How about your spouse? Who is better at saying these phrases? I reiterate, these are very important phrases to be stated in order to have the loving relationship that you desire.

Scorekeeping Can Ruin A Relationship!

Are you a "scorekeeper" in your relationship? What do I mean by that? A "scorekeeper" keeps count of what each person does on behalf of the relationship, sometimes on a day-to-day basis. This person wants to be sure, without a doubt, that his/her partner is doing his or her part. This person's tally always makes sure the partner comes up a little short. This mindset and behavior can be both exhausting and frustrating to both individuals.

There certainly is a place for responsibility, sharing, and accountability with regard to the various needs and demands of the partnership. Hopefully over the course of the relationship each person recognizes what needs to be done and steps up and does what is necessary.

Sometimes, or perhaps often, one person does not understand or appreciate what the other does on behalf of the couple's well-being. Most of the time this misunderstanding person is the husband, who surprisingly enough is usually the "scorekeeper." Many a time I have heard husbands castigate their stay-at-home wives for not doing enough.

Have you ever heard the song 'Mr. Mom' by Lonestar? It is about a man who has lost his job. His wife gets a job and he will stay home with the kids and "watch TV and take long naps; go from hard working dad to being Mr. Mom." After being Mr. Mom for a very short time he concludes that he "thought there was nothing to it. Baby, now I know how you feel. What I don't know is how you do it. Honey, you're my hero!"

Relationships go through many manifestations over the course of time. Job demands, children's needs, meals, home upkeep, etc. all call for attention from someone. Who answers the call and to the extent that the needs are met invite judgment. Be careful. Usually—

not always—each person is doing the best that she/he can. If you honestly feel that the other person is not doing his/her share, bring it up in an assertive, but non-judgmental, manner. Encouragement, gratitude, and compliments are the best response. Focus on what is being done, not what is missing. With such a complimentary and supportive couple environment, each person will probably do even more to ensure that she/he is contributing to the overall needs of the family.

During the course of a committed relationship, one person may in fact be doing more than the other. During another stage of the relationship the other person may be doing more. Don't keep score, be grateful that you have a partner that is there for you and the family and will rise to the occasion based on the presenting needs of the time.

"My Spouse Wasn't Like That When We Married!"

The above words are mentioned in most every counseling session I have with a married person. Duh, of course he wasn't—on the outside. You never would have married him if he (or she) did not show his (or her) best side during the dating ritual. From your perceptual stance at the time this person was a dream come true for a marriage partner. Sometimes, however, the dream was actually a nightmare in disguise. Outward appearances, behaviors, can be deceptive and not reveal well what is inside.

When you go look to buy a car, do you buy it because it looks nice on the outside? No. You also check out the inside—the mechanical parts that run the car. So too, should it be when looking at a potential spouse. Look at his interior mechanics—brain—to see what kind of shape it is in. The brain drives behavior based on how it is wired from life experiences. A person's family of origin carves deep emotional imprints that are deep and lasting and significantly affect the marriage experience, far beyond what most people understand.

If a person is sharp she/he can figure out what behavior is needed to win your heart. In the early dating period the emotional part of your brain can easily be caught up in the infatuation/sexual chemicals of the brain. These PEA (phenylethylamine) chemicals are intoxicating and exciting. Alas, they fizzle out after a while, usually within three years. At this point a deeper emotional attachment is built resulting in an endorphin-like loving closeness OR a negative disintegration process develops destroying the loving feeling that once was present. The determining factor as to which direction the connection/disconnection goes is dependent on the intimacy (vulnerability) issues in the marriage, based on trust and respect. These issues rarely surface before marriage. Within the marriage certain habits, behaviors, and attitudes develop that either result in each person feeling safe, secure, and loved. Or their opposites.

The direction here is contingent upon each other healing the interior wounds of the other, which were not vulnerably present in the dating process. The wounds can only be triggered by the vulnerability within a marriage relationship. If the necessary healing does not take place, a couple distances, because these raw wounds are then exacerbated. Everyone has some or many wounds from their early family and childhood experiences. (I encourage you to read the works of Dr. Harville Hendrix to get a more amplified understanding of this). I see these dynamics occur in every counseling situation I have. It has also been a beneficial experience personally in my marriage.

Such an understanding of this interior dynamic is critical if you want to have a good marriage. You only find this information out by a therapeutic process facilitated by a trained Marriage and Family Therapist. (It's like asking a mechanic to check out the used car you are contemplating to buy. The mechanic may even have to show you how to run the car efficiently and take care of it over the long haul.)

"You don't know what you don't know." But you can find out. A wise person is aware of what she/he does not know and goes about finding out knowledge that is necessary for success. In this case I am talking about relationship "due diligence."

Repeatedly in relationship counseling, after going through this process, individuals will say to me, "Now I understand why we were destined to fail." If people discover this soon enough, success can result. The deeper emotions, which are often defensed, surface and are capable of being healed and thus intimacy and deep connection can occur.

Do you know your deepest emotional core wiring? Your spouse's? Potential spouse's? I am willing to bet that you do not. Such knowledge and subsequent behavior will make or break a relationship over time. Guaranteed!

"Irritants" Need To Be Addressed By Couples!

Couples disagree and argue with each other. Couples can get quite mad at each other. Research says that the big five of arguments are about money, sex, parenting, in laws, or housework. Had any such arguments? But there is another level of issues that pull couples apart. They are the little IRRITATIONS that just drive each other nuts. Little irritations can cause big disconnections. Petty problems can subvert love surreptitiously. That's the focus of this article.

Irritations exist in every couple's relationship. It is not possible to live with another human being whose every quirk, habit, and preference aligns perfectly with yours. The challenge when these irritants bother you is "figuring out how to negotiate and live with your partner's irritants in a way that doesn't alienate them and keeps the two of you connected," according to psychiatrist John Jacobs.

Each person develops an individuality from genetically influenced temperaments, belief systems, and experiences growing up in the family of origin. Certain patterns of behavior can be deeply rooted and difficult to change.

Irritants can range from superfluous to substantial. Leaving clothes on the floor, eating habits, hygiene preferences, leaving the toilet seat up, snide comments, flirting, not remembering what was said, over-talking or interrupting, chewing gum, talking too much on the telephone, taste in clothes or furnishings, driving too fast or too slow, etc. Add your own. I'm sure you have a few.

Most of the time a person is not willing, perhaps unable, to change an irritant. Thus, the only option is for you to change how you think, feel, and react to it. What is the meaning or significance that you attach to the irritant? Do you make it bigger than big? An ice cube becomes and iceberg? Do you get paranoid and think your partner is deliberately trying to annoy you? Do you make the irritant intensely personal such that your partner doesn't care about you and what you feel? Do you sometimes think that "if you really cared about me you would stop driving me crazy with these habitual irritants."

Psychologist Michael Cunningham states, "The simple fact is that people engage in automatic behaviors that are habitual or self-focused without taking the other person into account." Cunningham's research found that people suppress their irritating behaviors early in the dating process but allow them to emerge once they're in a committed relationship. Too often people bring their best behavior in the dating process and then after marriage let some things slide. Certainly this is disappointing, and irritating to the partner who experiences such change in the other.

I encourage you, Respected Reader, to be aware of what irritants your partner perpetuates. If it seems significant to you, address it with your partner. Perhaps she/he can change the behavior. Perhaps not. How you deal with it is what is most important. If it truly is just an irritant find a way to live without it becoming a major issue to you that gets you all whacked out. Perhaps, too, you can examine your own "irritants" that you might want to change. The connected relationship is more important than the irritant. If it is not, then you might well examine the relationship!

Do You Bring "Sunday Morning Sunshine" To Your Mate?

Music is important to me. I use it for inspiration and mood movement. Since I am not particularly a "morning person" (Am I the only one? I think not!) I often listen to music to get me up and going on a positive energetic note.

One of the songs I use for early rising mood setting is 'Sunday Morning Sunshine' by Harry Chapin. One of the lyric stanzas goes like this:

"You brought your Sunday Morning Sunshine
Here into my Monday morning rain.
You taught me happiness ...
It keeps on coming back again."

The lyric strikes a positive chord (catch the pun?) for a couple of reasons—"morning" and "sunshine."

As admitted, I am groggy in the morning, slow to warm up to where I want to be—both for myself and for my wife. My wife, Sherry, on the other hand, is the total opposite. She truly is "Sunday morning sunshine" every day. She wakes up happy, smiley, and eager to connect. I am grateful that she restrains these gifts of her "sunshine" until I can open up the curtains of my mind and mood to be receptive.

Respected Reader, you may ask, "where is he going with this"? My message is threefold:

1. It is important to know yourself well, which would include knowing what your moods are at various times and what you may need to do to alter them, both for your own well-being

as well as what you bring forth to your partner and others who are special to you.

2. Music can be a vehicle to help you get there. Find music that brings you fuller into life, that evokes a smile, a happy feeling.

3. It is incumbent on you to attempt to bring your best self, your "sunshine" to your partner. Do you do it? When you go to your job I'll bet you do a pretty good job of turning up your positive style to others, no matter how you feel. Otherwise, you may well get fired. Does your significant other deserve less effort?

I am blessed to be married to a positive person who consistently brings her "sunshine" to me in many different forms. I attempt to reciprocate. I have a long ways to go, but I'm working on it every day!

Maybe tomorrow, I will surprise Sherry with these lyrics from "Good Morning, Sunshine":

"Good morning sunshine,
I wish for your heart.
You're a symbol to all that you meet,
'Cause you keep on shining.
You're extraordinary"

Oh wait, I can't sing. Guess I'll just read it to her—after my cup of coffee! I need to give it my best shot because this week she celebrates a significant birthday!

Are You Putting Your Marriage First? Ask Your Kids, They Will Tell You!

In my profession I have learned a lot—to say the least! One of the more important things that has consistently shown up is that your marriage, if you choose it, needs to be your first priority—after your own well-being and becoming the best SINGLE person that you could be.

Hopefully, you have seen the value of optimal personal development. Few people do. If you decide you would like the marriage state then do your research, due diligence, as to what type of person is the best fit for you as you travel through life. If you are already married perhaps you can do some tweaking, or major reconstruction if needed, to get your marriage into good shape.

Thus, if you are married, make your partner your priority. Develop a rich, solid, loving marriage. If you have kids, or plan or having them, let them see your bonded love, that you are a "we" in making decisions going forth. In doing this you will be giving your kids the best gift that you could give them. This "gift" is two parents who love each other and continually make thoughtful compromising decisions that result in a good marriage model and a solid security blanket for your kids.

I think one of the best compliments I have ever received is when our two kids, individually have stated, "Dad you guys always put your marriage first. We could not divide you for our personal gain when we were kids. Ultimately this did give us security for which we are grateful. You two are the role models for our marriage and family." Wow, it doesn't get any better than that! They have chosen good partners, have solid loving marriages, and are raising their children with the model they witnessed growing up.

To put your marriage first is to recognize and do the things that reflect that commitment. It may not be easy, but it is important with significant ramifications. Too often people put their job, kids, animals, friends, etc. ahead of their spouse. Costly mistake!

The Importance Of Nurturing Your Marriage While Raising Kids

I have written previously on how children affect and change a marriage. Too often many of this generation of parents get all goggle-eyed about having kids and focus too much on them to the detriment of their marriage relationship. The marriage becomes parent centered and the core of the marriage relationship suffers.

Tina Cettina has written a quality article based on the challenges that she and her husband Greg faced when their two girls were born. They were trying to do everything possible to be perfect parents, but nurturing their couple relationship was not on their "to do list." They were out of balance. She became less fun loving. They had more squabbles. He distanced himself from her. The relationship became like many other new parents—roommates instead of romantic partners.

Cettina offers the following suggestions taken from Carol Ummel Lindquist, Ph.D. in her book, *Happily Married With Kids: It's Not Just A Fairy Tale.*

- **Create Warm Welcomes:** As each of you comes and goes, greet each other with a smile and a kiss. Make the arriving spouse feel genuinely welcomed. This not only helps nurture the relationship but it models something that the kids will remember and practice in their own adult lives.
- **Try 20 Minute Reconnects:** Find twenty minutes here and there to talk, walk, connect in some fashion as two adults who love each other and are co-creating a family.
- **Set Early Bedtimes:** Put the kids down early when they are young. When they get older send them to their rooms while you share some end of the day special time together.

- **Share The Load:** There are a number of chores that need to be done for the kids and overall home maintenance. Each person should do their share. When our kids were very young, our family "domestic manager," my wife Sherry, would give me the option of doing the dishes or bathing the kids!

- **Encourage Your Kids' Independence:** Teach your kids to do certain things for themselves, as well as learning to entertain themselves. A parent does not necessary have to do every single thing for a child. Obviously this is age and competence related. Some insecure parents want their kids to be dependent on them far more than what is really good for the kids.

- **Revive Your Past:** Talking about some of the good ol' days together can bring a shared closeness, plus it may remind you to do again some of the fun things that you did early in your relationship.

- **Put Sex On Your Schedules:** Yes, spontaneity would be nice; however, too often people forget, are too tired, have too many other things that are pressing, etc. Cuddling and shared sensuality help to keep the emotional closeness alive.

- **Fight As If The Neighbors Can Hear You:** Your kids and your neighbors do not need to hear you hurling verbal insults at each other. If you have anger and frustrations—and every marriage does—be respectful in discussing them. Another way to keep the disagreements civil is to turn on the tape recorder when you are about to talk about a heated subject. Try it sometime; you will see how much your voice and style changes.

- **Remember: Dad's Way Works, Too:** Dad may have some good ideas about parenting or doing things in a certain way.

Empowering him may get him more involved than he normally would be.

- **Have Cheap Dates:** Husbands and wives need to have regular dates, but they don't all have to be over-the-top events. Working in a lunch together or going out and getting coffee or a pizza together can be occasions for getting together without the kids.

- **Know The Various Stages Of Marriage:** Marriages have an up and down rhythm to them depending on various factors such as your age, length of marriage, age of kids, physical and mental condition, finances, stresses, etc. Each stage moves on to another phase, hopefully with most of them getting better with age.

There will be a time of "empty nest"; may this period be one of a sense of accomplishment knowing that you have nurtured your marriage well while having raised healthy, responsible, and wise children. Your loving "team" did it by putting your marriage first!

Empty Nest? Need To Push Re-Start And Adjust Buttons?

Wonder if this profile fits you—or perhaps may in the future. You got married relatively young. You were in love (in lust?), enjoyed each other, and for whatever reason (and there are many) decided to get married. Maybe divorced, and married again.

Second chapter: Somewhere in the married journey you decided to have children, or "oops," a kid was on the way, ready or not. Then another—perhaps. You wanted to be a good parent, maybe better than the ones who raised you. You committed a lot of time and effort to raising the kids. You were involved, perhaps too much, in your children's lives.

You enjoyed the good times, survived the rough spots, particularly during the tumultuous teen years. The kids made it through high school and, hopefully, were on the way out of the nest. (If not, why not? In most cases they need to be, though these economical times have made things tougher).

And then, it was just the two of you. No practices to take the kids to or games to watch. The kids' friends no longer came over. Just the two of you. *Just the two of you.*

Good news, "free at last" or..."what do we do now?" There are basically two types of "empty nesters."

In the first type a couple has continued to prioritize and develop their marriage. They have continued to grow as a couple, adjusting to each other, taking time to be alone without kids, and nurturing the relationship. They have interests, separately and together, which have brought a sense of accomplishment and satisfaction into their lives. The "empty nest" has not been a great adjustment, rather more of a freeing up of time to continue to enjoy and experience their lives. This type, however, is more the exception than the rule.

The second type, unfortunately, became a parent-centered marriage. By that I mean that this couple was consumed by parenting—everything was about the kids. They did not continue to do the things that were necessary to maintain closeness of feelings and shared couple activities. They grew apart as a couple.

That is why you see so many divorces when the children are leaving home. (Some opt out early, which usually is regrettable because of the impact on the young kids.) The couple relationship got lost along the way in these relationships. Of those who did not divorce it is a challenge to re-unite as a loving couple sharing a richness of relationship and enjoyable activities.

For those of you still together, I commend your fortitude. Now, as a song suggests, "let's be us again." And how is that done? Sometimes you have to start again to really know each other. You each have changed in significant ways over the years. Careers, moves, various life adjustments have resulted in two transformed people with different needs and capacities to be enriched. Good communication and a revitalized energy to live life fully, both together and with individual interests, can create a desirous synergy between the two of you. It is worth the effort. You have worked hard all your life. Time to share the rest of your life with someone who has shared the burden—and the memories—and can love you the way you desire to be loved!

Examine Your Relationship Before "It's Too Late"!

One of the most heartbreaking elements of my profession is to witness the end of a relationship and/or to see one that is in really bad shape. There is so much hurt present in each person. And it did not need to come to that in most cases. Individuals in a relationship too often procrastinate and postpone working on the relationship, whereas in other areas of their lives they get right to it.

Most people, if they feel a sharp pain in their stomach, will quickly have it checked out by their physician. They do not wait and wait, hoping that it will get better while, in fact, it worsens. Most people, when they sense that their car is acting up and/or the warning light goes on, will have it checked out by a mechanic. People don't want to keel over and die or have their car die or leave them stranded.

But their relationship is different. Most people passively sit and watch their relationship deteriorate and march down death's row. Why? It doesn't make sense.

A failing, or failed, relationship has incredible ramifications for mental health, children, finances, and lifestyle. I reiterate, most relationships can flourish or at least get a lot better than what exists at the present time. Less you think I am naïve in this proclamation, let me note that certainly some relationships cannot be fixed, probably never should have been in the first place. But those misfits are the minority.

One of the main reasons for this column is to invite, beg, and cajole people to look at various facets of their life. Hopefully, an idea will strike a cord and a person will see the need to work on an area or two of his or her life.

In the world of relationships most often it is the female who will first recognize that something is amiss in the relationship and will see the need for professional assistance. Rarely is it the male who initiates the counseling process. Over and over I hear stories from women who say that they asked their husbands to go to counseling only to be rebuffed. Finally, they came alone. Together we look at ways to invite the husband to come in and share his perspective—to deal with it. Too often the man runs away from the marriage emotionally by working harder, drinking more, having an affair, vegging out before the tube, or living in porn city on the internet.

All too frequently when the man refuses to come to counseling the woman will give up. She goes to an attorney and papers are filed. The husband then will get angry and threaten the wife with various off-the-wall comments or, sometimes, he will decide to be open to counseling. By that time it may be too late and/or the scars are so deep that limited remediation can take place.

The words of Carole King's ominous song recounting the death of a relationship come to mind:

"There's something wrong here, there can be no denying
One of us is changing or maybe we both quit trying.
It's too late, baby, now it's too late...
Something inside has died and I can't hide
And I just can't fake it ...
It's too late baby."

Relationship issues are complex and various conflicting perceptions and perspectives exist between a couple. It is vitally important to get on the same page as soon as possible. Examining the past to get a look at the issues, recognize unfulfilled needs, enhance communication, set goals, compromise, be accountable all are factors that can move a couple forward toward an enhanced union.

Are you waiting too long? Does the relationship still have a heartbeat? Have you missed an opportunity to fulfill your marriage's potential? "If the shoe fits," please quit stalling and begin to work on one of the most important elements of your life. You deserve that! So does your partner.

Dead Marriage: What Are The Options?

Sometimes in my practice I am present to a "dead marriage." It is "dead" because:

1. It should never have been born. It was a poor fit from the git-go. The couple was too young, naïve, and/or just plain mismatched. It was not a good fit! In some cases the couple saw the mismatch early on, divorced, and started over. Others took longer to realize that they were not a good combination, and then they went to divorce.

2. Another type of "dead" marriage is one that could have been kept alive, but the couple beat it to death. This beaten up marriage tried to survive the on-going torture it received, but the tormentors refused to get quality assistance to heal and resurrect it. Or perhaps they tried counseling but the counselors or the therapeutic strategies presented were inept.

Thus, what did the couple with the dead marriage do?
Options:

1. They agreed that the marriage was a mistake, did not blame the other, got divorced, and continued their partnership in a respectful manner if children were involved. If no kids, "out of sight, out of mind," or "never the twain shall meet" as Kipling would say.

2. They parted as enemies, chose warriors (attorneys) to help them continue to hurt each other in new and painful ways. Both were bloodied and, if children were involved, continued to wound their offspring repeatedly. The financial and psychological "cost" of such a war was, and remains, devastating.

3. They wanted to dissolve their marriage in a humane and fair manner. They mediated their marriage dissolution, taking the warring tactics out. This significantly minimized the "costs" involved.

Respected Reader, you may have fallen into one of the above categories or are "fixin'" to. Breaking up a marriage is challenging and very difficult to pull off with the best of intentions. Perhaps that is already your experience. If possible do all you can to heal the damage done, especially if children are a part of the mix.

If you are on the brink of considering divorce seek out competent assistance to know what your realistic options are and then tread carefully into the potential pitfalls. Life is too short to inflict or receive unnecessary pain from a marriage partner, past or present.

Others of you who have not yet gone through the experience of a "dead" marriage, learn more about yourself and what you need/want in a marriage partner. If you are in relationship where marriage is a possibility, seek relationship counseling to assess the strengths and potential weaknesses that may exist is this relationship. There are few pains greater than going through the "dead" marriage process. You definitely can lower the odds of having such a painful experience

Chapter Seven: Family

Family Life Affects Us Deeply—Past And Present!

Over the years in my profession I have learned much from working with people and assessing research. One of the most significant insights has been the understanding of how impactful the family is on the core development of a person. Beyond one's basic genetic imprint, the family "programs" an individual deeply and profoundly.

Two authors in particular, John Bradshaw and Phil McGraw, have written about the impact of the family and ways to help the family be as healthy as possible.

John Bradshaw has been a pioneer in this area through the book and video series entitled *The Family*. In it he addresses what the basic needs are of children growing up in the family. He is one of the pioneers who have described the family as a system and showed how what affects one person in the family vibrates to affect every other member. He points out that when basic needs of a child are not met the family system becomes dysfunctional.

Bradshaw stressed the importance of the family facilitating the development of one's true "self," which can so easily be stifled by families that are compulsive, hurtful, negligent, co-dependent, etc. He offers checklists and roadmaps for developing a self that is empowered and spiritual. This is challenging and powerful reading.

Phil McGraw, aka "Dr Phil," has published an outstanding book, *Family First*. This book is the most comprehensive and readable book I have read relative to creating an optimal family, including strategies for divorced or blended families. Some of his key emphases are:

- The family's impact is with you forever
- Helps you realize how you were raised and its impact on your parenting style
- Offers an inventory to help you know your parenting style
- Helps you develop purpose and strategies for your parenting style
- Helps you identify your child's type
- Offers ways to create a mentally stimulating environment for your kids
- Assists you in developing kids with self-esteem, social confidence, emotional stability and spiritual growth.

McGraw also offers "tools to parent with."

1. Purpose
2. Clarity
3. Negotiation
4. Currency (reinforcement)
5. Capacity to change
6. Harmony
7. Good example

To be the best parent you can be you need to start by being the best person you can be. Robert Fulghum has a good quote along this line: "Don't worry that your children never listen to you; worry that they are always watching you."

Healthy Family: Characteristics And Resulting Strengths

Do you have a healthy family? Did you come from a healthy family? Do you know what a healthy family is so that you can answer the first two questions? I would like to share with you my version of what a healthy family is.

Characteristics:

1. **Actively Love Each Other:** There are daily hugs and "I love you's" shared. Loving words and hugs help to make the home a place to feel secure. Security, physical and emotional, is a basic building block for healthy development.
2. **RESPECT And TRUST:** Lying doesn't happen. Privacy is respected. Independence is fostered. Consistency is the norm.
3. **Communicates:** Individuals: ASSERT their thoughts and feelings. LISTEN to each other. THANK one another. FORGIVE one another. RECONCILE.
4. **WORKS And PLAYS TOGETHER:** Goals are established and reached. Fun happens. Laughter exists.
5. **Expectations:** Rules and responsibilities are understood and carried out. Consequences, positive and negative, are consistently enforced.
6. **Flexibility And Adaptability:** Things are not rigid. The family is developmental as it goes through the various ages and stages. Change is welcomed.
7. **Values And Morals:** Spirituality and ethical behavior is taught and lived. Boundaries are clear and respected.

Strengths:

1. **Insight/Awareness:** Individuals are tuned into what is going on around them. Perceptions are stated, questions are asked.
2. **Independence:** Physically and emotionally. A strong sense of self, not needy or dependent.
3. **Relationship Capability:** Able to develop healthy and appropriate relationships in various situation and stages of life, i.e., work, play, friendship, romance.
4. **Initiative:** Seeing an opportunity and doing something positive about it.
5. **Creativity:** Be able to create when needed or desired.
6. **Humor:** Be able to laugh.
7. **Integrity:** Have an informed conscience and be able to put it into practice. "Walk the talk."

Well, Respected Reader, what do you think? Is this the family you came from? Is this the family you are, or will be, creating? I hope this treatise has given you further insight and motivation to create and participate in a healthy family!

What Healthy Families Do—And The Strengths That Emerge For Kids!

Do you come from a "healthy family"? Are you creating or have you created a "healthy family? Do you know what a "healthy family" looks like? The following is my explanation of what the characteristics of a healthy family are and the wonderful strengths that emerge in the kids from such a family.

Characteristics:

- Have clear priorities. Family is important. Each person is valued.
- Actively love one another. Mom and Dad love each other and show it. There are hugs and "I love you's" shared. Loving words, compliments, and appropriate touch are important. The family is a secure place to be.
- Communicates. Listens to what other family members are saying, both verbally and non-verbally. Asserts as members state their perceptions and needs.
- Respects and trusts one another. Lying is not tolerated. Privacy and growing independence is valued. Boundaries are set and respected.
- Works and plays together. Things are accomplished. Fun happens. A sense of humor exists in the family.
- Forgives and asks to be forgiven.
- Expectations are clear. Consistency exists. There are roles, rules, and responsibilities. There are consequences, positive and negative, for performance.
- Thanks and expresses gratitude to one another.

- Flexibility and adaptability are present. Things are not rigid. The family is developmental as it goes through different ages and stages. Change is welcomed.
- Have clear values and morals.
- Sees and fosters the unique gifts of each family member.

Emerging Strengths In Kids:
- Insight and awareness. Individuals are tuned in, state their perceptions, ask tough questions.
- Independence, both physically and emotionally. A strong sense of self, not needy or dependent on someone else for happiness.
- Capable of developing appropriate relationships with others in various situations and stages in life—school, work, play, friendship, and romance.
- Initiative: Seeing an opportunity or problem and doing something positive.
- Creativity: Be able to create or make happen something special.
- Humor: Be able to see the light side of things.
- Be moral. Have an informed conscience and put it into practice.

I hope this presentation offers some insight and direction for those of you who have an interest in better understanding a healthy family. The impact of family cannot be overstated. Do you best to make a "healthy family" happen!

Your Relationship With Your In Laws Is Important

Life transitions and developmental stages are important concepts in understanding life's journey. To live joyously and effectively it is important to realize the effect on you of some of these transitions.

One of the milestone transitions of life is marriage—yours and those of your children. Among the many ramifications of marriage is that you now have an "extended family." You did not choose these people, nor did they choose you, but by law they have become related to you. This extended family can be a boon or a bane to your life.

The extended family members, created by law, are either in laws or what I call your "out laws." Legally, they are in your family life. However, you do have a choice to make, depending on their personhood and character, of letting them "in" or of keeping them "out" to some extent. You have a right to have a personal boundary relative to them. How much interaction do you want with these individuals?

The reason for this article is that very often in therapy I hear angry or sad accounts about how this or that in law has caused pain or destruction. Some of the stereotypical "in law" situations would include:

- The dreaded interfering mother-in-law who can't keep her nose out and mouth shut.
- The alcoholic father-in-law who ruins family events with his excessive drinking.
- The sister-in-law who feels left out, behaves badly, and saps the energy out of everybody present.

- The brother-in-law who is a family disgrace and embarrassment.

The parents of your son or daughter may be people welcomed or dreaded. You will share the wedding and other family occasions with them. Hopefully, you can cultivate a good relationship with them.

And, what kind of new in law are you to the other family? May you be a person who is respectful of the married children, as well as their parents and other family members. Do not intrude, offer opinions unless asked, or impose "shoulds" and expectations on them. It is not your place. If you do these things you may well be put on their "out" list.

Personally, Sherry and I have been very fortunate. Our in-law parents are wonderful and additive to our lives and extended family. We are grateful for our good fortune! We like them and look forward to sharing extended family life with them. Our kids made good choices of spouses, who come from quality parents.

May you, Respected Reader, be as fortunate in gaining in laws that are additive. If not, may you be able to keep those "out laws" at a safe distance so that they do not pollute with negativity the loving family you are trying to create and maintain.

Chapter Eight: Parenting, Stepparenting and Grandparents

Parenting

Parents: A Message From Your Children

Are you raising kids? Did that? Will do that? Do you, or did you, have a manual for doing a bang-up job in raising kids? Did you, or are you going to, raise the kids the way you were raised? What might you do differently?

Raising kids, no matter what their age, is a two-way street. Kids have feelings, perceptions, and needs. Oftentimes, however, they are not the best in communicating with you, their parents. Or, perhaps, you parents are not listening well. Plus, there still are some stone age parents who believe that "kids should be seen but not heard."

Would you like to "hear" them? They have spoken to me and I am passing their words on to you. They are now a part of a handout I often use when teaching parenting classes. Here your children's words:

- Stand by us, not over us. Give us the feeling that we are not alone in the world, that we can always count on you when we are in trouble.

- Make us feel that we are loved and wanted. We want to love you, not as a duty but because you love us.
- Train us by being affectionately firm. You will achieve more with us through patient teaching than by punishment or preaching. Say "no" when you feel you have to, but explain your rules, don't merely impose them.
- Bring us up so that we will not always need you. Teach us how to take on responsibility and become independent of you. We will learn this faster and better if you will let us question you, your ideas and standards.
- Don't act shocked when we do things we shouldn't. It is going to take us time to learn how to grow into life properly.
- Try to be as consistent as possible. If you are mixed up about what you want from us, why shouldn't we be mixed up too, in what we give you?
- Don't try and make us feel inferior. We doubt ourselves enough without your confirming it. Predicting failure won't help us succeed.
- Say "nice work" when we do something really well. Don't hold back the praise when we deserve it. That's the way to spur us on.
- Show respect for our wishes even if you disagree with them. Respect for you will flow naturally from your respect of us.

Articulate little devils, aren't they! "Out of the mouths of babes…" Listening to kids is not easy, but it is worth the extra time. Just as it is for you and me, we like to be heard by significant others in our life. The earlier we can respond to our children's exhortations the better the results will be for us as the kids go through the challenging teen years.

There is no more important role or mission than to be a loving parent who works in concert with our mate, or ex-spouse, to nurture and mentor our children. Communication with them is essential and an important ingredient for any effective dialogue is to truly hear them. Adhering to the above nine points will go a long way in developing children of whom you are proud and they are appreciative. Give it your best shot, no matter what age your kids are. A loving family of well-connected adults is a wonderful reality and worth such effort.

Advice On How Best To Communicate With Your Children

Regularly I meet with parents and children/teens and observe the lack of communication going on. I feel fortunate that most kids open up to me and, thus, I am able to help their parents understand what is going on, as well as coaching them as to better ways to communicate with their kids. This article offers some tips on how to best communicate with your children. The tips come from the American Psychological Association, embellished by the comments of this author.

- **Be available for your children:** Notice times when your kids are most likely to talk; for example, at bedtime, before dinner, in the car. Start the conversation; it lets your kids know you care about what's happening in their lives. Find time each week for a one-on-one activity with each child, and avoid scheduling other activities at that time. Learn about your child's interests: for example, favorite music and activities, and show interest in them. Initiate conversation by sharing what you have been thinking about rather than beginning a conversation with a question.

- **Let your kids know when you're listening:** When your children are talking about concerns, stop whatever you are doing and listen. Express interest in what they are saying without being intrusive. Listen to their point of view, even if it is difficult to hear. Let them complete their point before you respond. Repeat what you heard them say to ensure that you understand them correctly.

- **Respond in a way that your children will hear:** Soften strong reactions; kids will tune you out if you appear angry or defensive. Express your opinion without putting down theirs; acknowledge that it's okay to disagree. Resist arguing about who is right. Instead say, "I know you disagree with me, but this is what I think." Focus on your child's feelings rather than your own during the conversation.

- **Remember:** Ask your children what they may want or need from you in a conversation, such as advice, simply listening, help in dealing with feelings, or help solving a problem. Kids learn by imitating. Most often, they will follow your lead in how they deal with anger, solve problems, and work through difficult feelings. Talk to your children—don't lecture, criticize, threaten, or say hurtful things. Kids learn from their own choices. As long as the consequences are not dangerous, don't feel you have to step in. Realize your children may test you by telling you a small part of what is bothering them. Listen carefully to what they say, encourage them to talk, and they may share the rest of the story. Your children may test you by telling you a small part of what is bothering them.

- **Parenting is hard work:** Listening and talking is the key to healthy connection between you and your children. But parenting is hard work and maintaining a good connection with teens, in particular, can be challenging, especially since parents are dealing with many other pressures. If you are having problems over an extended period of time, you may want to consider consulting with a mental health professional to find out if they can help.

Having read the above tips, how do you think you communicate with your child (ren)? Would you be willing to sit down with your kids, go over these tips, and ask for feedback from them as to how well you do in each of these communication areas? You could preface such efforts by saying to your kids that you want to communicate well with them and would welcome their feedback as to how well you are doing. Such a discussion could help them realize that there may be some room for improvement in their communication style as well. (Well, we can hope, can't we?)

It would seem to be apparent that these same tips are applicable to any communication between two people, including husband and wife. Each week I meet with people and the most common refrain is "we don't communicate well!" To communicate well you need to know what you are trying to say, have some sense of how the other person can best hear and receive it, and adjust your message and style accordingly to insure that you are heard.

I hope that these parent communication tips are helpful to you and that they will be utilized to strengthen the loving bond that you have, or could have, with your children. Give 'em a try!

Try to remember that, "The best gift you can give your children is two parents who love each other."

Fifty Things You Should Never, Ever Say To Your Kids

I came across an interesting article written by Charlotte Hilton Anderson for *Redbook Magazine*. I found it interesting, and for the most part, agreed with the list. I share it with you for you to ponder, perhaps discuss, and maybe even change a few things you say to your children. The reasons for not saying these things are available should you need an explanation.

1. I do everything for you!
2. You did great on your test, but why can't you do that all the time?
3. B is fine, but an A is better.
4. You make me so mad!
5. Don't eat that or you'll get fat.
6. You're fat.
7. Eat your peas; they're good for you.
8. I'm so fat! I need to go on a diet.
9. I used drugs/smoked when I was a kid.
10. Stop crying right now!
11. It's not that big a deal.
12. Calm down!
13. You're fine!
14. You're so lazy!
15. Hurry up and get ready!
16. Why do I have to tell you everything 100 times?
17. Big boys/girls don't get scared.
18. Stop being such a baby.
19. You're being ridiculous.
20. Stop being selfish and needy.

21. I'm disappointed in you.
22. You're making me sad.
23. Don't do that!
24. You better do what I say or else.
25. Don't make me turn this car around.
26. It's my way or the highway!
27. You live under my roof; you follow my rules.
28. That's the way I was raised, and I turned out fine.
29. I hate it when you (insert bad behavior here).
30. Shame on you!
31. Ugh, you're just like your father/mother.
32. I told you so.
33. I know you didn't mean to hit your brother/sister.
34. Don't be mad at your brother/sister.
35. I wish you would be more like your brother/sister (or other kid's name).
36. That's just not good enough.
37. You're my perfect little angel!
38. You're so smart!
39. You're way better than that kid!
40. Great job!
41. Aw, I can never say no to you!
42. You're playing that game wrong.
43. Let me help you with that!
44. Are you sure you can do that?
45. You can't do that!
46. You're an idiot!
47. I hate math; I was never good at it.
48. I don't know who ate your candy.
49. Mommy's not crying; everything is just fine!
50. You want another spanking? (I added that one)

Respected Reader, do you understand, and agree, as to why these comments are inappropriate to say to your kids? Sometimes it is the context or intensity that is the problem with what is said. Other times it is just plain wrong to say these things to your kids. Did your parents say any of these to you? Which ones? And you "turned out just fine," did you not?

Parent's Fighting Harms Children!

I have counseled thousands of marriages and families over the years. A couple of observations:

1. Many couples are committed to their marriage and doing what it takes to make it work.
2. Other couples have made a poor choice for a partner and have either stayed together in battle or have legally gotten rid of each other.

Children are significantly affected by their parent's marriage, positively and negatively. The negative impact of battling parents is particularly troubling—whether the parents stay together and fight within the same household or divorce and wage war from afar.

"Kids" from six to sixty have told me of the pain and scars caused by their arguing parents. I wish I had a videotape of each of these embarrassing conversations to show the parents who yell and scream at each other. I believe most would quit.

Kids tell me of their pain, fears, sadness, anger, stress, inability to concentrate (ADD?), etc. as they hear their parents fight or speak badly of the non-present parent. They do what they can to stop the bickering and get their parents back together. One eight-year-old told me his parents were driving him crazy and that he was running out of ways to stop his parents from yelling. He said that he was going to ask them to speak through puppet characters that night, hoping that they would be nicer to each other. He lost his childhood trying to be the "adult" stopping his parents from fighting.

Depending on where a child fits in the sibling order oftentimes foretells what his or her reaction to the fighting will be. Some kids try to be "perfect" so as to not displease their parents and cause fighting. Another child will become the "rebel" child so as to bring the parents together in a common focus on the child. Others will become learning or emotionally disabled as a result of the stress in the family. Maladaptive neurological pathways will be formed that limit academic and social performance.

Statistical evidence is clear that children and adults in families experiencing divorce are two to three times more likely to seek mental health treatment than families in which there has been no parental separation. One third of former spouses have notable difficulty in establishing healthy adult relationships with each other after divorce.

Many of the resulting symptoms in kids do not fully emerge until adolescence, when inappropriate emotional, social, behavioral, academic, and addictive problems become manifest. This is a critical intervention time for these teens to be seen by a family therapist that understands and can relate to teens. If there is not a good "fit" between therapist and teen, money and time are just being wasted.

A word of advice to couples in troubled marriages—don't fight, get help! Kids have "radar" and feel every emotion present between their parents. If you do not have the commitment, resources, or hopeful possibility of making a success of your marriage, at least separate or divorce with class and dignity. Do not embarrass or stress your children because you picked the "wrong" partner or you have given up. There are guidelines for helping children cope with divorce which space does not permit. If you would like me to send you a copy, please call me.

Want To Be A Better Parent? Then Don't Make These Mistakes!

Part of what I do as a therapist is work with families with regard to parenting skills. I have taught classes on the subject and assist parents on a regular basis in counseling sessions. Most parents know very little about parenting so they tend to do what their parents did—or drastically different if they did not like the model they grew up with. In a two-parent family there can be, and often is, disagreement between the parents on how parenting should be done. In stepfamilies the disagreements usually are more pronounced.

Parental "mistakes" are over and above certain desired prerequisites. The most basic needs of a child growing up in a family are:

- Two parents who love each other and demonstrate it consistently.
- Two parents who love their child, are able to demonstrate it consistently, and want to be the best parents possible.
- Two parents who have a clear, united understanding of their expectations of their child, state them clearly, and are consistent in rewarding or punishing the child dependent on the behavior of the child in meeting such expectations.

Unfortunately, these "prerequisites" are not present in every marriage. To the extent that they exist then the probability of raising a successful well-adjusted child is high. Beyond these desired "prerequisites" are other important factors for being a good parent. However, these "mistakes" hinder.

1. Protect, but don't overprotect. You need to keep your child safe but as she/he grows older the opportunity for

exploration needs to expand. The overprotected child will have low self-esteem and will either be unassertive and meek, or at some point, rebel in a destructive manner.

2. Always be the parent, not your child's best friend. When your children become an adult the friendship factor can be added. Being the parent does not mean to be overbearing, harsh, or demanding. It does mean that you are in charge, giving and receiving respect, while mentoring your child.

3. Help your child see the many positive possibilities ahead. Do not use fear as a motivator or tell them that they cannot do or be such and such. Age appropriate, let them make their choices and find out for themselves if it is good for them or not.

4. You are to be a role model for your child. Do not be a hypocrite. Do not be that parent that tells a child not to do something and then do it yourself. Abuse of food, alcohol, or drugs, lying and stealing, would be some of the salient examples.

5. Always be present to your child, but not invasive. Being present will vary according to the age and stage of your child. Kids need to know that you are there for them— forever. The parent-child bond is unique and so special.

This writing is a basic "starter kit" for being a good parent. Certainly there are many other facets for being the best parent possible. It is both an exhausting and rewarding vocation, never to be taken lightly. May you, Respected Reader, make a responsible choice to be a parent and do your best to put into practice the things that your child needs to thrive. There is not greater role in life!

Parents Teach Your Children To Be Independent, Or...You've Failed Them

Raising children is very challenging. It is a job that parents have agreed to do upon bringing them home from the hospital. (Some people who are not ready or capable recognize this inadequacy and give children up for adoption. Hopefully, the adopting parents are ready and capable of performing this most noble task). Like with any other worthwhile endeavor, goals need to be established. Goals reflect the various outcomes desired. Some of the appropriate goals for children should include:

1. Optimal physical health development.
2. Emotional well-being.
3. Capacity to learn and achieve.
4. Good morals.
5. Appropriate manners.
6. Being motivated for personal and professional success.
7. Independence

This article highlights *independence*. The challenge for parents is to facilitate and transform a young dependent child into a confident, secure, independent person. The transformed adult must be capable of living on his/her own physically, emotionally, and financially.

Kahlil Gibran, in *The Prophet*, says it well as he speaks of parents as the bows sending forth the arrow (child), guided by the spirit and intent of the archer.

> You are the bows from which your children as living arrows are sent forth.
> The archer sees the mark upon the path of the infinite,

and He bends you with His might that His arrows may go swift and far.
Let your bending in the archer's hand be for gladness;
For even as He loves the arrow that flies, so He loves also the bow that is stable.

Parents need to be stable and unified in their joint effort to send forth into the world a young adult capable of flourishing amidst the chaos and temptation that greets him/her as that person steps forth from the parents abode.

Parents need to find the balance point between over-controlling your child and not providing the necessary guidance through the various life stages. There are appropriate tasks to be mastered by a child at various developmental stages. Know what stage your child is in and find the appropriate parenting behavior to facilitate his/her growth to the next developmental stage. These stages are based on age and capacity.

When a child transitions from childhood into his/her teens on the way to adulthood, markedly different parenting approaches need to emerge. A different level of communication is called for. Negotiation is a new respectful reality. Clarification of expectations and consequences are necessary. A certain "letting go" but still "being there" balance needs to be attained.

As you "let go" the teenager needs to assume greater responsibility for his/her emerging life. If a parent over controls or abandons the teen then he/she either becomes weaker, less confident and dependent or acts out in rebellious irresponsible behavior.

When young adults finish high school they need to decide how they want to live their lives. Parents are to be there to help them clarify their choices, give advice (if asked for) emotional support and some transitional financial support if possible.

The goal of the independent person is to have the capacity to happily live on his/her own with a quality life and not feel needy, dependent, or lacking in confidence. Attuned parents have the capacity to make it happen, unless there are particular physical or emotional impediments existing in the child that may limit some potential.

Ultimately this independent self-sustaining adult will want a partner to share life's possibilities. Hopefully he or she will find another independent person that is a good fit so that they can establish a synergistic interdependent (rather than an energy draining co-dependent) relationship.

Wherever your kids are on the journey of life, may you be with them in a loving manner facilitating their growthful independence. They will be grateful and you will have a sense of accomplishment for taking your responsibility seriously and parenting productively. Also, you have given them a good model that they may institute when they are parents. Good luck! Or, congratulations if you have achieved your noble goal!

When Your Child Is Struggling, Be A Part Of The Solution

I counsel kids as a part of my practice. There are unique inherent challenges in working with young people, but I embrace them. Some of the challenges are:

1. Communicating with the child/teenager in such a way that she/he can like and trust me so that she/he is able to open up and share what his or her life is all about.

2. Helping the parents realize that they are both a part of the problem and of the solution. Many parents prefer to drop the kid off so that I can return the child to them "fixed." The child lives in a family environment which has contributed to the problem and the parents need to be involved in the counseling in some form or fashion.

3. Getting the parents to hear the message of what needs to be done to help the child through this struggling stage. Many parents do not want to hear that they might be doing things that are contributing to the problems. Also, many resist changing behaviors that are needed for a better outcome.

Being a parent certainly is not easy. When the child arrived she/he wasn't carrying a manual as to how best she/he should be raised! I believe most parents do the best that they are able to do. However, they need to know that the one model they have, from their own respective childhoods, may not be the best way.

It is important for parents to be vigilant and open minded regarding a child's problems. It is very challenging for children/teens to grow up in our society today. The pressures are unprecedented. Too often parents wait too long and, thus, compound the complexity and duration of the issues. Some parents just don't want to see what they don't want to see. To recognize there is a problem calls them to do something about it.

Insights on a child's life can be gained by his/her mood, friends, grades, attire, diary, etc.

Needless to say, if you choose to bring a child into this world, you have the opportunity and responsibility to help him or her through every developmental stage. If you do this you will see a child becoming an adult and developing his or her fullest potential.

A few basic keys to being the best parent possible in meeting the needs of kids are the following:

- Love (marital and parental)
- Safety/security (physical and psychological)
- Structure
- Positive modeling
- Reasonable expectations
- Consequences(positive and negative)
- Consistency

No more noble task is given to you, fortunate parent, than having the opportunity to create and develop a child into being the best human being possible! Give it your best shot.

Positive Phrases To Inspire Confidence In Your Child

The goal of every parent should be to raise a confident child. Confidence is one of the core essentials that lead to success in life. Parental verbiage to a child has a huge impact for building or destroying confidence in a child. Thus, it is incumbent upon parents to do all that they can to learn positive phrases for building confidence in their child. I will list some of them and you can decide whether they are already a part of your parental vocabulary or you have some learning to do.

1. **You are capable.** Parental phrases become the internal language of a child. Your child is capable. Let him/her know that. Do not focus on the negative such as, "You are going to hurt yourself" or "Don't fall."

2. **That was brave.** Kids like to feel brave, that they can conquer challenges. Verbalizing that to the child reinforces such a belief.

3. **You've got this.** When you know the child has the skills, your comment gives an extra boost to succeed.

4. **I believe in you.** This is a biggee. Knowing that parents are solidly behind a child inspires him/her to do their best.

5. **You can do hard things.** When the obstacles get larger, it is important to encourage your child to do the next "hard" thing.

6. **No matter what happens, I love you.** The most important one. Kids need, and thrive on, the consistent love of their parents.

7. **Let's try together.** A little helping hand can assist a child in getting to the next step. Knowing that the parent is there, if needed, is reassuring and confidence building.

8. **How'd you do that?** By asking that, you are helping them feel proud and it gives them an opportunity to show off and do it again.

9. **That sounds awesome; can you tell me more?** Kids want to be heard. By picking a particular topic and asking to hear more, the child gets the message that she/he is important and has something to contribute.

10. **Give it your best.** You don't want kids to think they need to succeed at a high level in order to earn your accolade. Rather, you want to impart the message that it is the effort put in, not necessarily the outcome. There will be plenty of good outcomes if the best effort is consistently given by your child.

11. **I know it's hard, but I've seen you do it before.** Sometimes your child isn't fully into something, or is momentarily losing confidence. Reminding the child that she/he has done it before can help get him/her over the hump.

12. **You make me proud.** I like this one a lot and have used it often with our kids. Now as young adults they tell Sherry and me that they valued that growing up, and still like to hear it. Deep down kids want their parents to be proud of them.

13. **I wonder what would happen if...?** This type of question evokes curiosity and a search for possibilities. Such mind expansion can be encouraging and confidence building.

14. **Sometimes we make mistakes, and this is how we learn**. Parents often can over dramatize mistakes which will lead kids to stop trying. To emphasize that no mastery occurs

without a certain amount of mistakes along the way can help kids to keep plugging away.

15. **How did you challenge yourself today?** Continuing to personally demonstrate, and encourage your child to take on challenges, helps your child have new successes and more positive self-esteem.

16. **Repeat after me, "I can do it."** This direct statement can be very additive to the brain wiring that is the goal here.

There are more positive phrases that could be included here. I just wanted to give you a taste of how certain types of phrases can lead to a child's increased confidence. Confidence is a critical variable in success. Try to be aware if your phrases to your child are positive and enhancing or do they emphasize the negative and, thus, wither away your child's self-confidence. Your child deserves the best parenting you can bring to his or her life!

Stepparenting

Strategies For Helping A Combined Family Blend Well!

People marry. People divorce. People re-marry, often after having kids. Such a subsequent marriage offers many challenges, which is why the divorce rate for them is significantly higher. One of the main reasons for such failure is the children factor—trying to combine two families. Not easy!

In my practice I face this issue often. It is one of the more complex, and often frustrating, situations that I encounter. There are many variables involved. I will try to touch some of the more prevalent ones. Dr. Phil has listed some good strategies. I will share them with you and add some of my own.

1. **Acknowledge The Challenge:** Some people are naïve and think that "love conquers all." It doesn't. Money, discipline, chores, religion, visitation issues, exes, age of children, schooling, etc. are some of the more common challenging areas. Unfortunately, most couples do not have good communication, compromise, and a plan when entering into such an arrangement. It is a pity that so few couples do not see a licensed Marriage and Family Therapist beforehand to understand the feasibility of such a union and develop a pro-active plan to meet the upcoming challenges.

2. **Come Up With A Realistic Plan:** When a family merges, some of the more specific plans that need to be developed are:
   - The role each parent will play in parenting each other's kids
   - The division of labor concerning the kids

- How much alone time the couple will have without kids
- How grandparents and other extended family fit into the picture
- Long-term goals
- Financial goals, short and long term
- Many more!

3. **Be Aware Of How The Children Involved Are Experiencing This Change:** The kids did not make this choice. It was made for them. What are their perceptions, desires, and feelings as to such disruption of their lives? Good communication is needed to be sure that they can participate and be heard.

4. **Do Not Argue In Front Of Your Children:** Your children have witnessed enough family conflict. Don't make it worse. When you argue in front of your children, you change who they are. When they see you fighting, they believe it is because of them.

5. **Stop Complaining And Be Specific As To Your Needs:** Be clear in your own mind what your needs are and be respectfully specific in pointing them out to your spouse. Mind reading is not a gift that your spouse possesses! Also, ask your spouse what needs she/he may have.

6. **Agree On Discipline Strategies For Kids:** This is vitally important. What are the mutual expectations for all the kids and what are the consequences for meeting or not meeting them. Generally, the biological parent should be the explainer and enforcer of such rules. Be fair and consistent.

7. **Create A Personal Relationship With Your Stepchild(Ren):** You are now a pivotal person in the child's life, having a significant impact in how she/he develops. How you accept and treat the child is very important.

8. **Support Your Spouse's Relationship With His/Her Child:** Never make your spouse choose between you and his/her child. Too often in counseling I hear the spouse say, "I'm not number one." Anger or hurt accompanies this statement. I believe that there can be two "number ones." Each is a different relationship with different emotions, behaviors and time spent factors.

9. **Form A Good Alliance With Your Former Spouse:** You and your former spouse have not ended your relationship. Your marriage has ended, but you have an eternal bond with the co- parent of your child. How you relate has an enormous effect on your child(ren). One of the more disheartening things I witness in counseling is when the parents continue to have an estranged argumentative relationship. Severe damage is caused by these parents who cannot ante up and relate well for sake of their child.

The list could go on and on. It is a daunting task to seamlessly blend children with another parent and any kids that may be a part of such a package. If you are contemplating such a union, or already in one, please get some professional help for the arduous task ahead.

Stepparenting Is One Tough Job

Again, people marry. People divorce. People re-marry. Often these people have kids. Kids need to be parented. Welcome to the task, new marriage partner. Major lifestyle changes are ahead—for all concerned!

The stepparent role generally is challenging, and often thankless, at least until many years later. The stepparent usually is not initially welcomed by the kids, and is often resented. "You're not my parent!" The stepparent often is impotent with regard to discipline. "You're not my parent!"

A marriage with a step-parent often fails. Too many competing pressures. Communication is often frustrating, especially regarding expectations, consequences, and consistency of implementation for the children. If the stepparent also had kids, it gets even crazier. Fairness of treatment toward each other's kids is often a source of disagreement.

Often the stepparent has to interact with the spouse's ex. Rarely is that an enjoyable experience. Being pals and co-parenting cooperatively is rare. Good communication here is worth any effort put forth.

If you are entering into a stepparent role, or have been in one for a while, it is important that you be realistic about your role, that you have the patience of Job, and that you limit your expectations. You probably will get limited ROI (return on your investment) in the short term. Long term it could be immensely gratifying, depending on how well the early-on step parenting process goes. If you can hang in there giving your time, energy and affection, you probably will be appreciated and feel rewarded in the long run for your noble service.

Your role as a stepparent is to co-parent with the biological parent (and his or her ex, if possible) in helping the kids to feel:

1. Safe and secure: Kids need to be able to count on their parents. They have already been upset by their parents' divorce.
2. Loved: Kids need and want affection. This may be a gradual process as they learn to trust you, your motivation, and ultimate staying power.
3. Seen and valued: They need to be heard and participate in the decision-making process affecting them appropriate to their age and maturity level.
4. Appreciated and encouraged: Their efforts need to be validated with positive feedback.
5. Limits and boundaries: These are necessary components to help them feel secure but probably will be resented initially and occasionally. Later they will see the value if implemented well.

Age differences:

Young children under ten: May adjust more easily because they thrive on cohesive family relationships. Are more accepting of a new adult. Feel competitive for their parent's affection. Have more daily needs to be met.

Adolescents, aged 10 to 14: May have the most difficult time adjusting to a stepfamily. Need more time to bond before accepting a new person as a disciplinarian. May not demonstrate their feelings openly, but may be as sensitive or more so than young children when it comes to needing love, support, discipline, and attention.

Teenagers 15 or older: May have less involvement in stepfamily life. Prefer to separate from the family as they form their own identities. Also, may not be open in their expression of affection or sensitivity, but still want to feel important, loved, and get attention.

There is so much more that could be added to this stepparent discussion. There are so many factors and variables involved. It is important to see a therapist who successfully works with stepfamilies. This person can offer support, insight, recommend-dations, and help you keep this new marriage viable and loving.

Stepparent, if you are doing a good job, you deserve the highest praise because your position is one of the most challenging of all relationships!

Stepparent: Some Tips For A Difficult Role

O f all the family relationships that exist the stepparent role may be the most difficult. There are so many factors and variables involved. I am going to give a few guidelines and directives to those of you who may have an interest in that complex position. I am aided here by Dr. Phil and the principles espoused in his book *Family First*.

1. The stepparent should not be the disciplinarian. That honor goes to the biological parent. If the stepparent disciplines she/he is in a lose-lose situation. The biological parent may be upset by what you did, how you did it, when you did it, and why you did it. Also, the kids will dislike you even more than they may already—plus they may confront you with your right to do so. It can get ugly.

2. The stepparent needs to have input, dialogue with, and agree with whatever discipline the biological parent ultimately adopts—and actively support it on a consistent basis. She/he is not to take any guff or abuse from the stepkids. Sending the kids to their room may be a necessary buffer step.

3. The stepparent should seek to define his or her role as an ally and supporter of the kids. Often insight and advice may be solicited and welcomed by the stepkids once a certain trust level is established. The stepparent is not to supplant the out-of-home biological parent who hopefully is still involved with his or her kids—but is additive.

4. The stepparent should not be naïve or overly optimistic as to the level of closeness or intimacy that can be achieved with the stepkids. It takes time to build a solid trusting relationship and usually many challenges must be met to

reach that goal. The stepkids usually have an ambivalent stance, sometimes hostile, to a stepparent coming into their lives. In most cases they are wishing and hoping that their absent biological parent will return and that this "interloper" will leave.

5. The stepparent should actively support the children's relationship with the biological parent who no longer lives in the house. There may be exceptions if this parent is unhealthy and detrimental to the children's welfare.

6. If you are a stepparent in a blended family such as "yours, mine, and ours," be particularly careful to not play favorites. Kids are very sensitive to this and often will raise the issue, even if it does not exist in actuality. This is probably the number one reason that second marriages such as this model fail.

A stepparent rarely receives his or her due, but if it occurs it most likely will be after many years into it. The child/adult must be capable of understanding and appreciating the sacrifices and valiant effort made.

If you are in the stepparent role or expect to be in one, "good luck! You will need it, as it is such a challenging position. Yet, it can be so significant in the lives of stepkids you help to parent. In most cases you deserve a gold medal. Thank you for offering yourself to this very significant role!

Grandparents

Grandparent Time Is Arriving! What Are The "Rules"?

I'm excited! Sherry and I are soon to be grandparents for the first time! Our daughter, Brittany, is pregnant and expecting on Labor Day (appropriate enough). Both Brittany and David are enthused about welcoming "Baby D" (Dixon is the family name) into their home. It is interesting to feel emotions not experienced before. They are powerful. "Daddy's Girl" is having a baby! I still remember watching *Father of the Bride* with her when she was eight. Time flies.

Recently Brittany sent us via e-mail a sonogram showing the child developing (size of a peach) and last week a video of her hearing the heartbeat. Interesting and affirming—picture and sound. Brittany is doing a great job of including us in her developing pregnancy, for which we are appreciative.

I wonder what kind of grandparent I will be. First, what to be called? "Grandpa" felt ancient. After sounding out a few other possibilities and getting feedback from family I settled on "Papa John." (Did you know I also started a pizza franchise?) Sherry has decided on "Nana." "Grandma" certainly doesn't fit this forever-young woman!

Next question I asked myself, "Papa John, are you going to practice what you preach?" Having counseled many grandparents, their kids, and their kid's kids, I know well most of the pitfalls that can exist in this new generational offspring's family.

My grandfathers were special to me in my growing up years. I felt loved and cared for in a special way by each of them. I hope to follow that grandfather tradition—and maybe add a touch or two!

I'd like to share with you a few of the do's and don'ts of being a good grandparent. A few pertinent "rules" would include:

1. Support your kids raising their kids. The grandkids are not your kids.
2. Don't give advice unless asked for by the parents.
3. Learn how to connect with, and be a positive influence in the grandkids' life, without usurping the authority of the parents.
4. Be there when needed, but do not impose. Do not be "used" by parents who abdicate their responsibility.
5. Don't spoil the kids. Stay within the parameters of behavior/discipline/rewards established by the parents.
6. Learn when to keep your mouth shut. Certain comments or observations are unnecessary and create bad feelings.
7. You are not the only grandparents; sharing and balance is needed with the other grandparents and members of the "extended" family.
8. Work through and with the parents, not around them.
9. Be familiar with the parents' priorities involving safety, health, feeding, discipline, hygiene, etc. and reinforce their desires through your actions.
10. Love 'em with all your heart!

I am enjoying this countdown period as I witness a special glow effervescent on Brittany's face—and on Nana's! I look forward to welcome our "Georgia Peach" (even if the birth will be in North Carolina). Sure hope I can follow the "Rules."

How about you? What are your thoughts about being a grandparent? How good are you in this role? Or will you be? It is a great opportunity to be a positive force in the development of another generation evolving—yours!

Chapter Nine: Communication Skills

Do You Need To Be "Right"—Or Want To Have A Good Relationship?

Power is an interesting reality. What is power? How is it best used? How can it be shared? Every relationship is an exchange of power. How a person utilizes power, or fails to use it, can greatly affect any relationship. For discussion sake here, I will address power exchanges in the personal realm—between committed partners.

Too often in the relationship there exists a dominant person and a submissive person. In such a dominant-submissive relationship, one person has to be "right," keeping him or her in control and psychologically safe. Thus, the other person has no choice but to be submissive—"wrong." It does not feel good to be the "wrong" person most of the time. Such a person keeps being whittled down, feeling bad about oneself. Perhaps, when she/he cannot take it anymore she/he explodes—usually inappropriately.

The goal in any healthy relationship is to create a "win-win" way of communicating, addressing problems, and living together harmoniously. And that is not easy! Most disagreements about who is "right" are subjective perceptions and experiences—not about objective facts. This opens the door to the power exchange.

How does the power exchange work within your primary relationship? (I mean besides the classic one with most couples:

338

Man controls money; woman controls sex.) Does one person have most of the power; she/he is the one that is "right"? This imbalance is unhealthy and sets up toxic communication and resentment. Or, is there a balance of power with the emphasis being on agreeing, not winning. When there are disagreements, does each person allow enough "wiggle room" so that there is not a winner and a loser, a "right" and "wrong" exchange?

In the relationship counseling that I do frequently, the power struggle is in full force. Each person righteously states what the issue was and how the other person was "wrong." Each person is angry and often belittling in style. I then intervene and say that since neither person brought along the videotape of this power exchange, we are wasting valuable time in discussing this past experience with widely variant subjective understandings. Instead, I try to teach a method of communication that allows each person to express a viewpoint, and where there are differences, have good communication and compromise be the outcome. This method can keep the relationship solid with a balanced power exchange. After all, the relationship is the most important factor, not the particular issue being argued over. In fact, most people (especially the men) don't even remember what the disagreement was about a few days later. Yet that clumsy interaction significantly damaged the relationship. Defenses went up. Emotional distance was created.

In a close relationship ego and pride get overly involved. Neither party wants to be vulnerable, so one aggresses or hides so as to not be perceived as "wrong" or the "loser."

The bottom line here is to do the right thing by not insisting on being "right." If you need to be "right" you will ultimately be wrong and have a rotten relationship. Who wants that? This suggestion is not easy, but it is worth striving for.

"I'm Sorry": Are These The "Hardest" Words To Say?

John Denver has written many songs. One of his lesser-known songs, 'I'm sorry,' caught my ear the other day. It got me to thinking about one of the challenges I have in working with couples. Too often neither party wants to own some undesirable behaviors or apologize for them if acknowledged.

In relationship counseling one of the first steps is to bring up and discuss past and present issues that have been destroying the relationship. These "mistakes" have one or both individuals upset. I do not spend a lot of time on these past misdeeds because each person has a different perspective on what has happened, and swear that their version is what "really happened." So I tell a couple that unless they bring me a video of the offending behaviors we are not going to talk about it in detail. We will talk about needs going forward. I'm hoping to get apologies from each and then move on to create a better relationship.

Too many individuals are not ready to own their undesirable behaviors and, thus, don't do a very good job of apologizing. Nobody likes to be "wrong," vulnerable to the other. Hopefully, the "sinner" can apologize to the "saint" and the "saint' can accept it, let go of it, and move on.

"I'm sorry" words can be great healers. Oftentimes when "ice," emotional separation, takes place, both individuals have been less than perfect. It would be nice if the person who first feels the "ice" would say "I'm sorry" or at least, "I didn't handle that very well." Upon hearing those words it would be nice if the other person responded with, "apology accepted" or "I didn't handle that well either." This allows the "ice" to melt and the heart to re-open.

One of my favorite sayings—reminders—is "begin each day with fresh forgiveness." This presupposes that both persons in the relationship are of good faith working on the relationship. If one person is not, and continues to do hurtful behaviors, then the person being hurt needs to do something more drastic to remedy the situation.

I started this theme with a singer/song title. I close with Elton John's song title, 'Sorry seems to be the hardest word.' Respected Reader, please don't make it so hard to say "I'm sorry" to your mate. Mate, please own your part, perhaps an "I'm sorry" is due from you as well. Apology offered and accepted. Then, let go, move on and create something wonderful between you and your partner. Perhaps it may be a good idea to add "I'm sorry" to your re-connecting communication skills!

How To Turn A Simple Argument Into A Disaster

Have you ever been in an argument and it escalated into something that you wish it had not? There are a number of things people do when emotions take over and deliver behavior and comments that raise tempers and stifle resolution.

A couple of behaviors that contribute to anger escalation are eye rolling, stonewalling, groaning, and walking away. These are disrespectful and certainly don't help in moving the communication forward.

Inappropriate comments also can turn respectful communication into hostile warfare. Here are a few.

- "You never..." Or, "You always ..." Such "all or nothing" phrases are typically exaggerations and are used to illustrate a point or elicit a response. The all or never comments, which are not true in most cases, make the other person defensive. Thus, anger escalates as the communication becomes intensely personal.
- "You're acting just like your mother." This personal accusing statement is a sign you are losing the argument. Thus, you get nasty as your defense. Button that one up!
- "I'll talk to you when you get rational." Again, this is a loser's defense. It is a put down, which makes the other angry. The result is poor communication and frayed feelings.
- "We're done, I'm outta here!" Leaving, abandoning the person and the problem may be the worst thing you can do to hurt the other person. Taking a clarified break, planning on return at a designated time, is acceptable—sometimes needed. But quitting with such bravado is more inappropriate behavior.

- "You are such a @#$%&!" Name calling is childish, mean, degrading, and ineffective for positively moving forward. Such personal attacks just make the other person mad and probably retaliatory. Try to stay on topic and not make it personal.
- "Why are you making such a big deal over nothing?" This zinger implies the upset person has no grounds for being such. It is another put down trying to make the other person look ridiculous and quit the discussion.
- "Not this again! Can't you just drop it and move on?" This one is similar to number six in that it tries to make the other person feel small and give up. This arrogant behavior does not elicit respectful communication.

Preferable words when things start to get testy would be, "Tell me more about how you feel." "I'm sorry you're upset." "I want to understand." "I don't think I said that well, let me try again." "I respect your opinion and think we can get this resolved."

Hopefully, Respected Reader, you are not involved in many arguments. But when you are, may these reminders serve you and the other person well and lead to a productive respectful resolution.

Healthy And Unhealthy Ways To Handle Disagreements

People disagree. That's a fact of life. Each person has a right to his/her feelings, opinions, and wants. No two people see everything eye to eye. Individuals and groups often differ as to how something should be handled, a direction to go toward. There are two or more sides to every story.

What is important is how disagreements are handled. Too often disagreements escalate into conflict, oftentimes hurtful and damaging to the participants. Relationships are often diminished when people disagree on issues.

There are healthy and unhealthy ways to deal with strong differences of opinion:

Unhealthy:
1. Ridicule the other person or position.
2. Make it personal; malign the character of the other(s).
3. Distort the facts.
4. Become intransigent; make it a right–wrong issue.
5. Assume ulterior motives in the other(s).
6. Talk behind the person(s) back and put the other down in order to gain support.
7. Divide and conquer is the misguided motto.

Healthy:
1. Respect the other person(s) and the position offered.
2. Communicate openly with no hidden agenda.
3. Hear the feelings and facts of the opposing person and position.
4. Check out the facts. Don't assume.
5. Don't let your ego/pride get in the way.

6. Compromise where possible, without violating principle.

7. Follow through on what you commit to.

8. Verify that the agreement is unfolding as understood.

9. Don't become bitter or hold a grudge if your position doesn't carry the day.

If you choose to try and settle a disagreement in the **Unhealthy** manner, you can be assured that:

1. Nobody will win.

2. Further distrust is embedded.

3. Greater difficulty in the future to be able to agree on differences of opinion.

4. Wounds and divisions inflicted may be difficult to heal.

The **Healthy** style leads to greater respect and trust. Thus, the individual or parties involved are more capable of handling future areas of disagreement. "Together, we can do remarkable things" is their motto.

"Changing The Channel" Is Good Brain Advice!

Recently I met with a client that I did some counseling with a number of years ago. He had some issues with anger and often used drugs and alcohol to assuage the pain underneath that anger. He improved greatly. The reason for this recent visit was that he had fallen in love with a woman and wanted to be sure that this marriage would work, especially since an earlier one failed. It failed for a number of reasons, starting with his ex wasn't a good "fit" for him.

When he came to see me this time he mentioned one of the unique tools that he got from our previous sessions was the ability to "change the channel." He said it has helped him immensely to cope with frustrating and hurtful situations.

"Changing the channel" is a method that I use personally and invite my clients to do. A little information here is necessary. The brain works like this: a thought comes to mind; the thought elicits an emotion, the emotion is the energy for the consequent behavior. Thus, what we think about, focus on, leads us down a path of positive or negative emotions, and then positive or negative behaviors. All of which then leads to positive or negative outcomes and consequences.

So, if your thought is the trigger mechanism that sets forth this chain of events, it, therefore, behooves you to be careful about what you think about. By becoming more attuned, becoming more conscious of what is going on in your mind, you then can take some control of what you think-feel-do.

"Changing the channel" is about changing the thought that is in your mind. "Changing the channel" is about getting rid of negative thoughts—past or present. The neurological pathway of the brain thickens, gets stronger, when you pay attention to a thought. When you stop paying attention to a thought it weakens, withers. Thus, the thoughts you focus on move you toward a more positive or negative way of thinking—and then feeling and acting.

An example here might help:

Perhaps a person in your past has hurt you deeply. When you think about that person, events that caused you pain come to mind. This then is followed by the negative emotion of fear, hurt, or anger. These emotions then affect your stress level and ultimately your immune system, weakening you in a number of ways. When you use the "change the channel" technique, whenever you think about that person or the events that hurt you, you switch your thought to something else.

A wise person seeks out tools and techniques that help that person think positive thoughts, feel good, and "do the next right thing" (positive). I believe this "change the channel technique is a worthy addition to good mental health and creating new brain cells so that you can continue living well and long. Give it a try; I think you will find it freeing and stress reducing!

"Veto Power": Spouses Can Use This For Good Reasons

When working with couples who have difficulty in making decisions regarding various facets of their joint life, I find that effective use of the "veto" can be helpful. Obviously, I do not use the word "veto" in the sense of government and constitutional power. One of the definitions of veto is to "prohibit from going forth." I think there is a productive use of a veto in a marriage. Let me explain why I choose such an emphatic term.

In a committed relationship there is an exchange of power. The goal in this exchange is to make decisions that are respectful of each person's interest and results in a win-win decision, not win-lose. Too often in marriage one person is more the controller, usually more self-centered than his or her pleaser type, who tends to give in on an issue.

The "veto" says that a suggestion, idea, direction is not going to happen. The person using the veto is establishing a boundary that prohibits any further consideration of a proposal.

Let me use a couple of examples that have come up in marriage counseling which have divided a couple and left each one "frustrated" (female) or "angry" (male). (Yes, this is a stereotype, but it fits so many couples.)

1. Buying an object for their home. Joe wants a deer head in the den. Sally doesn't like the idea. This argument could go on and on, but if Sally employs the "veto," it's over. The decision is made—no deer head in the den. Or, Sally thinks this feminine pink love seat would look great in the living room. Joe says, "Over my dead body" and yells "Veto"! Sally ponders his statement of his demise and then agrees to the veto and gives

up the idea of the preferred love seat. In each of these cases, once the deer head and the love seat were off the table, the couple was able to further communicate, compromise, and come up with something for the den and the living room that each could live with.

2. Where to go out for dinner. Sally wants to try out a new sushi restaurant. Joe says he doesn't eat "bait" and says he won't go to it. He plays the veto card. Sally is frustrated because she has heard some good reviews from her girlfriends. Joe says he wants to go to the sports bar so he can watch the ball games. Sally doesn't want that because she wants to have her husband's attention and some conversation. Veto is her response to that. As a result of each veto the couple's disagreement doesn't escalate and they find a nice Italian restaurant that both can live with.

These two situations may seem silly or mundane to some of you but I can assure you that so many arguments I witness in counseling are about these topics or other seemingly mundane issues. People get invested in their choices and often excessively push them on to their partner. Perhaps you can think of an example or two when you two disagree about what to do and each stridently tries to influence the other to agree to his or her way.

By employing the veto you can stop the argument from escalating and can rather spend the time looking at alternatives that each of you can buy into for a win-win solution. To do this effectively one of you (usually the most "enlightened" of you two) needs to say to the other, "I read this great idea from Dr. Stathas about using a veto to stop debate, and potential arguments, by using a veto when either of us proposes something that the other person cannot comfortably accept. Let's agree to do that."

"Yes, Dear."

When The Talk Gets Too Hot Try "Broccoli"!

Do you ever get in arguments with your spouse or significant other? You don't! Then you must be a Trappist Monk living the vow of silence all your life. Everyone else in the universe does have arguments, disagreements, differences of opinion in which a couple get angry, hot under the collar, pissed off at each other. Not a good place to be!

Such confronting moments can escalate to yelling, put downs, and maybe even into hitting. These moments lead to distancing, icy conditions, and resulting wounds. Mean words are remembered for a long time.

In couples counseling I often have to intervene when couples start escalating the rhetoric while making their individual cases as to why the other person is wrong, hurtful, a scum bag, etc. I remember once I even had to yell, "shut up" to get the couples' attention to stop the screaming. Emotions escalate when couples disagree and can spiral into a serious danger zone. So what might serve as an effective truce instrument?

"Broccoli" to the rescue! Over the years I have asked couples to promise each other and me that when they feel a discussion is getting out of hand and in danger of hurtful escalation to say the word "broccoli." Why "broccoli"? Because it is a nonsensical word in the context of an argument. Something must stop this couple before they reach the uncharted rough seas ahead. Take a minute, stop reading, and imagine an argument going on between you and a special person. Now say "broccoli." Did you not smile at the absurd thought? If you did not, you have no sense of humor or you are just a mean person that nothing can divert you from "winning" an argument at any cost.

So, when the argument is going on, who is the person to say "broccoli"? What I say to couples is this: the person who is the most aware of what is going on, that is the most loving, that is the most intelligent, the most caring person: that is the person who will be able to initiate the "broccoli" rescue. Now who would not like to be described in such a manner? Thus, may it be a race to see who can say it first.

When "broccoli" is used as an intervention, the couple has agreed beforehand in my office that when the word is used, both individuals must stop talking immediately—no "last word." They must go to separate rooms and chill down a bit. No further discussion on the topic can begin for a minimum of thirty minutes. Sometimes people need to wait to the next day. Sometimes people table the discussion because it is too flammable until they next meet with me.

When the individuals calm down a bit, I encourage each to come back to the other with the statement: "Sorry, I didn't handle that very well." When someone says that "I statement" defenses come down and each person realizes that the topic could have been discussed in a more mature manner. Too often, however, each person will come back by saying, "I wouldn't have done X if you hadn't done Y." The defensive offensive statement (understand what I mean here?) only re-engages the couple with angry disharmony.

Most arguments are over relatively trivial matters. After the dust settles from an argument, most couples realize that to have expended way too much negative energy on the given topic du jour. If there is a topic that is important and there is a significant difference of opinion, let me suggest a way to handle it. A would say to B that she/he wants to discuss an issue. A time that is suitable for each is agreed upon. This gives each person some time to calm down and rationally think through what his or her opinion is on the topic. Then each person should present the issue while the other person listens and does not interrupt. If no agreement is reached, agree to disagree for the moment. Next option would be to reconvene or bring it to a mediator. A disagreement should not significantly negatively impact the relationship, which is the most important factor.

Remember, if it gets too hot, chill with "broccoli"!

"Gaslighting" Ruins Your Relationships And Your Life!

Relationships of all kinds are complex, with a lot of dynamic variables permeating the interactions. All relationships involve an exchange of power. Knowing who has the power and how it is used in relationships is important. The goal of healthy relationships is an equitable, win-win exchange of power. There are a number of methods used to gain an unfair advantage in this relationship exchange. One of them is "gaslighting." It is important to understand this insidious modality and understand if it is eroding your relationship(s).

According to Professor Preston Ni, "Gaslighting is a form of persistent manipulation and brainwashing that causes the victim to doubt her or himself, and ultimately lose one's own sense of perception and identity. In its milder forms, gaslighting creates a subtle but inequitable power dynamic in a relationship, with the gaslightee subjected to the gaslighter's unreasonable, rather than fact-based, scrutiny, judgment, or micro-aggression. At its worst, pathological gaslighting constitutes a severe form of mind-control."

No matter the relationship, no person wants to be the "gaslightee"! Am I correct, Respected Reader? Here are some warning signs for you to examine just in case you might be being "gaslighted" in a personal or professional relationship. Following are techniques that gaslighters use to manipulate you, according to Dr. Stephanie Sarkis.

- **They tell blatant lies and exaggerate.** Example: "There's something wrong and inadequate about you." This begins the process of putting the gaslightee on the defensive.

- **They deny that they ever said something, even though you have proof.** This continues the process to have you question your reality and start accepting theirs.
- **They use what is near and dear to you as ammunition.** They look for and attack the foundation of your being.
- **They wear you down over time.** Gaslighting is done gradually over time. A lie here, a lie there, a snide comment every so often ...and then it starts ramping up.
- **Their actions do not match their words.** When dealing with a Gaslighter, watch their actions. Do not pay attention to what they say.
- **They throw in positive reinforcement to confuse you.** Most of the time the Gaslighter is cutting you down, but occasionally there is some praise offered. This is a calculated attempt to keep you off-kilter, keep you in the game, and have you question your reality.
- **They know confusion weakens people.** Remember, the goal is to weaken you so that you are vulnerable to be manipulated by the Gaslighter.
- **They project.** They accuse you of what they, in fact, are doing. This is done so that you start defending yourself and are distracted from the Gaslighter's own behavior. "The best defense is a strong offense." I see this technique often in counseling sessions.
- **They try to align people against you.** Gaslighters are masters at manipulating and finding the people they know will stand by them no matter what—and they use these people against you.
- **They tell you or others that you are crazy.** This dismissive judgment is powerful and again puts the Gaslightee on the defensive with self-doubt.

- **They tell you everyone else is a liar.** This manipulative technique gets you to turn toward the Gaslighter for truth.

Respected Reader, this Gaslighting focus is aimed at helping you become more aware of your various relationships and the dynamics involved. Are any of your relationships "Gaslighters"? They may not be using all of these techniques, but they may be using some of them. Be aware!

The Art Of The Re-Connect For Couples

D o you know the importance of the "re-connect" in order to have a successful relationship? The "re-connect" need arises when two people, who usually are emotionally close, become distant. It happens in every loving relationship, whether they are lovers, family members, or friends. Words are spoken, actions taken that move us emotionally apart from each other.

A "dis-connect" occurs when feelings are hurt. When our feelings get hurt we react generally in one of two ways, we get angry or we withdraw into our shell. The "dis-connect," or emotional gulf, is very awkward and disturbing. We are not in contact with someone who is important to our well-being.

We want to get back to our closeness, but often do not know how to "re-connect." We do not want to be blamed, nor do we want further distance or rejection. After a period of clumsy silence or, perhaps, bitter arguing, someone has to break the ice. What is said? What is done? Do you address the distance head-on or do it subtly? Do you initiate contact quickly or allow for some cooling off time?

In your relationship:

1. What are typical examples of disconnects? Issues?
2. How often do you dis-connect?
3. How long is the time lag usually?
4. Who is the initiator? How is it done?
5. Who is the most stubborn, cynical, angry, or shut down?

When there is need for a "re-connect," try to be the initiator. The initiator generally is the more loving of the two, more capable or rising above the fray and facilitating closeness. To be a good initiator one must do it in a way that lowers the defenses of the other. Instead of saying, "Why do you always do that?" say "I'm sorry we are fighting; I want us to be closer." Judging, blaming, criticizing, over explaining, defending are wasteful efforts in this process. Generally, the sooner the efforts are made, the better it

will go. Occasionally a period of cooling off and feeling the emptiness of the distance can be helpful. Openness, being positive, asking forgiveness, seeking a hug are elements that facilitate an emotional reunion. "Re-connects" are the bridge of an enduring relationship. Try to cross it often!

Quality Conversations Enhance Good Communication

Good communication can be a challenge. Conversation is one of the main forms of communication. Are you aware of your conversational style? Might you be guilty of conversation blunders?

I came across an article by Rich Santos in which he describes conversational types that need correction to enhance quality communication. I would like to share a few of them with you and add my own embellishment. See if you recognize yourself or someone else familiar to you.

1. **Conversational Hijacker (CH)**: A person shares something with the CH and the CH takes over without really listening to you or commenting on what you said. The CH wants you to listen to him/her. The CH takes over and dominates. A conversational imbalance results.

2. **Eye contact style:** Some people continually stare a hole through you as you converse; others barely look at you or in your eyes. Eye contact should have an easy rhythm to it.

3. **Ghost Listener (GL):** This person continually asks you to repeat what you said. The GL is not really into you or interested in what you have to say. The GL's mind is someplace else but periodically re-connects by asking you to repeat what you said.

4. **Tasteless Jokester (TJ):** The TJ just has to be heard and resorts to tacky, tasteless jokes to get attention. The TJ is boorish.

5. **Shameless Self-Promoter (SSP):** The SSP is a me, me, me person. SSPs take over and talk about themselves ad nauseam. An SSP does not ask about the other person's world. Again, a conversational imbalance results.

6. **Negative Person (NP):** The NP finds something negative or wrong about most everything. The NP sucks the positive energy out of a conversation. A conversation with an NP invites the listener to find an excuse to move away.

7. **Dead-end Answerer (DA):** The DA answers with a yes or a no or a single sentence. This illustrates that the DA has no personality or is detached and wants to get out of the conversation. Conversation with a DA is going nowhere. Exit .

8. **Word Machine (WM):** The WM talks and talks and talks and/or questions and questions and questions. The WM is exhausting and draining.

9. **Vacuous Person (VP):** The VP is shallow. The VP is not informed or interesting. Conversation is very boring with a VP.

10. **Pseudo Intellectual Person (SIP):** The SIP is a conversational snob—above it all. The SIP tends to be condescending, sometimes belittling. The SIP needs to be one up on the conversational partner.

Conversation is one of the chief ways that we get to know another person. A conversation that has appropriate sharing, balance, and rhythm facilitates a deeper relationship. It is worthwhile for you, Respected Reader, to see if any of these descriptors apply to you. If someone important to you is guilty of such you might want to have them read this article—or see that they receive it from an anonymous source!

Life Lesson: See And Tell The Good—Sincerely!

A confession. I am a 'Type A' personality. I'm genetically wired like that. There are plusses and minuses to that personality profile, as there is to any other. Over time I have tried to maximize the benefits of that personality and minimize its down side.

As you probably know Type A's are competitive drivers. Being successful, winning, is important. To "win" one must seek out every competitive advantage at hand. This style includes finding the weakness in the opponent, whether it be a person, team, or business. To do that you look for any flaw, a vulnerability, that may exist and use it to your advantage.

In relationships the same modus operandi exists, perhaps even amped up because of the emotional vulnerability that can exist in a deeper relationship. This can lead to a detective-like search for the other's flaws—and scorekeeping—one-upsmanship—"The best defense is a strong offense."

This competing, find the weakness in the other, style may work to some degree in sports and in business, but it is absolutely fatal in personal relationships, especially between spouses.

A turning point in my life's lessons journey took place in a graduate class that I took early on in my doctoral studies at Georgia State University. The class consisted of an ongoing small group whose primary agenda was to get to know people in the group, seek out and find positives of fellow group members, and then sincerely offer the observation to the appropriate person. Such a process began with the superficial, i.e., "I like the outfit you have on." As time wore on, and we began to know each other better, a positive comment like, "You come across as a very caring and empathic person" would be offered and comfortably welcomed. The goal was to get to know the person at a very personal level, see the positive of that person, and offer the compliment. (We developed some nice friendships out of that group!)

My point in this is to say that this experience significantly modified the way I perceive and interact with people, both personally and professionally. I have re-trained my brain to look for, see, and say the positive that exists in another person. The more I know the person, the richer and deeper the positive statement. The emphasis here is on sincerity.

Sincerity is critical. No BS, no superficial flattery, no excessive sucking up. I must be honest, objective as possible, while stating the positive. That is not to say that I cannot point out that which may be lacking in another—if in a professional capacity or if such an observation is requested or warranted. No Pollyanna in me!

I enjoy seeing the positives in another person. In my profession I have the privileged opportunity to look into the deepest parts of people, their soul, inner core, and find that for the most part most all people are pretty special—even when they may do something stupid or hurtful things.

Bottom line, Respected Reader, do you look for, see, and then share what you perceive to be positive with another person? It is a better way to live!

Non-Verbal Communication Can Say A Lot!

Various researchers and pundits have speculated that anywhere from 55 to 90 percent of our communication is non-verbal. Thus, you might want to be concerned with the message you are sending non-verbally. Beyond being aware, you may also want to be intentional as to the non-verbal message you want to send. The intent of this article is to assist you to be intentional and loving with the messages you send to someone you love.

Winifred M. Reilly, licensed Marriage and Family Therapist, has written about this topic and has some suggestions on how you can say "I love you" without saying a word. I will list many of these suggestions and add further commentary. I would like to be able to read your mind as you react to reading these suggestions. Do you find them silly, unimportant, thought provoking, inspiring, etc.? Most of them fit within the categories of gestures of kindness, generosity, attention, and touch.

1. Do the stuff neither of you wants to do but needs to be done by one of you.
2. Give your partner some slack when she/he messes up. You are not a parent or judge.
3. Flirt. It can be fun and bring forth good stuff.
4. Be patient. Take a few deep breaths and relax when your partner is not "up to speed."
5. Pay attention, full-on and undivided when something of import in being imparted.
6. Clean up beyond the call of duty. Not your dirty cup? Who cares? Put it in the dishwasher.
7. Stay present. Don't run away, physically or emotionally.

8. Let your guard down. Vulnerability and intimacy is the same thing.
9. Receive and welcome loving efforts by your partner. Perhaps an acknowledging smile.
10. Stop a fight in its tracks. Stay calm when your partner is all upset. Don't escalate.
11. Leave enough gas in the car, enough hot water for a shower, milk for the coffee.
12. Initiate a kiss. Hug back. Warm smiles are nice.
13. Give your partner some space.
14. Stay in touch. A text here and there saying hi, or I'm thinking of you, is thoughtful.
15. Support the dreams and desires of your partner. "Thumbs up!"
16. Be the first one to reach out after a disagreement. Be the classy one.
17. Make your relationship your number one priority. Date nights, getaways—keep the fire burning.
18. Turn off your phone when together unless some significant reasons suggest otherwise.

Respected Reader, do you do some of these? All? Keep it up. If not, step it up! Your non-verbal really does speak loudly to your partner and is an indication of how tuned in and caring you are.

What Do You Say About Your Spouse?

In front of other people? Behind his/her back?

What a husband or wife says about his/her spouse to others speaks volumes about the relationship, and one's character, tact, and sensitivity—or lack thereof. Stay with me on this one and see what you think about it.

Perhaps you have been out for dinner with another couple and one of them takes a cheap shot by saying something negative and personal about the other. Other social events also can serve as a platform for a cut or insult. Often such a comment is delivered through an attempt at humor. This is tacky and poor taste. One, it is none of the other couple's business. Two, if something needs to be addressed, it should be done in private, not in front of other people.

Another example of inappropriate spousal comment is when a partner reveals personal information about his/her spouse to another. This group usually involves women. (Men generally only make the generic comment that he doesn't get enough sex and that his wife spends too much money.) Women are generally more likely to share more specific personal details about their husbands, usually their shortcomings or idiosyncrasies. Every person has some failings or oddities that only a spouse would know. Such information is private and should be kept that way.

An important aspect of a good husband—wife relationship is a "protection" factor, psychological security. This special partnership should include an understanding that each one will keep personal issues, frustrations, and behaviors private, unless one is given permission to share. By honoring such an understanding a greater bond of trust will be established. When that happens, each person can share more and be more vulnerable to the other. The evolving result is greater closeness at all levels of connection.

The marriage relationship needs to be a sanctuary where each person can be himself or herself, and with caring feedback and support can grow into being an even better person and spouse. Spouses, along with a therapist, if needed, are the most potent change agents of another. If you are becoming a better person, healing past wounds and defenses, give a lot of the credit to your loving spouse. I hope your marriage has this or will develop it!

Be Careful What You Say To Your Spouse!

When I do marriage counseling I usually begin by asking each person to tell me some of the positive attributes of the other. Each one then says some very nice things. They remember, momentarily, special qualities that were present at one time and were some of the reasons that they came together and married.

Then I ask them why they are seeing me, and the other side of the coin shows its face. Each person goes on and on saying what is wrong with the other. It is amazing how what had started out so tender and sweet has become harsh and bitter. (All couples don't do this. Some couples come in recognizing that they have a decent enough marriage, but some issues have arisen, some tweaking is needed. I wish more couples would do this so that less damage would be done during the downfall. The earlier a couple addresses their issues, the better chance of long- term marital success.)

Spousal comments greatly affect the quality of the relationship. I wonder what the comments between spouses would be if they knew there was a hidden recorder present. For sake of discussion let's presume that there is such a hidden video recorder that records the statements uttered by each marriage partner. After recording, the machine analyzes whether it was a positive or negative statement, and how high or low it was on the praise meter. For example what number do you think would be assigned to the following statements? (The scale is 0-10, with 10 the highest.)

1. Thanks for taking out the garbage.
2. I wish you would pick up your stinky shorts.
3. That was a wonderful meal.
4. I wish you would bathe more regularly.
5. Are you frigid?

6. You are a wonderful parent.

7. I wish I had married your brother!

8. Why did you let your body go?

9. I love being married to you.

10. You are a lush just like your old lady.

11. Why do you cut me down in front of other people?

12. Your breath smells.

13. You're as mean as yo' Daddy.

14. You are so handsome.

15. You eat/drink too much.

16. You're as beautiful as the day I married you.

17. Your beer gut gets in the way of our lovemaking.

18. You're so stupid.

19. I can see why your ex divorced you.

20. I'm so fortunate to share my life with you!

(Please feel free to add your own)

The emphasis here is that what comes out of your mouth to your spouse is either positive or negative, with varying intensity, and either enhances or hinders the relationship. Those observations that are positive should be aired. Everyone appreciates a compliment. All negatives do not need to be shared; some restraint is warranted, especially related to things that can't be changed. If a negative needs to be offered, kindness optimizes the probability that your spouse will hear and address the issue.

Bottom line: look for the positive in your spouse and sincerely share it. It is a better way to help a marriage thrive!

Pot Shots At Your Spouse In Front Of Others—Bad Idea!

Are you a very observant person? Have you ever been out and witnessed a spouse being critical of his/her spouse in front of you and/or others? What an uncomfortable place to be for everybody—except the clueless criticizer. Maybe you have done it yourself. Perhaps your spouse/significant other has done it to you. Cheap-shot artists. Poor taste!

Pot shots while in the company of others is a passive aggressive act which comes from pent-up anger and frustration at the other. Most couples have some issues and irritations that exist over the period of their lives together. It is not easy to live with someone day in and day out in complete harmony.

In the course of counseling couples over the years this issue usually is included in the list of "grievances" that are brought up to be dealt with in a session. The one who has been criticized felt embarrassed on these occasions. The person is tempted to come back with a "zinger" of his/her own. This, of course, just raises the arsenal of shots going back and forth.

Why do people do this? Usually it is because the person is too timid to bring up the issue to the other person face to face without others present. Perhaps she/he is fearful of retaliation and figures that if she/he does it in front of others such a reaction is less likely. Or perhaps she/he has such anger built up that she/he wants to hurt and embarrass the other in front of other people. Another possibility is that she/he has tried everything to change the behavior of the other person and now resorts to the court of public opinion. She/he feels that maybe the listening party will take his/her side and help convince the "offender" that she/he is wrong.

What I am talking about here are people who consistently do this type of backbiting in front of others. Most people on occasion have slipped and said something less than kind about their spouse/significant other in front of others. Hopefully that person realized the mistake made and apologized. Perhaps she/he needs a kindly reminder that such an offense happened. Liquor often allows the lips to speak where it would have been better to restrain.

If you are characteristically guilty of this, please stop. You really embarrass yourself more than the person you are taking pot shots at. If you are with a couple where this behavior exists, are you going to say anything at the time? Not that it is easy to do that. At least a change of topic would help.

Whatever issues and concerns that exist between a couple should stay between a couple. Airing one's dirty laundry in front of others is not the outlet needed. Try to communicate assertively and kindly to your spouse if you have a particular concern. Sometimes, you just have to suck it up regarding some behaviors that the other person is not able to change, or just plain won't. If it is a major issue, get some counseling and work to resolve the issue. Your relationship is worth the effort!

What Do You Think And Say About Others?

Every once in a while certain events or situations arise that engender thoughts that I feel might be additive and edifying to you the reader—and a reminder to myself. "What comes out of your mouth about others" is about what you, and I, say about others. Being mortal imperfect beings, most everyone says some things that are hurtful to or about another person. Some people assume it as a lifestyle.

These articles are meant to educate, or remind, you and me that there is room for us to grow as a person. What comes out of our mouth is probably the most obvious way to advertise to others who we are.

Put downs, hurtful comments, slander, negative gossip, crossing the line comments, etc. occasionally mouthed or consistently verbalized, are not reflections of the kind of person most of us aspire to being. We are better than that.

Let's look at a few scenarios and possible behavioral directions:

1. If you are a person who consistently looks for the flaws in another person and tells others of such findings, consider changing what you are looking for. Generally those who look for the weakness in another are trying to shore themselves up by putting others down. It is amazing what wonderful qualities most people have if you focus on finding them, rather than looking for the flaw.

2. If you are a person that occasionally "crosses the line" and says things, perhaps in jest, that hurt, embarrass, or disgust another, take a peek in the mirror. Every person has unique sensitivities that reflect how she/he hears particular comments. A commentator needs to be aware as to what

are sensitive areas for another person. Something said to one person may be "crossing the line" to that person and perfectly fine to another.

3. If someone has hurt you by something she/he has said, consider bringing it up to the person and telling that individual that you were hurt or angry at what was said. Give the person a chance to respond by explaining or apologizing. Perhaps the person was not aware of what she/he said or that it hurt you.

4. If you are a person who feels that a particular person has hurt or betrayed you, and you feel that you cannot address it with that person for whatever reason, learn to "let go, let God." Don't engage in a vendetta against that person. Why do you need to continue to rip that person? Examine your true motives and agenda. Take the high road if you can do so.

5. If you are a negative person who focuses on finding what is wrong with everyone and everything, turn over a new leaf. That negative energy is hurting your health and your friendships. This is not to suggest that people need to become "Pollyanna's" who are "excessively and blindly optimistic." Naiveté' and not seeing and dealing with real issues are not healthy ways to live either.

May each of us become more aware as to what comes out of our mouth toward others. Words spoken cannot be retrieved and the consequences can be hurtful. The bottom line needs to be respect—given and received.

Couples Should Address The "Elephant In The Room"

You have probably heard the expression, "there's an elephant in the room and nobody's talking about it." If not, you may be thinking that this is a pretty dumb title for an article. It still may be so, but hopefully it got your attention to an important communication factor that may often elude your attention.

A definition of "elephant in the room" is "an important and obvious topic which those present are aware of, but which is not discussed, as such discussion is considered to be uncomfortable." It represents a major communication miss going on between people. A major event, behavior, problem, attitude, or feeling is present and nobody is addressing it (the elephant).

Such "elephants" exist in a number of settings. For the purpose here let's focus on couples. When I meet with couples I try to find any "elephants" that exist in the relationship. And I find them! Besides grievances, concerns, hurts and angers that exist, there often is a major issue that has not been addressed. Typical "elephant" topics are related to finances, sex, alcohol or drug consumption, parents, and kids.

Do you, as a couple, have an "elephant in the room"? Is there some concern that you are aware of but fearful of bringing up, one that is affecting you and the relationship? Some topics are hard to bring up for fear of a negative response from your spouse or your own awkwardness or embarrassment in trying to address it. In such cases a therapist can be of assistance as she/he facilitates, perhaps mediates, a constructive discussion about the topic.

I am not saying here, however, that every thought, feeling, want, or issue should be discussed with a spouse. Some things are better left unsaid for sake of the relationship. There needs to be a "cost-benefit" assessment of whether bringing up the topic ultimately is additive or harmful to the equation. Sometimes it may be important to "suck it up" and not bring up the topic. Or, you may want to schedule an individual session with a therapist who can help you think it out. She/he can help you determine whether you should address the "elephant" and if so, how it would best be presented. Delivery is important in bringing up sensitive issues. Some individuals think that every single thought, feeling, desire and experience needs to be talked about. TMI (too much information) does not help a couple communicate well.

The bottom line here is to ask you if there is an "elephant in the room," perhaps pushed "under the rug" that should be addressed for the overall betterment of the couple relationship. When you hold back something that you really need to get out you are hurting yourself and oftentimes building resentment. Ask yourself, and your partner, "Is there an elephant in the room?"

Seeing The Positive And Reinforcing it: A Better Way To Go!

Most of us know when we screw up. How we need to apologize and change the behavior is a different complicated story! I'm in a change profession. My life has been passionately devoted to helping people—and myself—become a better person. Such a life would include being a person who prospers in the chief roles of life, i.e., spouse, parent, provider, etc.

Being a change-oriented, results-driven, pragmatic-idealist therapist, I employ what works. What is the ideal desired and how close can the client and I work together to approximate the goal through wise strategic planning?

Criticism does not work. One more time, *criticism does not work*. Depending on the personality type, the criticized person either lashes back defensively with anger or poutingly withdraws and stays resentful.

A preferred approach that I suggest consists of three parts. First, state what you would like from the other person, perhaps with a rationale. Second, be aware and notice such an effort by the other. Third, serve up a compliment—a positive reinforcement of the behavior.

Too many people are not attuned (psychological term for being aware, or noticing) to the behavior of the other person—except when it is wrong or undesired. Then, usually a swift criticism occurs. What I am suggesting, Respected Reader, is that you enhance your radar to look for, find, and tell the cared for person that you appreciate what she/he has done. Such observation and complimenting skills can be acquired and developed with intentional practice.

The result of your compliment is that the other person will appreciate it, feel validated, and is most likely to continue the affirmed behavior. Plus, she/he will feel more positively toward you. Think about it. When you feel criticized, how do you feel toward the other person? On the other hand, when you are complimented, how do you feel? Point made, I hope.

Along the journey of life too many of us were made aware of when we did the wrong thing in some manner or form. Such a negative approach did not, and does not, bring out the best in us. Positive reinforcement does, no matter the relationship.

As an aside, I am waging a war against the negativity present in social media comments and posts. There are too many people who seem to enjoy putting people down. They ridicule people, particularly in the political realm, or make derogatory and often hurtful comments about others. What I enjoy seeing and posting are the positive things going on in peoples' lives. Offering congratulations and support and posting fun and loving pictures sure is a more enjoyable and positive way to participate in social media.

Bottom line, be the kind of person who looks for, finds, and offers something positive. May it be a personal comment, written note, or post in social media. The recipient will be grateful for such acknowledgment and will be inclined to continue such a behavior, and maybe offer in kind back to you. Plus, you will be viewed in a better light! And who would not want that?

Relationships Need Perceptual "Wiggle Room" To Thrive

Have you ever been in a situation where you told your spouse something and later she/he said that you did not? Also, has your spouse said to you that she/he told you something and you swear she/he did not? What couple has not experienced this communication mishit?

Much of the counseling that I do with couples involves listening to each of them telling me what was said or what happened between them. Both proclaim that they were right and the other was wrong. I don't let this kind of "he said, she said" go on very long. I tell them that if they cannot bring in the video tape, we won't discuss it. Subjective revisionist history is a waste of time and money.

Each person has a view of reality—his or her perception of what has gone on between them. Each then has ego investment in it, and the couple has a power struggle that can only end up in a win-lose condition or severe argument where both people get mad. Neither wants to lose.

In order to avoid such destructive communication battles, I encourage people to give each other "wiggle room." When a couple disagrees about what was said or done, each person can say, "I thought I said or did that, maybe I did not." The other gives "wiggle room" by saying, "Maybe you did say or do that; maybe I missed it."

When you give "wiggle room" you give the other person respect and thus lower the other's defenses. This communication adjustment eliminates someone being righteously victorious or demeaned into defeat.

Usually the "he said, she said" differences of opinion are about trivial things, sometimes more serious. The most important element involved, however, is the RELATIONSHIP. No difference of opinion or communication failure should get in the way of the relationship staying on track. That is why a couple dare not let the different perceptual reality escalate into an argument. It isn't worth it!

For those couples that have trouble giving "wiggle room" and continue with ugly communication, I offer another suggestion. If you know a topic to be discussed is volatile, then turn on the video or audio recorder, and proceed. Knowing that the conversation will be recorded greatly influences the way each person talks to the other. Even if you are in the middle of a "hot one," one of you could have the presence of mind to turn it on. That will change the tenor of the communication!

"Wiggle room" and/or a recorder can help when communication reflects different views of reality. Try these suggestions and you won't argue as much or as heatedly. It doesn't pay to "win" or "be right" at the expense of the other person's dignity or of the relationship.

The Remarkable Power Of Touch

To touch or not to touch, that is the question these days. Touch is powerful. Touch can be good or bad, healthy or inappropriate. The focus here is on the many wonderful benefits that accrue from appropriate touch.

Touch is vitally important right from the git go. Touch is the first of the five senses to develop. Babies need it to thrive. It is essential for a baby's physical, emotional, and eventual social development.

Karen Young has written an excellent article about the power of touch. I am sharing her salient points, while adding my own. Her words, "The power of touch is profound—whether it is an accidental glazing from a stranger, the strong kneading of a professional masseur, a gentle hold from someone close, a reassuring squeeze of the hand, an 'I see you' caress, an encouraging touch on the back, a quick kiss on the forehead or one that is slower, more tender and more anticipated. It can strengthen connections, heal, communicate, influence, and soothe." Benefits of appropriate touch include:

1. **More Nurturing Touch, Less Violence:** Research shows that when there is greater physical affection during childhood, the rates of adult physical violence are lower. On the other hand when touch is limited, physical and verbal aggression is higher.
2. **Communication Without Words:** Oftentimes touch can convey a caring message better than words.
3. **Reduces Stress:** Touch has a calming effect as it reduces cortisol.
4. **Brings People Closer Together:** Oxytocin is affectionately called the "cuddle chemical." Affection that is wanted causes

the release of oxytocin. It helps to nurture feelings of trust and connectedness.

5. **Communicates Compassion:** Touch activates the body's vagus nerve which is intimately connected with our compassionate response.

6. **It Makes People Nicer:** Those who are touched in ways that feel appropriate and safe are more likely to cooperate and share resources.

7. **Nurtures Growth:** Babies that are consistently touched have more advanced visual motor skills and more advanced gross motor development.

8. **Not Just For Babies:** Touch can suppress pain, ease the symptoms of depression, and it improves couple relationships.

9. **Helps People With Alzheimer's:** Such touch reduces stress and depressive symptoms and helps them make emotional connection with others.

It is unfortunate that because of all the inappropriate touching that exists in our current culture, many people have backed off of healthy touching because they do not want to be cited for crossing an individual's boundary. When not sure a person should ask permission so as to not offend.

Respected Reader, I hope that you have been the recipient of very little, or no, inappropriate touch. May your life, past and present, be one where you are in your comfort zone for both giving and receiving a touch that is additive, meaningful, and healing. May you give and receive touch that feels good, appropriate, and maybe even loving!

Why You Need To Give Compliments To Your Significant Other!

Too often in my therapy sessions do I hear the words, "I don't feel appreciated," "my spouse rarely gives me compliments." The related feelings are of hurt and sadness, or anger. People need attention, recognition, affirmation. Whether it be in the workplace, the family, or in a marriage, this need is present. Compliments serve this purpose.

Let me give some underlying theory to back up this premise. Two prominent psychologists, Alfred Adler and B.F. Skinner, have given a credible theoretical basis for this human need.

Alfred Adler, an early contemporary of Sigmund Freud, emphasized that when we are encouraged, we feel capable and appreciated. This contributes to a feeling of connectedness and, therefore, one becomes more cooperative. Is this not a desired end game in any human interaction?

B.F. Skinner is the founder of the operant theory of conditioning. He showed that positive reinforcement led to repeated behaviors. If reinforcement did not occur, the behavior died out or was extinguished. Does it not make sense to reinforce a person for doing desirable things, understanding that more of that will be forthcoming?

Given such a theoretical framework it makes great sense to develop the skill set of giving compliments. In a marriage, where individuals are particularly vulnerable to the thoughts, feelings, and behavior of one's partner, this is a very important. In every marriage each individual wants to "feel capable and appreciated … having a feeling of connectedness … and more cooperative." And if you want certain behaviors of your spouse to continue, reinforcement is the vehicle.

Part of my training in graduate school was learning to look for and find positive qualities in another person and then give him or her a sincere compliment based on that observation—emphasis on being sincere. I have found that skill to be of great value, both personally and professionally.

I love to give compliments, as well as receive them! I am fortunate personally in that my wife Sherry is a pro at giving compliments, as well as our two adult kids, Kris and Brittany. This shared gift of complimentary communication is one of the main reasons we love each other so well and feel so connected.

So, please, Respected Reader, look for and find positive qualities, behaviors, etc. that you like in your spouse and give those compliments—over and over again. Certainly you can find some of these to share. If not, see me. You are in trouble! Your spouse wants and needs that from you. Also, you may show this article to a non-complimentary spouse and ask him or her to give you some of the "good stuff" compliments that you would like to receive. Doesn't hurt to ask.

Chapter Ten: Divorce

13 Factors That May Lead To Divorce In Your Life— Know Them!

I'm would guess that along the way you have said, "I didn't know what I didn't know." Had you have known you probably would not have made the mistake that you did. So, Respected Reader, I thought I would throw out for your consumption some of the things I have observed in my practice that have led to a couple's disabled relationship and potential divorce.

1. **Time:** How you spend your time reflects your priorities. There's only so much time in a day. Jobs, kids, errands, friends, parents, socializing, etc. all can be time eaters. Easy to get caught up in these presenting concerns, demands, and opportunities. Quality time together as a couple is paramount as a divorce inhibitor.

2. **Money:** How money is discussed, handled, saved, and spent is a major factor leading to divorce. This is huge. Practically every couple I have worked with has money as one of the factors that has divided them. It is a delicate topic, usually not handled well.

3. **Family Of Origin:** Too often the husband or wife's parents, siblings, or extended family members are a factor in discord. Time with, money spent, or involvement in family issues of

one sort or another can lead to disagreement with high emotional intensity. I so urge couples to put their marriage first, their kids second, and then find a place where to put parental involvement.

4. **Selfishness:** One of the major adjustments in a marriage is to give up being totally independent, the "it's all about me" perspective, and become interdependent as a couple. Forming a "we" relationship moving forward is critical.

5. **Intimacy:** Emotional and physical connection is vital for maintaining and deepening a loving relationship. Anything that sabotages this needs to be removed. It is an important lifeline to marital happiness.

6. **Kids:** Too often kids, as wonderful as they may be, get in the way of the marriage. One of my frustrations as a therapist is to see "kids first" marriages. Too much time and effort related to the kids leaves the marriage on the back burner. And then the kids grow up and leave. What's left? Not much, because the marriage was not nurtured along the way. Thus, another "empty nest" divorce.

7. **Addiction:** Alcohol, drug, sexual addiction all tear apart a marriage connection. The need for this addictive lifestyle supersedes the need or ability for marriage first. If this behavior starts to develop, nip it in the bud. It's dangerous.

8. **Abuse:** Physical or emotional abuse, and/or neglect fracture a relationship. If it happens, re-prioritize, get healthy, and focus lovingly on each other.

9. **Different Paths:** Each person is an individual with unique hopes and dreams for a life of personal fulfillment and happiness. Such personal direction pulls may divide a couple who cannot find the balance between individual and couple

fulfillment. Lifestyle choices are so important here. How do "I" and "We" intersect?

10. **Friends:** Friends can be allies and supportive of a good marriage or they can be dividers. How much time spent individually and together with friends says much about the marriage connection. Also, whether these friends are "healthy" or not is important.

11. **Holding On To Yesterday's Hurts:** Hurtful "stuff" happens between couples. Sometimes an individual can't get past them, can't let them go. Hopefully, the offender has acknowledged and apologized for the hurt and it has been accepted. Hit the "reset button" and move forward! "Begin each day with fresh forgiveness!"

12. **Not A Team:** "You and me, babe, forever" are not thoughts/words shared with enough couples. A couple needs to develop the "we" team. Any significant decision involving each person, or as a couple, needs to be made together. Being "left out" is a feeling leading to hurt and anger and is fuel for divorce.

13. **Personal Dissatisfaction:** If one person in the marriage is significantly dissatisfied with his/her life, then a drag on the marriage surfaces. When such bumps come along, hopefully, they are recognized early on, and productively handled, with the other spouse offering love and support.

Clearly this list is not exhaustive, but perhaps it may hit on most of the challenging ones. May it serve its purpose of raising the awareness of such unhealthy detours to a good marriage.

Divorced Men And Women Reveal Why They Got Divorced

Divorce happens. Too often. It is painful. It should be avoided in most cases. Hindsight often offers clues and insights as to why a marriage did not work. The following is offered in hopes that by reading what divorced people say as to what caused the demise of their marriage, you may glean wisdom pertinent to your marriage to be, present relationship, or how to avoid another divorce.

Huffington Post divorce editor, Brittany Wong, asked readers to submit the real reasons why their marriage ended in divorce. The following answers resulted. I add my commentary.

1. **We Didn't Speak The Same Love Language:** "We are both so different that we didn't speak each other's love languages." (Laura) "Opposites attract." Yes, to a point, but there needs to be sufficient connecting points that bring a couple together so that their "love language" unites, not separates. What is important to one person may not be very important to the other.

2. **My Ex Didn't Prioritize Our Marriage:** "He never made our relationship the most important thing in his life." (Bren) If I have learned anything over the years doing marriage counseling is that both persons need to make the other number one. This is your life partner. Kids, other people, jobs, etc. are transitory and move on.

3. **A Lack Of Trust Led To Lack Of Intimacy:** "We had an 'open marriage' and lost that incredibly special foundation of trust and intimacy with each other. We became more like roommates than intimate partners." (Amy) Trust and respect are the bedrocks for a solid marriage.

4. **We Didn't Discuss Big Life Decisions With Each Other:** "We didn't have the ability to communicate well... I made independent decisions ..." (Chris) Marriage is a partnership, and both persons need to be able to communicate openly, honestly, and respectfully in order to arrive at mutually agreeable decisions.

5. **There Was No Friendship:** "We weren't friends. Everyone and everything was always more important." (Tamara) A basic core friendship is an enduring need in a relationship that can survive the various challenges that present themselves over the course of time.

6. **I Got Lazy:** "I could have been better. I could have found a way to keep us on track. I could have done more." (Al) You cannot half ass a marriage. Be prepared to be your best self and give it your best shot—or don't bother, cuz, it ain't going to work!

7. **My Spouse Let Me Do All The Work:** "There was no dependability or attention. ... I didn't want to be the diligent strong woman all the time." (Susan) Here again, marriage is a partnership where each person does his or her fair share after each agreeing as to what the responsibilities are.

8. **There Was No Sense Of Adventure:** "We never really did anything. The same things got old, and since that is what our marriage consisted of, sadly our marriage started to feel old." (Chelsie) A couple needs a sense of adventure, something to look forward to, something new. This need not be expensive per se, but does have to have some creative, look-forward to, energy. Stale and "old" just doesn't get it.

9. **We Were Too Stubborn:** "Our marriage became a staring contest and neither one of us was blinking. We were locked in stubbornness." (Bill) Being flexible and able to give in are

important traits for staying aligned and not in separate stubborn corners.

10. **We Married Too Young:** "We were the poster children for marrying too young; the lack of maturity resulted in a tumultuous marriage. ...We lacked the tolerance, patience, and understanding that is critical for all healthy adult relationships ..." (Nicole) Age at time of marriage is a very real factor for the durability of a marriage. Lust and fun together at a young age are not enough of a foundation for an enduring marriage.

11. **We Didn't Envision The Same Future:** "One of the biggest qualities that was missing from my marriage was the desire to mutually grow. ...Without a shared vision, the journey failed." (Bill) Here, again, maturity, compatibility, good communication, and awareness of needs/wants are basic qualities needed to determine a shared vision for the future.

What impact do these voices of the divorced have on you? These are not the only reasons, but in my experience they are "right on" to explain the divorce of so many. "If the shoe fits!"

Reflections And Regrets From Some That Have Divorced

And again—people marry. People divorce. Some people should not have married the persons they did. Some people did not work hard enough at their marriage to get through the rough times and create a solid marriage.

This writing focuses on a blog written by Brittany Wong. Ms. Wong solicited opinions from divorced persons as to any regrets they might have. I will present the regrets in italics and offer my commentary.

1. **"I regret not realizing he was broken and that I couldn't fix him."** One thing that dismays me is that so few people do an appropriate and exhaustive due diligence on a prospective mate. If people would do as much research when choosing a mate as they do buying a car there would be much less "buyer's remorse" about the mate chosen. The second part of this that said "I couldn't fix him" says a lot. Spouses don't "fix" each other. They may assist through love and support in helping this person heal and improve, along with the help of a Marriage Therapist, but "fix"—not!

2. **"My biggest regret? Staying seven years."** Ah, the "seven year itch" finally got to this divorcee. The cliché "he who hesitates is lost" may be pertinent here. It didn't take seven years to see that there was a problem. This person needed to get help early on and if the desired response was unbearable—move on!

3. **"I regret looking past all the signs. I was 'in love.' I thought you gave without reservations. I gave up on me."** Two fatal mistakes here. One, not paying attention to the "signs."

Second, not voting for herself and not developing a win-win partnership.

4. **"I regret that we didn't wait longer before we got married. We didn't take the time to get to know each other beforehand."** One of my favorite mottos, borrowed from an old Holiday Inn slogan, is "the best surprise is no surprise." Before making a significant commitment such as marriage a person needs to know the other person in depth from many vantage points. May the "surprises" be few and those that occur be positive ones.

5. **"I'm sorry I didn't see the umbilical cord still attached."** Too many newlyweds never have cut the psychological "umbilical cord" to Mommy or Daddy. They are still dependent personalities who have not become independent and, thus, capable of forming an adult interdependent relationship with another.

Ms. Wong has a few others but they basically all relate to the above themes. Too many people make the above mistakes and, thus, have serious regrets.

Where are you on the relationship continuum? Regrets? Lessons learned, or continuing to make the same mistakes over and over? If so, make an enlightened effort to know what you don't know and proceed forth to create the awesome relationship that you want and will deserve!

"The Seven Deadly Sins Of Divorce"

I ran across this article recently and it reminded me that I might write again an article on divorce and some of its ramifications. Divorce does happen often, especially during the summer when kids are out of school, and divorced couples often add to their separation pain by doing, or failing to do, certain things that are in their best interest, as well as for any children that may be involved. So let me share "The Seven Deadly Sins of Divorce" as seen through the pen of Natasha Burton as she gleans insight from a book entitled *Last One Down The Aisle Wins* by family therapist Shannon Fox and divorce attorney Celeste Liversidge. An interesting collaboration.

Before getting into the "Sins" Ms. Burton cites an interesting study from the University of Pennsylvania which correlates age of marriage and education with marital happiness. The study found that 81 per cent of college graduates who wed during the 80's, at age 26 or older, were still married twenty years later. That number decreased to 65 per cent for college grads who married before age 26. There are a number of studies pointing out that the more education you have and being older than 25 increases the probability of marriage success. And the "Sins" are:

1. **Forcing your kids to take sides:** "The last thing a parent wants to do during a divorce is to cause more pain for the children. Unfortunately, more often than not, the way a parent acts during the divorce makes things worse for the kids than necessary... Using your kids as pawns in the process will cause irreparable damage to them. Don't force them to take sides or to prove their love to you by defying their other parent... Remind them that both of their parents love them and always will have a relationship with them."

2. **Using your attorney as a therapist:** "Your attorney may be a whiz when it comes to the law... but he or she is not a trained mental health professional... and you are on the clock. And that's a pretty pricey sounding board."

3. **Spending $10,000 to get $1000:** "Time and time again we've seen couples make the mistake of fighting to the bitter end of who gets the.... By the time you pay your lawyers to duke it out, who do you think ends up the winner? That's right, the lawyers. Making your lawyers rich off your refusal to back down is definitely a losing proposition."

4. **Taking a laissez faire approach to your case:** "You do yourself a huge favor by staying on top of your case and holding your lawyer accountable for his or her hourly billing and timeline for finishing your case. Request a weekly email update from your attorney."

5. **Refusing to mediate:** "You may not be able to settle all the issues in your case without hearing from the judge but even knocking out a few issues through mediation can really save you time and money.

6. **Demonizing your ex:** "When you trash a child's mom or dad, you are trashing a part of them. This is their one and only dad/mom. If your ex is a bad person, your children will discover it on their own. Their relationship should remain unencumbered by your relational baggage."

7. **Jumping into a rebound relationship:** "Refrain because you are nowhere near ready to give another person what they deserve in a relationship. Refrain because your kids will be further traumatized by bringing in a 'new parent' into their lives when they are reeling from the loss of their intact family. Refrain because you will never learn from the mistakes you made in your first marriage if you don't take

time to figure out your responsibility in the failure of the relationship."

I hope that the above material is helpful for those of you divorced, contemplating it, or know someone in that position. For a more complete elaboration on the above "sins" and further issues that you might consider I refer you to my web site: drstathas.googlepages.com. There you will find a number of articles related to going through a divorce and the impact on children.

Divorce: Minimize The Pain And Damage, Especially To Kids

D ivorce happens. Marriage is a challenge and some people are not equipped to meet that challenge. Others decline the opportunity to develop such a capacity. Divorce results. Many of those who divorce came from households where they themselves experienced divorcing parents. When a couple divorces, and how they do it, has lasting implications.

On occasion I am called upon to mediate a divorce because the couple wants to:

1. Save money and not give it to warring attorneys
2. Have as amiable a divorce as possible
3. Learn what each person did to sabotage the marriage
4. Learn how to co-parent as effectively as possible
5. Minimize the damage done to their children

Children are deeply impacted by divorce (as well as by living in a tension-filled argumentative home). The following are some of my suggestions to divorcing parents.

- Meet with the children together to tell them of the divorce. Emphasize that you have tried to make the marriage work, that you both love them very much, that the divorce is not their fault, and that you both will be co-parenting and very involved in their lives. Ask them if they have any questions.
- Do not blame or talk negatively about the other spouse at any time. Your children love each parent and do not want to hear either one disparaged by the other.

- Explain to them the living and visitation arrangements of each parent and how it will affect them. Try not to move the children from their home or school.
- Try to spend individual time with each child. Each kid needs one-on-one time.
- Speak directly with your ex; do not use your child as a pawn, spy, or messenger. Never make them choose sides. "Take the high road!"
- Have agreed up expectations and consequences for your children that each of you enforce consistently. Consistency offers them security and helps them realize that they cannot play one parent off against the other.
- Do not introduce your children to a new "significant other" until such point as you are near re-marriage with that person. A parade of dates is harmful. Attachment and separation is damaging to your children.
- If you re-marry be very clear what the stepparent's role is and is not. You should be the primary communicator to your children.
- Try not to involve your children in any negative emotions you may have toward your ex-spouse, the situation, child support, etc. Your emotions are not their business.
- Be cordial to each other, especially when your children are present. Go to all their events if at all possible. It helps them with their "abandonment issues."

There are many other suggestions that can assist a divorcing couple so that the damage to the children may be minimized. Be assured, however, that they will be affected for their lifetime in the neurological wiring of the emotional areas of their brain. These facts are not meant to guiltify, rather to inform. This is serious stuff!

Strategies For Divorced Parents With Children

The reality in our culture is that roughly fifty per cent of married couples divorce. Those in their second marriage have about a seventy percent probability of divorce. Usually there are children involved in these marital changes.

It is plenty challenging to raise children today under the best of circumstances with a traditional first marriage model. Divorce, re-marriage, and stepparents all impact kids significantly. Research and clinical experience confirms the facts that children of divorced families on average have higher anxiety and depression, more behavior and addiction problems, get lower grades, and have a higher divorce rate when they marry than kids who come from stable two parent families. There are exceptions of course.

This is not to say that some people with children should not get divorced. There are some valid reasons. Nobody should ever judge someone who gets divorced. By the same token someone who chooses to divorce should be able "to look at yourself in the mirror and honestly say that you've done everything possible to rehabilitate and save your marriage." (Dr. Phil McGraw from his book, *Family First.*)

Dr. Phil and his researchers and fellow contributing clinicians offer some facts and suggestions that I would like to note here and amplify for divorced parents. Some people in this situation may be ignorant, in denial, or want to challenge these assertions. But I can assure you with the utmost confidence that my clinical experience confirms these comments.

- Even before a divorce children have internalized parental conflict and may already be exhibiting behavior problems.

- Divorce shakes a child to his core and likely has traumatizing effects. Two overt symptoms, depending on genetic predisposition and sibling order, are clingers or anger-based aggressors.

There are at least six basic needs of children going through their parent's divorce:

1. Acceptance of their new reality. Reassurance that they still are a part of a family.
2. Assurance of physical and emotional safety.
3. Freedom of guilt or blame for the divorce. Children often feel they have caused it.
4. Need for structure. When the family is falling apart there is an even greater need for this. Structure gives them a sense of security.
5. Need for at least one stable parent who can take care of the business of running the family.
6. Need to continue to be a kid. Sometimes a child takes on the role of a caretaking "parent" figure.

Divorced parents need to take the "high road" in the continuing relationship with each other. These acts are destructive:

- Sabotaging your child's relationship with the other parent.
- Using your child as a pawn to "get back at" or hurt your ex.
- Using your child to gain information or to manipulate and influence your ex.
- Transferring your hurt and anger feelings toward your ex onto your child. Never talk bad about your ex to your child. You are just showing your immaturity.

Proactively, sit down with your ex, perhaps in the company of a Marriage and Family Therapist, and develop a game plan on co-parenting your children. Communicate regularly and respectfully as you inform and make decisions regarding your children.

There is more to be said but space limits for now. Know that positive interaction and communication are critically important for the well-being of your children—both in the short and long term. May both parents be persons of integrity and not let past hurts get in the way of raising your children.

"Gray Divorce": Older Couples Are Increasingly Getting Divorced. Why?

It is a fact that older Americans are increasingly getting divorced. Since 1990 the divorce rates have doubled for those over 50 and have more than doubled for those over 65. In 2010 one in four divorces was between couples 50 or older. A research study from Bowling Green University said that the reasons for these divorces were not usually from "severe discord," rather "the couples had simply grown apart." People change and often in a different direction from their partner. Couples, post children and diverging interests no longer have enough connecting points to live a happy shared life together. Different visions of how they want their future life to be are significant contributors to these divorces. Mortality issues emerge and many individuals wonder if this marriage and lifestyle is what they really want down the line.

Besides the significant factors of physical and emotional abuse, these seven factors lead to the "gray divorce."

1. Frequent fighting: Couples don't communicate well and issues over things like money, sex, and lifestyle escalate into intolerant fighting.
2. Sexual desire discrepancy: one partner wants sex; the other does not. One feels neglected; the other feels put upon.
3. One partner's drinking and/or drug abuse: Many individuals as they age get more and more dependent on alcohol and/or drugs to mask their depression or anxiety—or just to "have a good time."
4. A difference of opinion on work-life balance: How much one works and recreates affects a couple's relationship.

Retirement issues present new challenges. "Live to work or work to live."

5. Financial stress: How much money is earned and available, how it is spent and by whom causes turmoil in many a marriage.

6. Weight issues: As people get older they tend to gain weight. Rarely is that attractive. Some people are more tolerant of a partner's weight gain than another might be. Many of the older generation are working hard to stay in shape and not gain weight. If one's partner chooses to not do that, then another reason for the parting of ways develops.

7. Arguments related to adult children: If a couple does not see "eye to eye" on children related issues, or cannot find an acceptable compromise, then conflict flares. Adult children issues are becoming more and more prevalent during these times.

If a couple is fighting more, disenchanted with one's partner, rarely having sex, preferring to spend time with others rather than spouse, dreading weekends, and/or fantasizing about another lover or lifestyle, or being happily alone, help is needed. A Marriage Therapist who can bring some objectivity and direction to this "falling out of love" phenomenon can be of great help. The marriage may be rehabbed into something quite wonderful. Or, a respectful and peaceful dissolution of the marriage may be mediated. Plus, a person may get some insight as to what has been done wrong that has helped to deteriorate the marriage.

Chapter Eleven: Therapy

Can People Really Change? Yes!

Often I am asked these questions: "Can you help this person?" Can you help me?" Can a person really change? My answer is "Yes—if certain steps are followed."

As a therapist I am presented with many concerns by people who want themselves or someone they care about to get better, to get healthier, to be a better functioning person. There are many variables in the quest for personal growth and healing Success depends on these basic factors.

First there needs to be an ASSESSMENT of what appears to be the problem. Does the patient/client recognize that there is a valid concern? Who are the people involved with the issues presented? Identification of the issue to be worked on in therapy needs to be stated and understood by those involved. Anxiety, depression, alcohol and drug abuse, anger management, communication issues, marital strife, parenting concerns, physical and sexual abuse, attention deficit disorder, fear issues, divorce, separation, addictions, sexual compatibility, money management—all would be illustrative of some of the types of presenting concerns worthy of therapeutic assistance.

Secondly, does the patient/client recognize that there is a problem? AWARENESS is a necessary step in problem solving. If she/he is not attuned to the issue, what needs to be done to help this person realize this concern?

If progress is to be made a COMMITMENT to the appropriate therapeutic modality is necessary. Progress cannot be made without the appropriate people committing to work through a process toward a solution. Sometimes people have too much fear or anger to overcome in order to commit. Others just want to "keep their head in the sand" and deny that there is a problem. And some stubbornly say that they are not ready to deal with it. And, last but not least, there are those who "shoot the messenger" because they do not have the gumption to be open and to recognize the problem. Therefore, they decide to blame the therapist diagnosis and/or solution modality.

If the patient/client will not accept that fact that she/he has a problem and refuses to commit to therapy, the concerned and caring persons involved need to change their behavior toward him/her in order to get this person to realize that she/he needs to get better or there will be significant changes in his/her life.

In some cases appropriate medication may be needed to facilitate the therapeutic process. It is here that I collaborate with some of the outstanding medical doctors available.

People need to know the complexity of their unique brain wiring and how it affects their various feelings, thoughts, and behavior. How does their brain—beginning with family genetics and affected by life experiences—work for or against them in the challenge of everyday living. Without this knowledge appropriate intervention and change is not possible.

So, Respected Reader, you can see that the answer to the question as to whether or not people can change is complex. I would not be in my profession as a Counseling Psychologist, Marriage and Family Therapist, if I did not see and effectuate real and lasting change in the people I work with. I am blessed to be in this profession and grateful to see what individuals, couples, and families can become!

Some Reasons That You Might Consider Counseling

It is 2019! Good news. Fresh start. Lots of energy. New goals set with an action plan to achieve them. Yes, that is how you are feeling as you begin this new year. *What*, you're not feeling this burst of optimistic energy? Enthusiasm is not abounding? Then what is your present mood as you look at this new year and its challenges?

Perhaps you might consider some counseling to help you clarify and assess your moving forward in life. Lindsay Holmes has written a provocative article suggesting eleven areas where you might consider counseling. I share those along with my additional thoughts.

1. **You're Experiencing Unexpected Mood Swings:** If you are noticing, or others are telling you, that you've taken on a more negative mood or thought process—and it's persistent—it might be worth talking to a therapist.

2. **You Are Undergoing A Big Change:** Relationship change, job switch, moving, etc. can be challenging and unnerving. Talking to a trained objective person can clarify and help you make the necessary adjustment moving forward.

3. **You're Having Harmful Thoughts:** Suicide and self-harm are preventable with treatment by a licensed psychotherapist.

4. **You're Withdrawing From Things That Used To Bring You Joy:** Loss of motivation to do the "fun stuff" could well signal that you are falling into depression and/or have developed social anxiety.

5. **You Are Feeling Isolated Or Alone:** By talking with a therapist you will feel more connected with yourself, understand better that you are not alone, and develop some

insight and skills to better connect with the people that are important to you.

6. **You're Using A Substance To Cope With Issues In Your Life:** Abusing alcohol, drugs, or other addictive substances or behaviors are inappropriate and ineffective means to run away from depression.

7. **You Suspect You Might Have A Serious Mental Health Condition:** Something just seems "off." You are not functioning like you feel you should. Check it out with a therapist.

8. **You Feel Like You've Lost Control:** Being out of control never feels good. Stop this as soon as possible.

9. **Your Relationships Feel Strained:** An objective trained relationship therapist can help you sort out your relationships. Some may need to be altered or let go. Others just need some clarification and direction. Perhaps better communication skills can be of benefit.

10. **Your Sleeping Patterns Are Off:** Sleep patterns often can help you understand what might be going on in your life. Too little or too much sleep can be effective warning signs that a therapist is warranted.

11. **You Just Feel You Need To Talk With Someone:** Sure, a friend is available. But is this person objective, will she/he bring a bias, or is she/he just plain nosey?

Respected Reader, do any of these reasons hit home for you personally? Or for someone you care about? It is worth looking in the mirror for these factors. The earlier you catch a developing problem, the better chance you have of healing it. Therapy can be a useful, productive, even enjoyable experience for those who begin with good faith and a commitment to be the best person possible. A noble objective for 2019. N'est pas?

Couples Therapy: Why, When, How And With Whom

As significant part of my practice involves couples therapy. It is an aspect that I enjoy, especially if I can meet with a couple before one or the other persons checks out, gives up. While I do divorce mediation also, I would prefer to meet with a couple early on if it has the potential to be a good relationship. It is not easy for two people who have chosen to be a couple to live "happily ever after" on an everyday basis. "Stuff" happens that make couples attack or retreat from each other. Emotional distances arise and make it difficult for a couple to connect. Yet, too often couples do not utilize this marriage saving vehicle, or they wait too late.

Why do couples need marriage counseling? If a couple has difficulty communicating, making joint decisions, making love, agreeing on financial issues, parenting together, etc. they would be wise to seek marital counseling. Many issues may exist that trigger anger, fear, sadness, or guilt. An objective voice needs to be introduced to such situations.

When should couples seek marriage counseling? Earlier than they do! Most often couples begin such counseling—if they do at all—later than they should. Much damage has already been done to the relationship. Most typical is that a wife will suggest it and the husband will initially resist and maybe relent later. Sometimes a spouse will not agree to go to counseling. I ask the willing party to come and see me so that I can empathize, support, and create a strategy to get the reluctant spouse to enter into the counseling process.

How does couple counseling work? There are different therapeutic approaches. I share mine. A couple comes in to meet with me and shares each of their unique perspectives as to what is wrong in the relationship. Of course, the problems mostly exist *because of the other person*! This can be a very heated part of the process. I ask each person to be respectful in the way they present and react to the various accusations. At the end of the initial session I give extensive "homework" for them to do and return to me. Next, I meet with each individual separately to help me understand each person's brain wiring and previous relationship-related experiences. Then I meet with them together for the purpose of developing a "game plan." To make the "game plan" work a few things need to happen. First, and very important, is for each person to own his or her mistakes, ask for and receive forgiveness. Next is a commitment by each to do certain things, refrain from others, while starting to grow closer through better communication. We then meet with some agreed upon regularity to address accountability.

With Whom should couples seek counseling? A licensed Marriage and Family Therapist is required here. They are trained in a particular way that they can have the most significant impact on a couple. There are many "counselor" types who have good intentions but lack the necessary training to maximally assist couples under duress. The old adage certainly applies here: "You get what you pay for."

Respected Reader, I would be interested to be "in your head" when you finish this reading. Does it apply to you and your marriage? Anyone you know that might benefit from being reminded that quality marriage counseling is available? The quality of your marriage affects you in so many ways. It is a major source of happiness or depression. Choose well!

Don't Choose A "Rent-A-Friend" Therapist!

- Are you unhappy with some aspect of your life and looking for answers?
- Do you have issues with your spouse?
- Are your children acting out and you are wondering why?
- Is your career frustrating you?
- Is retirement causing some anguish?
- Is depression or anxiety challenging you?
- Might you have an addiction that is getting in the way of healthy living?

If you have said "yes" to any of the above, you may have sought, or need to seek counsel for support and expertise in working through these concerns. Where will you find this help?

Some people ask their **Preacher**. Some preachers believe in, and work with, psychotherapists. They see the value of spiritual and psychological integration from trained professionals in each discipline. Others try to counsel when they have had minimal training and/or just ask you to have faith and pray more. Good intention, poor result.

Some people ask **Physicians.** Most physicians respect, collaborate, and refer patients to competent therapists (although they often keep it in the MD "club," meaning psychiatrists instead of including Ph.D. professionals). Some physicians, however, go beyond their training and expertise and try to either counsel or preach to the patient. Not good "practice."

Some people ask a **Friend.** This can be a good source for support, but usually not for objective advice.

The **Yellow Pages**. Good luck. Perhaps a clever advertisement. Beware.

Once you decide on a particular therapist, ask him/her some questions about his/her qualifications, experience, theoretical methodology, and personal life. Yes, personal life. It helps to be working with someone who "walks the talk."

A side note, recent research concluded that therapists as a whole have poorer marriages than their contemporaries based on matching demographics. That is why I encourage you to learn about the past history and present reality of the therapist. If the therapist balks, that's a red flag. Personal life can influence professional practice.

Once you have started therapy, are you willing to hear what you may not like, or are you trying to "rent a friend" therapist who will give you the answer you want? There are some of those therapists around who make you feel good by agreeing with your pre-conceived desires. These therapists are either:

- Hurting for business
- Weak "pleasers" who want you to feel good and like them
- Or they over-identify with your concerns due to their own personal experience

Nobody wants to hear "bad news." People who won't "run away" from the physician who says they have a heart condition will "run away" from the therapist who says they have a debilitating emotional disorder and/or are making unhealthy choices in their lives. They will seek out therapists who give them the "answer" they want. There's always a therapist or two who will accommodate.

Don't "rent a friend" therapist for any concern. Find a competent therapist who can earn your trust and, thus, assist you with your particular concern. Sometimes it is painful to hear what you do not want to hear, but at least you can be on the road to a better life if you stick with it and work it through.

What Couples Say After Receiving Quality Marriage Counseling

Marriage counseling can be enormously successful in helping couple to develop a loving and sustainable marriage, communicating well as partners. This will result if:

- They find a qualified and licensed Marriage and Family Therapist
- They are truly committed to work on the relationship, spending the necessary time and money for this priority
- They don't "shoot the messenger" therapist because the counseling process causes them to initially feel defensive when the therapist asks them to change certain behaviors

Brittany Wong, Huffington Post divorce editor, has written an article about this and presents quotes from couples who participated in marriage counseling. She lists eight healthy habits learned by the participants.

1. **Recognize When You're Telling A "Story":** "Sometimes we tell ourselves stories because we want things to be or sound a certain way. We want to be viewed as the main character. The thing is, in a healthy relationship both people are equally important and both sides of a story matter. These days I try really hard to notice when I'm building a narrative and make sure it aligns with what's real. I recognize that my husband's story may be as legitimate as my own."
   - When I work with clients I discuss subjective perceptions that lead to a story. If there is no recording of what happened, it is just one side of the story. Always two sides!

2. **Listen More Than You Talk:** "I am a talker. Therapy has taught me and my husband to listen more than talk. Active listening helps us to feel heard and understood."

3. **Create Couple Time, Even If It Means Waking Up Earlier:** "Through going to therapy with my wife, I've learned that date nights and scheduled time together creates structure and improves emotional engagement. More importantly, it builds a sense of togetherness."

4. **Don't Assume You Know Everything About Your Partner:** "My husband and I have been together five years now and sometimes it's tempting to assume I know everything there is to know about him—which isn't true—especially when it comes to conflict."

   People are complex with many sides and nuances.

5. **Give Up The Right To Be Right:** "I feel I am usually right, although I sometimes let my husband think he is. While the truth is probably somewhere in the middle of us. We have learned to not allow the need to assert our 'rightness' get in the way of loving each other. Who cares who is right?"

   - This is one of the most important. The marriage is more important than who may be right on a particular issue.

6. **Call A Timeout If Things Are Getting Too Intense:** "There is a ground rule to avoid escalation. If for whatever reason a discussion or disagreement escalates to a high degree and you feel overwhelmed, you have the right to ask for a 'timeout.' … But be sure to reschedule a time to talk about the subject within 23-48 hours."

   - I tell clients that whoever is most aware of the escalation to say "broccoli." This is a weird/funny way to get attention and to stop the hurtful words at the present time.

7. **You Can Be Honest Now Or Honest Later, But Eventually, You Have To Tell The Truth If You Want To Move On:** "I'm a people-pleaser at heart, so in relationships I frequently feel the need to hide information. ... I quickly learned in therapy there's no other path forward but an honest one. You're actually wasting time and money if you show up to a counseling session without being willing to share your truth."

   • My clients tell me that I am very direct. True. I get to the point and ask couples to do the same. Don't waste time and money!

8. **When All Else Fails, Give Each Other A Hug Or A Kiss:** "Therapy has emphasized the importance of physical touch in our marriage. It is healing. When all else fails, kiss. It works like a charm."

   • Often at the end of an emotional session, I will invite the couple to embrace. Usually with tearful eyes in each a warm hug is shared.

Respected Reader: Might any of these lessons be pertinent in your relationship? Is there a need for some fine-tuning on these or other lessons that need to be learned?

Why People Quit Psychotherapy Prematurely

People come to see a therapist for various reasons. Over the course of my thirty years of doing psychotherapy I have consistently worked with patients/clients who have these types of issues: anxiety, depression, compulsive behaviors, addictions, ADD/ADHD, phobias, anger issues, abuse (physical, emotional, sexual), relationship issues (including marriage, children, parents, relatives, co-workers, etc.) career clarification, divorce and death adjustments—and others that may present on occasion.

Therapy is not easy, unless you go to a "rent-a-friend" therapist who you just want to help you to feel good during that therapy time. Therapy invites and challenges you to look at your current situation and the healthy choices that may lead to a better and happier life. However, a competent therapist will want to go beyond short term "cosmetic" counseling—which does not endure—and get to the deeper roots that are causing the distressing situation existing.

At the end of the initial get-to-know you session where the issues of concern are discussed, I give some in-depth "homework" for the individual(s) to work on. The content of this homework invites the patient/client to bring into consciousness many past and present factors that have led up to the present distress issues. This "homework" is not easy. It takes time and effort, and often brings up deeper painful emotions. Some of these emotions have been buried in the unconscious but, nevertheless, have been a factor related to mental health concerns, inappropriate choices and behaviors.

Some people leap right into the "homework," despite it being painful. Others procrastinate, not wanting to address these underlying factors. Some people, usually men, can't remember some of the key events that have been formative of their emotional core. And then there are those that recognize that therapy is hard work and decide to cop out, or are just too scared to venture forth. They quit.

The second phase of therapy after the initial session, and hopefully after completed "homework," we begin further understandings of how earlier life experiences have wired the brain in certain ways which relate to the presenting concerns. Next we look at possible choices and direction needed to clarify/ change/remediate/heal them. This is where it can again be challenging for the patient/client. S/he may not want to make the necessary therapeutic changes needed. Operative word here is "change." As Albert Einstein said, "Insanity is doing the same thing over and over and expecting different results." Therapy involves change.

Here is where the "rubber meets the road!" Tough choices need to be made and sometimes a person can't or won't make the appropriate choice. I will never forget many years ago when I was working with a couple for marriage counseling. They both did phase one well. However, when I encouraged the husband to look at, feel, and understand the implications of his father's "abandonment" of him, he balked. This was a critical factor holding him back from emotionally connecting with his wife with empathy and love. He was closed off. Tears came to his eyes (usually he was pretty stoic, with the only emotion being anger) and he said, "This is too painful, I can't go there." He quit therapy. He would not deal with his emotional withdrawal and occasional temper. Thus, the couple got divorced because he couldn't deal with his underlying driving emotions.

It bothers me when I see a patients/clients quit therapy prematurely. They usually find some "excuse" to justify that decision, but usually it is because the therapeutic process dug too deep and they did not want to address it and its implications. I wish more people were "ready" to deal with the factors that are getting in the way of a better life in a particular area of life. Good therapy works if people stay the course!

About The Author

Dr. John J. Stathas is a successful Psychotherapist, licensed Marriage and Family Therapist, and newspaper columnist. Dr. Stathas is happily married for forty years to his beloved wife, Sherry. Together they have joyfully raised their two children, Kristopher and Brittany, who are healthy and successful in their respective marriages and careers. Dr. Stathas is passionate about helping others to be happy, fulfilled and productive in their relationships and life choices.

Made in the USA
Columbia, SC
18 May 2019